"十四五"國家重點出版物出版規劃項目

The Tsinghua University Warring States Bamboo Manuscripts: Studies and Translations 6

《清華大學藏戰國竹簡》研究與英譯 6

Lady Wu of Zheng Admonished her Child and Other Related Texts

《鄭武夫人規孺子》諸篇

Rens Krijgsman

[荷] 武致知 著譯

Edited by the Research and Conservation Center for Unearthed Texts, Tsinghua University

清華大學出土文獻研究與保護中心 編

清華大學出版社
Tsinghua University Press
北京

内容简介

2008年7月，清華大學從境外搶救入藏了一批戰國時期竹簡，學界稱之為"清華簡"。清華簡的內容多為早期的經史類典籍，其中除了可與《尚書》等傳世古書對照的篇目外，更多的則是已失傳兩千年之久的前所未見的佚篇，對於準確認識先秦古籍的原貌、重建中國早期歷史均有重要學術價值。清華簡所帶來的新知識以及對傳統文化認識的更新，已經引起了海內外學術界以及社會各界的廣泛關注，對中華優秀傳統文化的傳承與創新性發展具有重要的意義。

本書的主要內容是對清華簡中見於《鄭武夫人規孺子》或與之體裁相近篇目（《鄭文公問太伯》《子犯子餘》《晋文公入於晋》《趙簡子》《子儀》）的英譯及背景知識介紹，同時對戰國時期歷史敘事的文學特征提供了一些見解。主要讀者為海內外從事早期中國研究的學者以及對中國古代文明有興趣的一般讀者。

北京市版權局著作權合同登記號　圖字：01-2024-4673

版權所有，侵權必究。舉報：010-62782989，beiqinquan@tup.tsinghua.edu.cn。

圖書在版編目(CIP)數據

《清華大學藏戰國竹簡》研究與英譯.6,《鄭武夫人規孺子》諸篇：英文 / 清華大學出土文獻研究與保護中心編；(荷)武致知(Rens Krijgsman)著譯.—— 北京：清華大學出版社，2024.10.—— ISBN 978-7-302-67233-3

Ⅰ.K877.54

中國國家版本館CIP數據核字第2024KS9833號

責任編輯：梁　斐
封面設計：王紅衛　劉星池
責任校對：薄軍霞
責任印製：楊　豔

出版發行：清華大學出版社
　　　　　網　　　址：https://www.tup.com.cn, https://www.wqxuetang.com
　　　　　地　　　址：北京清華大學學研大廈A座　　郵　　編：100084
　　　　　社　總　機：010-83470000　　　　　　　　郵　　購：010-62786544
　　　　　投稿與讀者服務：010-62776969, c-service@tup.tsinghua.edu.cn
　　　　　質量反饋：010-62772015, zhiliang@tup.tsinghua.edu.cn
印　裝　者：三河市春園印刷有限公司
經　　　銷：全國新華書店
成　　　品：155mm×235mm　　印　張：18　　插　頁：8　　字　數：318千字
版　　　次：2024年10月第1版　　　　　　　　　　印　次：2024年10月第1次印刷
定　　　價：188.00元

產品編號：102181-01

本叢書獲得了國家社科基金重大項目"清華大學藏戰國竹簡的價值挖掘與傳承傳播研究"（20&ZD309）的資助。本卷的撰寫獲得了古文字與中華文明傳承發展工程項目"中國出土文獻的西方傳播與研究"（G1817）以及北京市外籍高層次人才資助計劃（J202132）的資助

This book series has received support from the Paleography and Chinese Civilization Inheritance and Development Program and the National Social Science Fund Key Program "Research on the Value and Transmission of the Tsinghua University Warring States Bamboo Manuscripts" (20&ZD309). The writing of this volume has received generous support from the "Western Dissemination and Research of Chinese Unearthed Texts" (G1817) project funded by the "Paleography and Chinese Civilization Inheritance and Development Program" and a grant from the Beijing Municipal Foreign High Level Talent Support Plan (J202132).

Contents

General Preface I　　Huang Dekuan 黃德寬..1

General Preface II　　Edward L. Shaughnessy..8

Conventions..22

Preface and Acknowledgements...27

Introduction to Volume Six 32

Chapter One　　Narratives about the Past..42

Chapter Two　　Dialogue Dynamics 58

Chapter Three　　Image-based Language 70

Chapter Four　　Conclusion...94

Chapter Five　　*Zheng Wu Furen Gui Ruzi* 鄭武夫人規孺子 *Lady Wu of Zheng Admonished her Young Child* 98

Chapter Six　　*Zheng Wen Gong Wen Tai Bo* 鄭文公問太伯 A & B *Lord Wen of Zheng Asks Grand Elder*...........................125

III

Chapter Seven   *Zi Fan Zi Yu* 子犯子餘 Mr. Fan and Mr. Yu 159

Chapter Eight   **Jin Wen Gong ru yu Jin* 晉文公入於晉 *Lord Wen of Jin Entered Jin* 183

Chapter Nine   **Zhao Jianzi* 趙簡子 **Zhao Jianzi* 201

Chapter Ten   **Zi Yi* 子儀 **Mr. Yi* 222

Works Cited 252

Index of Concepts 270

Index of Proper Names 275

Index of Text Titles 278

Images of the Manuscripts 281

General Preface I
Huang Dekuan 黃德寬

Since the beginning of the twentieth century, a series of important archaeological discoveries has greatly enriched contemporary scholars' understanding of ancient China. Among the many archaeological excavations, several discoveries of Warring State, Qin and Han manuscripts stand out as milestones: the Han-dynasty bamboo-slips unearthed at Yinqueshan 銀雀山, the silk manuscripts unearthed at Mawangdui 馬王堆, and the Warring States Chu 楚 manuscripts from Guodian 郭店. The publication of these ancient manuscripts has attracted the greatest interest from the scholarly world, and has had a profound influence on the development of contemporary Chinese scholarship. Scholars both at home and abroad have approached these new documents from different scholarly backgrounds to explore such different topics as ancient history, ancient literature and paleography, bringing manuscript studies to the forefront of contemporary scholarship.

The profound influence that the discovery of these manuscripts has had on contemporary Chinese scholarship is a sign of their extraordinary significance for the study of ancient China. As one of the great civilizations of the world, Chinese civilization has had a long and unbroken history, and its writing system is the only one in the world that is still in use today and that still maintains its ancient form. For this reason, there is a continuous tradition of literature written in Chinese characters, making China the richest source of literature in the world. Even though Chinese history saw the calamity of the burning of the books during the Qin dynasty (221–207 BCE), after the establishment of the Han dynasty Emperor Hui of Han 漢惠帝 (r. 194–188 BCE) abolished the Qin proscription on literature and thereafter there were continuous efforts during the remainder of the dynasty to restore pre-Qin literature. This established a firm foundation for the transmission of classical literature over the next two thousand years, throughout which time the sacred place of classical literature was never shaken.

In modern times, the prestige of the ancient classics was called into question by the rise of the new historiography of the "doubting antiquity" movement. Nevertheless, against the background of the "doubting antiquity" movement's attack on classical literature, repeated discoveries of such paleographic sources as the oracle-bone inscriptions and Western Zhou bronze inscriptions, as well as the Warring States, Qin and Han manuscripts had an especially important significance. In 1925, while teaching the course "New Evidence of Ancient History" at Tsinghua University's Institute of Sinology, Wang Guowei 王國維 (1877–1927) announced his famous principle of "dual evidence." In this, he found a middle ground between traditional scholars' excessive belief in antiquity and the modern excessive doubting of antiquity. What is more, he also demonstrated the value of combining "paper sources" and "underground sources."[1] Some of the Warring States, Qin and Han manuscripts discovered since the 1970s correspond to texts in the received literature, and these manuscripts have resolved certain questions of long standing concerning those texts; some have confirmed the authenticity and date of texts that have been doubted, while many others provide hitherto unknown sources for the literature of the period. More important still, these unearthed manuscripts allow an entirely new understanding of how ancient texts were created, transmitted, modified, and systematized.

These discoveries have also furthered the development of contemporary Chinese scholarship, especially as represented in the fields of history, literature and paleography. This has prompted the scholarly world in general

---

1 Wang Guowei 王國維, *Gu shi xin zheng: Wang Guowei zuihou de jiangyi* 古史新證——王國維最後的講義 (Beijing: Qinghua daxue chubanshe, 1994).

to rethink the history of Chinese scholarship. For instance, Li Xueqin 李學勤 (1933–2019) spoke of "leaving behind the doubting antiquity period,"[2] and proposed instead to "rewrite the history of scholarship" "based on new materials, new viewpoints, new methods, new heights, and under new historical conditions."[3] He also argued that "rewriting the history of scholarship should especially include a renewed emphasis on the history of twentieth century scholarship."[4] Qiu Xigui 裘錫圭 has proposed "reestablishing classical studies," suggesting that "the first of the recent reestablishments of Chinese classical studies began in the 1920s," when "doubting antiquity gradually became the main current of classical studies, to a considerable extent replacing traditional classicism." According to Qiu, because of the great amount of paleographic materials unearthed beginning in the 1950s — and especially of manuscripts discovered beginning in the 1970s — Chinese scholars then "began the second reestablishment of classical studies."[5] This rethinking of Chinese scholarship has not only had an enormous influence on scholars within China, but has also attracted the notice of Western scholars. In the Preface to his book *Rewriting Early Chinese Texts*, Edward L. Shaughnessy said:

> "[Professor Li's call to leave behind the doubting antiquity period] has had a resounding effect in China, numerous books and articles published in the intervening ten years featuring the word 'rewriting.' Even in the West, the notion of rewriting Chi-

---

2 Li Xueqin 李學勤, *Zouchu yigu shidai* 走出疑古時代 (Shenyang: Liaoning daxue chubanshe, 1994).
3 Li Xueqin 李學勤, "Yigu sichao yu chonggou gu shi" 疑古思潮與重構古史, *Zhongguo wenhua yanjiu* 中國文化研究 1999.1: 4; rpt. Li Xueqin, *Chongxie xueshushi* 重寫學術史 (Shijiazhuang: Hebei Jiaoyu chubanshe, 2002), 2.
4 *Ibid.*
5 Qiu Xigui 裘錫圭, "Zhongguo gudianxue chongjian zhong yinggai zhuyi de wenti" 中國古典學重建中應該注意的問題, *Beijing daxue Zhongguo guwenxian yanjiu zhongxin jikan* 北京大學中國古文獻研究中心集刊 2 (2001): 4; See also, Qiu Xigui 裘錫圭. *Qiu Xigui xueshu wenji: Jiandu boshu juan* 裘錫圭學術文集：簡牘帛書卷. (Shanghai: Fudan daxue chubanshe, 2012), 334–344, esp. 335–336; "Chutu wenxian yu gudianxue chongjian" 出土文獻與古典學重建, *Chutu wenxian* 出土文獻 4 (2013): 1–18.

na's early history, if not the word itself, inspired the recently published *Cambridge History of Ancient China*."[6]

Expressions such as "leaving behind the doubting antiquity period," "rewriting the history of scholarship," and "reestablishing classical studies" surely show the great significance of these discoveries of Warring States, Qin and Han manuscripts.

In this context, the appearance of the Tsinghua University Warring States bamboo slips (commonly referred to as the "Tsinghua manuscripts") can be said to have "met the moment," and to have provided a further impetus to the "rewriting" of Chinese scholarship. In 2008, Li Xueqin encouraged Tsinghua University to salvage this corpus of invaluable manuscripts from the Hong Kong antique market. Based on AMS ^{14}C analysis, the bamboo slips can be dated to about 305±30 BCE, which is to say toward the end of the middle of the Warring States period. This is consistent with the opinion of the group of experts that Tsinghua University convened to evaluate them. As of the end of 2021, after more than ten years of work preserving, editing, and studying the more than 2,500 separate slips, eleven volumes, including sixty-one different texts, have already been published. We have already finished two-thirds of the editorial work, and the overall picture of these manuscripts is already perfectly clear.

The contents of the Tsinghua manuscripts are extremely rich. Just the texts already published include long-lost texts of chapters of the *Shang shu* 尚書 *Exalted Scriptures* and *Yi Zhou shu* 逸周書 *Leftover Zhou Scriptures*, Western Zhou poems not seen in the *Shi jing* 詩經 *Classic of Poetry*, historical materials of the Three Dynasties period through the Springs and Autumns and Warring States periods, as well as astronomical and hemerological texts. These texts touch on the core topics of Chinese civilization, and their publication has received the attention of scholars in all the related

---

6 Edward L. Shaughnessy, *Rewriting Early Chinese Texts* (Albany, N.Y.: SUNY Press, 2006), 1.

fields and has added invaluable new materials for the rewriting of ancient Chinese history.

After having been buried for more than 2300 years, the Tsinghua slips have now finally been exposed to the light of day, allowing us to see something of the intellectual culture of the pre-Qin period; how fortunate this has been for those of us who study ancient China! Nevertheless, it is disappointing that these slips did not come to us by way of archaeological excavation, but rather were robbed from some unknown tomb, destroying the context from which they were taken and losing whatever other objects may have been buried in the same tomb. This has given us many problems in terms of preserving, editing and studying the slips, but the team at Tsinghua University's Research and Conservation Center for Unearthed Texts (清華大學出土文獻研究與保護中心) has worked very hard to preserve and edit them. We have made use of the most advanced technology to produce enhanced images of the texts; we have made every effort to put the slips, most of which came to us in great disarray, back in order; and, to the extent possible, we have attempted to return them to their original appearance. On this basis, the editorial team has produced transcriptions of the text, as well as notes on disputed characters, all of which has been published in the formal volumes that have made it possible for other scholars also to study the texts.

The publication of each of these volumes has stimulated wide attention within China and even abroad, such that both Chinese and foreign scholars have produced a great many studies of the manuscripts. At the same time that foreign scholars have written articles about the Tsinghua manuscripts, they have also translated some of them into foreign languages, making them available to those who are unable to read Chinese. However, these translations have been occasional, based on individual scholars' own interests. This suggested to us the need to organize a systematic effort to translate all of the manuscripts. But this is truly an intimidating project. After all, these texts are over 2300 years old, and even if the basic editorial work has been relatively well done, there are still many characters and phrases that still have not been explained, and for some of the manuscripts there is no scholarly consensus at all regarding their meaning. Because of this, one can imagine just how difficult it would be to translate these texts into a foreign language, not to mention one of a completely different culture. It demands that the translators not only thoroughly understand the language of the texts, but also their historical background. This requires the very greatest of scholarly competence.

Fortunately, the internationally renowned scholar Edward L. Shaughnessy has already succeeded in translating some of the Tsinghua manuscripts, and his translation of the *Yi Zhou shu* texts has allowed us to see the dawn of this work. In 2019, while Shaughnessy was visiting Tsinghua University, we proposed this translation project to him and invited him to join us in a cooperative effort. After careful deliberation and much communication back and forth, Shaughnessy has organized a team of translators and is working together with us to bring this giant project to fruition. At the beginning of 2020, when this effort was just taking shape, we agreed to work together to make available the results of our research on the manuscripts and to provide the best possible conditions for the translations. I myself organized the editorial team at Tsinghua University's Research and Conservation Center for Unearthed Texts to produce revised editions of the manuscripts, to reorganize them according to their contents, to provide more detailed notes, and to translate them into modern Chinese, to be made available to the English translators. Shaughnessy has been responsible for organizing the team of excellent international scholars to undertake the translations, and is responsible for the quality of their work. After considerable consultation, we have settled on the principles of translation, the format, the framework of the series, and the publisher. As of the end of 2021, this project is finally on the way forward, with the Tsinghua team and the English translation team both making progress toward the publication of the revised editions of the manuscripts and of the translations.

The translation and publication of the Tsinghua manuscripts is an enterprise of great significance, but it is also one that will require a long-term effort. We hope that this effort will advance still further the scholarship on the Tsinghua manuscripts, and we hope too that it will also contribute to scholarly cooperation between Chinese and foreign scholars. We sincerely hope both that all scholars will give enthusiastic aid and support to this project, and will provide criticism and suggestions.

For my part, I am extraordinarily pleased and honored to have the opportunity to work with Shaughnessy and his team to undertake this English translation. As the first volume of the series becomes available to readers, I am happy to express my highest admiration and gratitude to Shaughnessy and the international team of translators he has assembled. I also express heartfelt thanks to Tsinghua University for its wholehearted support of this project, as well as to Tsinghua University Press and to all those friends whose hard work has made possible the publication of these English translations.

General Preface II
Edward L. Shaughnessy

Early in 2006, rumors about an important new cache of ancient bamboo-slip manuscripts began to circulate on the Hong Kong antiques market. This was but the latest in a rash of antiquities coming on the market as a result of tomb robbing in China that began in the early 1990s. Reprehensible though tomb robbing is, robbing both the ancients of their dignity and also modern science of knowledge about the context from which the antiquities came, cultural organs within China, especially museums and universities, have taken it upon themselves to "rescue" and repatriate these products of traditional Chinese civilization. This has been especially true of bamboo-slip manuscripts, the writings on which are regarded as the highest expression of this civilization. Thus, in 2008, Tsinghua University of Beijing dispatched a small group of select scholars led by Li Xueqin 李學勤 (1933–2019), at the time universally acknowledged as the leading expert on all aspects of early Chinese cultural history, to go to Hong Kong to examine this new cache of manuscripts. According to an account by Liu Guozhong 劉國忠, now a member of Tsinghua University's Research and Conservation Center for Unearthed Texts (出土文獻研究與保護中心), once Li determined the slips to be authentic, the university moved quickly to arrange for their purchase.[1]

The bamboo slips, totaling nearly 2,500 slips or fragments of slips in all, arrived at Tsinghua University in July 2008. When the plastic wrapping in

---

1   Liu Guozhong, *Introduction to the Tsinghua Bamboo-Strip Manuscripts*, tr. Christopher J. Foster and William N. French (Leiden: Brill, 2016), 51–54. Tsinghua University claimed that the slips had been donated by an anonymous alumnus.

which the slips had been transported to Beijing was opened, scholars there discovered that a form of mold was developing on many of them. They immediately commenced intensive efforts to preserve the slips; these efforts, which required almost three months, were ultimately successful.[2] A preliminary inventory conducted during the preservation work identified 2,388 slips or fragments bearing writing, to which unique serial numbers were assigned. Subsequent work with the slips turned up writing on another hundred or so pieces, such that the total number of fragments bearing writing is close to 2,500. Also at this time, pieces without writing were sent to the Peking University Accelerator Mass Spectrometry (AMS) Laboratory for ^{14}C testing; the result was a date of 305 BCE $\pm$ 30 years. This matched well the evaluation of both Tsinghua researchers and also a group of China's senior-most paleographers, who were brought to Beijing to evaluate the slips in October of 2008; they agreed that the calligraphy and format of the slips is consistent with other slips known to date to the end of the Middle Warring States period or the beginning of the Late Warring States period, i.e., roughly 300 BCE. The final step in the preservation work was the making of high-resolution photographs of the slips; thereafter, it was from these photographs that the Tsinghua editorial team would work, while the original slips were sealed away in a climate-controlled environment submerged in trays of distilled water.[3]

---

2 For a detailed narrative of this preservation work, see Liu, *Introduction to the Tsinghua Bamboo-Strip Manuscripts*, 54–69. Liu was one of three researchers tasked by Tsinghua to work with the original slips, and he kept a detailed diary of all of their efforts, so his account should be authoritative.

3 The tomb from which the slips came was almost certainly filled with water, providing an anaerobic environment conducive to the preservation of organic material such as bamboo. It is for this reason that slips such as these, once unearthed, are generally preserved submerged in water.

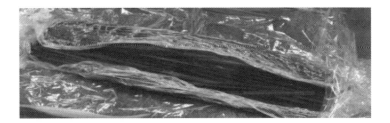

Tsinghua Slips arrive at Tsinghua University; 15 July 2008

Tsinghua Slips before and after being returned to natural color

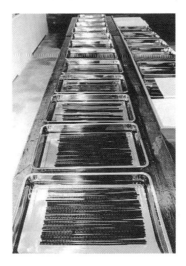

Tsinghua Slips in trays of distilled water

During the preservation and photographic work, the editorial team was able to arrive at some preliminary understanding of the content of the slips. Nevertheless, it was only after that work was completed that editorial work could begin in earnest. The first order of business was to identify how many different discrete texts there were, and which slips belonged to which texts. Because the slips had been robbed from a tomb, when they arrived at Tsinghua University, they had become largely separated from their original context. Thus, the identification of texts depended on the sort of typological analysis that archaeologists usually employ: placing slips of similar length and width together; noting the locations of the straps that were used to bind them together (sometimes leaving a distinct mark on the bamboo, and usually marked as well by small notches on the side of the bamboo intended to keep the strap from sliding up and down on the slip); identifying paratextual features of the slips (placement of text above or below the top and bottom binding strap, the presence or absence of numbers indicating the sequence of the slips, the use and types of punctuation, as well as features on the reverse side of the slips including the presence or absence of titles, diagonal slash marks presumably made during the preparation of the slips, and occasional "ghost" characters left imprinted from other slips); and examination of the calligraphy (assuming that a discrete text would feature a consistent calligraphic hand). After placing slips into groups of these features, the editors turned finally to their content. In this regard, they were often able to rely on comparisons with received literature to identify text that continued from one slip to another. Often of crucial importance in this respect was sequence numbers found on the bottom or reverse side of numerous slips, a feature seen for the first time with the Tsinghua manuscripts.

In the course of this editorial work, the original approximately 2,500 fragments of slips have been rejoined into a total of 1,811 discrete slips, which the editors have further grouped into seventy-five different texts. The texts run the gamut from chapters of the *Shang shu* 尚書 *Exalted Scriptures* (also known as the *Classic of Documents*) and the *Yi Zhou shu* 逸周書 *Leftover Zhou Scriptures* to an anecdotal history of China from the early Western Zhou

(c. eleventh century BCE) to the early fourth century BCE and a chronicle of the capitals of the state of Chu 楚, from collections of poetry to an extensive handbook on milfoil divination, and include a great many discrete texts concerning the political philosophy of China's classical age, the Spring and Autumn and Warring States periods. The first volume, which includes nine of these texts, was published toward the end of 2010. Since then, the Tsinghua University Research and Conservation Center for Unearthed Texts has published the manuscripts at the rate of one volume per year, under the general title *Qinghua daxue cang Zhanguo zhujian* 清華大學藏戰國竹簡 *Warring States Bamboo Slips in the Collection of Tsinghua University*.[4] These are deluxe editions with full color photographs, exacting transcriptions, careful annotations, complete concordances for each volume, and tables of information regarding the physical features of each slip. Each new publication has generated great scholarly interest both in China and also abroad.

As just one indication of the great interest that the Tsinghua manuscripts hold, the first volume includes two texts that correspond to chapters of the *Shang shu*. These have conclusively resolved the greatest outstanding debate in the entire history of Chinese textual criticism: the question of the authenticity of the so-called *guwen* 古文 or "ancient script" chapters of that text. One of these manuscripts is entitled by the editors **Yin gao* 尹誥 *Announcement of Yin*.[5] It corresponds with the chapter "Xian you yi de"

---

4   For Volume One, see Li Xueqin 李學勤 ed.-in-chief, Qinghua daxue Chutu wenxian yanjiu yu baohu zhongxin 清華大學出土文獻研究與保護中心 ed., *Qinghua daxue cang Zhanguo zhujian (yi)* 清華大學藏戰國竹簡（壹）(Shanghai: Zhong Xi shuju, 2010).

5   *Qinghua daxue cang Zhanguo zhujian (yi)*, 4–5 (full-size photographs), 41–43 (double-size photographs), 132–134 (transcription and notes). In a similar manner, Volume Three of the Tsinghua manuscripts contains a three-part text, each part of which is self-titled as *Fu Yue zhi ming* 傅敓之命 *Fu Yue's Command*. This text corresponds with "Yue ming" 說命 "Command of Yue" chapter found in the *guwen Shang shu*. However, the contents of the Tsinghua *Fu Yue zhi ming* are completely different from the "Yue ming" chapter, again showing the spurious nature of the latter. See Li Xueqin 李學勤 ed.-in-chief, Qinghua daxue Chutu wenxian yanjiu yu baohu zhongxin 清華大學出土文獻研究與保護中心 ed., *Qinghua daxue cang Zhanguo zhujian (san)* 清華大學藏戰國竹簡（叁）(Shanghai: Zhong Xi shuju, 2012), 2–7 (full-size photographs), 29–51 (double-size photographs), 121–131 (transcription and notes).

咸有一德 "Both Had a Singular Virtue" found only in the *guwen* version of the *Shang shu*. A passage from the text is also quoted in the classic *Li ji* 禮記 *Record of Ritual*, where it is referred to as "Yin ji" 尹吉 (though *ji* 吉 "auspicious" is clearly a mistake for the graphically similar *gao* 告 "to announce" [itself an abbreviated form of the word *gao* 誥 "announcement"]).[6] This *Li ji* quotation is included in the *guwen Shang shu* version of the text, and is found also in the Tsinghua manuscript. However, everything else in the Tsinghua manuscript is completely different from the *guwen Shang shu* text. This seems to confirm that the *guwen Shang shu* text was fabricated, probably in the early fourth century CE, on the basis of this one early quotation and other materials then circulating, a hypothesis first proposed almost three hundred years ago.[7] The Tsinghua manuscript, on the other hand, represents the authentic early version of this chapter. The resolution of this question alone would serve to make the Tsinghua manuscripts one of the great discoveries of Chinese history. But there is much, much more as well. The panel of experts convened by Tsinghua University to examine the manuscripts in October 2008 was not exaggerating in the least when it said this about them:

> These Warring States bamboo slips are tremendously valuable historical artifacts, whose contents speak to the very core of

---

6   *Li ji zhengyi* 禮記正義, in *Shisan jing zhushu* 十三經注疏 (Beijing: Zhonghua shuju, 1980), 55 ("Zi yi" 緇衣), 420 (1648). It should be noted that there are two different early manuscripts of this text, and both of them write the name of the text quoted as *Yin gao* 尹誥; see Jingmen shi bowuguan 荊門市博物館 ed., *Guodian Chu mu zhujian* 郭店楚墓竹簡 (Beijing: Wenwu chubanshe, 1998), 17 (photograph), 129 (transcription); Ma Chengyuan 馬承源 ed., *Shanghai bowuguan cang Zhanguo Chu zhushu (yi)* 上海博物館藏戰國楚竹書（一）(Shanghai: Shanghai Guji chubanshe, 2001), 46 (photograph), 176 (transcription).

7   The first detailed presentation of this hypothesis was made by Yan Ruoqu 閻若璩 (1636–1704) in his *Shang shu guwen shuzheng* 尚書古文疏證, in *Huang Qing jingjie xubian* 皇清經解續編 (Jiangyin: Nanjing shuyuan, 1888), vols. 6–10. For Western-language studies of the issue, see Paul Pelliot, "Le *Chou King* en caractères anciens et le *Chang Chou che wen*," *Mémoires concernant l'Asie Orientale* 2 (1916): 123–177; Benjamin Elman, "Philosophy (*I-Li*) versus Philology (*K'ao-cheng*): The *Jen-hsin tao-hsin* Debate," *T'oung Pao* 2nd ser. 69.4–5 (1983):175–222.

traditional Chinese culture. This is an unprecedented discovery, one which will inevitably attract the attention of scholars both here and abroad. It promises to have a lasting impact on many different disciplines, including but not limited to Chinese history, archaeology, paleography and philology.[8]

Tsinghua University established the Tsinghua University Research and Conservation Center for Unearthed Texts to study and preserve these manuscripts. Its first director was Li Xueqin. While the Center has very admirably fulfilled these responsibilities, in his Foreword to Liu Guozhong's *Introduction to the Tsinghua Bamboo-Strip Manuscripts*, Professor Li stressed that the further study of the manuscripts requires a collective endeavor.

> The significance of the Tsinghua slips cannot be overstated. It has fallen on us to preserve, edit, and eventually publish these manuscripts; what exciting research may come from these efforts is a question that must be answered in turn by the entire academic community.[9]

Liu Guozhong himself returned to this point in the conclusion to his work:

> The content of the Tsinghua slips can be very difficult to decipher. These are not manuscripts that can be explicated by only a handful of people over a short duration of study, but rather any comprehensive understanding of this collection will require careful analysis that spans a much longer period of time. Research on bamboo and silk manuscripts is at times very pragmatic and detail-oriented. Piecing together one slip, or one fragment of silk sheet, interpreting just one character or one

---

8 "Report on Authentication" (鑒定意見), quoted at Liu, *Introduction to the Tsinghua Bamboo-Strip Manuscripts*, 72.
9 *Ibid.*, xii.

sentence — each of these tasks requires much time and effort. Publication of the first volume of the Tsinghua slips was only possible due to the combined efforts of many scholars, who put much care and research into this project already. However, for this reason, publication of our editing report should mark only the first stage of research on the Tsinghua slips. Really it is only just the beginning. We hope that now many more scholars will conduct research on these remarkable artifacts, that you will join our team and help to bring study of the Tsinghua slips to a whole new level.[10]

It is in this spirit that early in the year 2020, the Research and Conservation Center for Unearthed Texts of Tsinghua University organized two separate projects to extend still further the research on these manuscripts. The first project, undertaken by scholars at Tsinghua University, is to produce "collated interpretations" (*jiaoshi* 校釋) volumes devoted to one or a group of related individual texts, summarizing scholarship on the texts published (largely, though not exclusively, in Chinese) in the years since their original publication; these volumes will not feature the same groupings of texts as the original publication *Tsinghua daxue cang Zhanguo zhujian*, but rather will group the texts based on various relationships (whether of content or codicology).[11] We expect this project to be complete in eighteen volumes. The second project is to produce English-language translations and studies of the manuscripts. These translations will be produced by a team of Western translators, the translator of each volume hand picked for their expertise with the contents of that volume. Each of these volumes of translation will mirror the "collated interpretations" volumes in terms of content, though the translations will not necessarily reflect the interpretations of the Tsing-

---

10 *Ibid.*, 208–209.
11 Huang Dekuan 黃德寬 and Xia Hanyi 夏含夷 (Edward L. Shaughnessy) ed.-in-chief, *Qinghua daxue cang Zhanguo zhujian jiaoshi* 清華大學藏戰國竹簡校釋 (Beijing: Shangwu yinshuguan, 2024).

hua editors, either in the original volumes or in the "collated interpretations" volumes. While the different contents of the different volumes will require somewhat different approaches, each volume will feature a general introduction placing the contents of the volume in their scholarly context, followed by carefully annotated translations of the individual text or texts. Each text will also be provided with a brief introduction discussing its significance, and will also feature translations of related texts from China's traditional literature when relevant. These volumes will be the work of the individual translator responsible for the volume, and will appear under his or her name.

In short, through the international collaboration of these two teams of scholars, and with the active support of the Tsinghua University Press, we look forward to sharing these Tsinghua Manuscripts with readers throughout the world. In closing, it is fitting to echo the sentiment of Liu Guozhong quoted above: "We hope that now many more scholars will conduct research on these remarkable artifacts, that you will join our team and help to bring study of the Tsinghua slips to a whole new level."

A Note on the Authenticity of the Tsinghua Manuscripts and the Ethics of Preserving Looted Cultural Artifacts

The publication of each successive volume of *Qinghua daxue cang Zhanguo zhujian* 清華大學藏戰國竹簡 *Warring States Bamboo Slips in the Collection of Tsinghua University* has demonstrated anew the conclusion reached by the panel of experts convened in October 2008 to evaluate the value of the manuscripts: "These Warring States bamboo slips are tremendously valuable historical artifacts, whose contents speak to the very core of traditional Chinese culture." Nevertheless, it cannot be denied that the value of the manuscripts is diminished by virtue of their having been robbed from some unknown tomb and then smuggled onto the antique market, with any information of either their provenience or provenance being unknown. Doubts have been expressed both in China and abroad about other collections of looted manuscripts, such as those of the Shanghai Museum and

Peking University,¹² though these have been met both in China and abroad by extensive discussions of authentication techniques.¹³ With respect to the Tsinghua manuscripts, although as noted above Tsinghua University sent pieces of bamboo without writing to the Peking University Accelerator Mass Spectrometry (AMS) Laboratory for ^{14}C testing, and also invited a group of China's senior-most paleographers to authenticate the slips, both sorts of tests agreeing that the slips date to roughly 300 BCE, the publication of the first volume was also met by some doubts about the authenticity of the manuscripts.¹⁴ As the volumes of *Qinghua daxue cang Zhanguo zhujian* have been published, there has developed a consensus among other scholars in China that the manuscripts are authentic, and do indeed date to the Warring States period.

Artifactual and archaeological evidence in support of the authenticity of the Tsinghua manuscripts has subsequently become available, corroborating the scientific and paleographic analyses. In 2010, Sun Peiyang 孫沛陽, working with the Peking University Han slips, discovered for the first time lines cut into the verso side of the slips, a feature that was subsequently found also on archaeologically excavated slips, such as those at Guodian 郭

---

12 For doubts regarding the Shanghai Museum manuscripts, see Xing Wen, "New Light on the *Li Ji* 禮記: The *Li Ji* and the Related Warring States period Guodian Bamboo Manuscripts," *Early China* 37 (2014): 522–523; and for those about the Peking University manuscripts, see Xing Wen 邢文, "Beida jian *Laozi* bianwei" 北大簡《老子》辨偽, *Guangming ribao* 光明日報, 8 August 2016; "Bianzheng zhi mei yu sandian toushi — Beida jian *Laozi* zai bianwei" 辯證之美與散點透視——北大簡《老子》再辨偽, *Guangming ribao*, 12 September 12 2016.

13 See Hu Pingsheng 胡平生, "Lun jianbo bianwei yu liushi jiandu qiangjiu" 論簡帛辨偽與流失簡牘搶救, *Chutu wenxian yanjiu* 出土文獻研究 9 (2010): 76–108; Christopher J. Foster, "Introduction to the Peking University Han Bamboo Strips: On the Authentication and Study of Purchased Manuscripts," *Early China* 40 (2017): 167–239.

14 Jiang Guanghui 姜廣輝, "'Qinghua jian' jianding keneng yao jingli yige changqi guocheng — Zai tan dui *Bao xun* pian de yiwen" "清華簡"鑒定可能要經歷一個長期過程——再談對《保訓》篇的疑問, *Guangming ribao* 光明日報, 8 June 2009; Jiang Guanghui, "*Bao xun* yiwei xinzheng wuze" 《保訓》疑偽新證五則, *Zhongguo zhexueshi* 中國哲學史 2010.3: 30–34; Jiang Guanghui, Fu Zan 付贊 and Qiu Mengyan 邱夢燕, "Qinghua jian *Qi ye* wei weizuo kao" 清華簡《耆夜》為偽作考, *Gugong bowuyuan yuankan* 故宮博物院院刊 4.168 (2013): 86–94; Jiang Guanghui, with Fu Zan, "Qinghua jian *Yin gao* xian yi" 清華簡《尹誥》獻疑, *Hunan daxue xuebao (shehui kexue ban)* 湖南大學學報（社會科學版）28.3 (2014): 109–114.

店.¹⁵ While the exact function of these lines is still a topic of discussion, it is generally agreed that the lines were made in antiquity in the production of slips from the original bamboo stems. These verso lines are also found on the Tsinghua slips, and since they entered into the collection of Tsinghua University in 2008, two years before Sun Peiyang's discovery, this constitutes almost incontrovertible artifactual evidence for the authenticity of the slips.¹⁶

Even better evidence of the authenticity of the Tsinghua slips has come from a subsequent archaeological discovery. On 30 October 2020, archaeologists at the Jingzhou Museum 荊州博物館 excavated a tomb, numbered M46, at the Zaolinpu 棗林鋪 Paper Factory, with at least 535 inscribed bamboo slips in it. These slips can be divided into five different types, with nine discrete texts. One of these, which the excavators have given the title *Wu Wang Fuchai qi shi fa Yue* 吳王夫差起師伐越 *Fuchai, King of Wu, Raised Troops and Attacked Yue* matches very closely the Tsinghua manuscript entitled by the Tsinghua editors *Yue Gong qi shi* 越公其事 *May the Lord of Yue Attend*.¹⁷ These are both lengthy texts, the Tsinghua version being written on seventy-five slips and the Zaolinpu version written on seventy-nine slips. While there are a number of variants between the two manuscripts, there is no doubt that they are one and the same text. Since the Tsinghua *Yue Gong qi shi* manuscript was published prior to the excavation of the Zaolinpu manuscript, the authenticity of which is beyond question, it could not have been copied from that text and so it too is almost surely authentic.¹⁸ And since the slips of this one Tsinghua manuscript were embedded in

---

15 Sun Peiyang 孫沛陽, "Jiance bei hua xian chutan" 簡冊背劃綫初探, *Chutu wenxian yu guwenzi yanjiu* 出土文獻與古文字研究 4 (2011): 449–462. See, too, Li Tianhong 李天虹, "Hubei chutu Chu jian (wuzhong) geshi chuxi" 湖北出土楚簡（五種）格式初析, *Jiang Han kaogu* 江漢考古 2011.4: 102–106.

16 See Jia Lianxiang 賈連翔, *Zhanguo zhushu xingzhi ji xiangguan wenti yanjiu: Yi Qinghua Daxue cang Zhanguo zhujian wei zhongxin* 戰國竹書形制及相關問題研究——以清華大學藏戰國竹簡為中心 (Shanghai: Zhong Xi shuju, 2015), esp. 82–102.

17 See Zhao Xiaobin 趙曉斌, "Jingzhou Zaozhi jian *Wu Wang Fuchai qi shi fa Yue* yu Qinghua jian *Yue Gong qi shi*" 荊州棗紙簡《吳王夫差起師伐越》與清華簡《越公其事》, in *Qinghua Zhanguo Chujian Guoji xueshu yantaohui lunwenji* 清華戰國楚簡國際學術研討會論文集, Beijing, November 2021, 6–11.

18 It is interesting to note that the Zaolinpu text shows that the title given the Tsinghua text

mud together with the other slips when they arrived at Tsinghua University in 2008, it furthermore stands to reason that they too are authentic.

In addition to questions about the authenticity of the Tsinghua manuscripts, other scholars have raised questions about the ethics of working with looted materials. For instance, Paul R. Goldin has argued "when a looted artifact is repatriated by being purchased at great cost, the process only encourages more looting in the future,"[19] and he has suggested that scholars ought to refuse to study such materials. Scholars at the Research and Conservation Center for Unearthed Texts of Tsinghua University join scholars throughout China and abroad in decrying the scourge of tomb-robbing that has plagued the country for the last three decades. But they view the work they do to preserve, edit, and publish the manuscripts in their collection as both a scholarly and a moral responsibility. What is more, it is entirely consistent with the United Nations "Convention on the Means of Prohibiting and Preventing the Illicit Import, Export and Transfer of Ownership of Cultural Property" of 1970, Article 7 of which states:

> The States Parties to this Convention undertake:
> (a) To take the necessary measures, consistent with national legislation, to prevent museums and similar institutions within their territories from acquiring cultural property originating in another State Party which has been illegally exported after entry into force of this Convention, in the States concerned. Whenever possible, to inform a State of origin Party to this

---

by the Tsinghua editors was based on a faulty understanding of the final slip of that manuscript. The last four characters of the text are "*yue gong qi shi*" 越公其事, which the Tsinghua editors interpreted as the title, even though these characters followed immediately after the preceding phrase, and were not separated by a blank space as usually seen with titles. The Zaolinpu manuscript also writes "*yue gong qi shi ye*" 越公其事也 together with the preceding text, and what is more follows it with a section ending ┗ mark. See Zhao Xiaobin, "Jingzhou Zaozhi jian *Wu Wang Fuchai qi shi fa Yue* yu Qinghua jian *Yue Gong qi shi*," 11.

19 Paul R. Goldin, "*Heng Xian* and the Problem of Studying Looted Artifacts," *Dao* 12.2 (2013): 158.

Convention of an offer of such cultural property illegally removed from that State after the entry into force of this Convention in both States;

(b) (i) to prohibit the import of cultural property stolen from a museum or a religious or secular public monument or similar institution in another State Party to this Convention after the entry into force of this Convention for the States concerned, provided that such property is documented as appertaining to the inventory of that institution;

(ii) at the request of the State Party of origin, to take appropriate steps to recover and return any such cultural property imported after the entry into force of this Convention in both States concerned, provided, however, that the requesting State shall pay just compensation to an innocent purchaser or to a person who has valid title to that property. Requests for recovery and return shall be made through diplomatic offices. The requesting Party shall furnish, at its expense, the documentation and other evidence necessary to establish its claim for recovery and return. The Parties shall impose no customs duties or other charges upon cultural property returned pursuant to this Article. All expenses incident to the return and delivery of the cultural property shall be borne by the requesting Party.[20]

This international convention, to which China is a party, is concerned exclusively with the exportation of cultural artifacts beyond national boundaries. Since the Tsinghua manuscripts originated in China, it is the respon-

---

[20] "Convention on the Means of Prohibiting and Preventing the Illicit Import, Export and Transfer of Ownership of Cultural Property of 1970," at: https://www.unesco.org/en/legal-affairs/convention-means-prohibiting-and-preventing-illicit-import-export-and-transfer-ownership-cultural.

sibility of relevant Chinese cultural institutions — such as Tsinghua University — to make every effort to ensure that they do not leave the country. Within the country of origin, cultural and scholarly organizations have the right — and the responsibility — to preserve and make these manuscripts available to the broader public. It is this spirit that motivates the various publication projects of Tsinghua University's Research and Conservation Center for Unearthed Texts, very much including this series *The Tsinghua University Warring States Bamboo Manuscripts.*

Conventions

Manuscripts are based on Li Xueqin 李學勤 ed.-in-chief, Qinghua daxue Chutu wenxian yanjiu yu baohu zhongxin 清華大學出土文獻研究與保護中心 ed., *Qinghua daxue cang Zhanguo zhujian* 清華大學藏戰國竹簡, Vols. 1–8 (Shanghai: Zhong Xi shuju, 2010–2018) and Huang Dekuan 黃德寬 ed.-in-chief, Qinghua daxue Chutu wenxian yanjiu yu baohu zhongxin 清華大學出土文獻研究與保護中心 ed., *Qinghua daxue cang Zhanguo zhujian* 清華大學藏戰國竹簡, Vols. 9–15 (Shanghai: Zhong Xi shuju, 2019–) as the publication of record. Titles of texts are generally given as in that publication, with the following qualification: when a title is specified on the manuscript, it is rendered as written; when no title is specified on the manuscript, but has been assigned by the modern editors, the title is given as they have it, but preceded with an asterisk (*) to indicate this difference.

The contents of individual volumes follow those of Huang Dekuan 黃德寬 and Xia Hanyi 夏含夷 (Edward L. Shaughnessy) ed.-in-chief, *Qinghua daxue cang Zhanguo zhujian jiaoshi* 清華大學藏戰國竹簡校釋 (Beijing: Shangwu yinshuguan, 2024), hereafter "*Jiaoshi*," and do not necessarily follow the contents of the individual volumes of *Qinghua daxue cang Zhanguo zhujian*. These volumes have been reorganized to reflect conceptual coherence. When there is evidence that two or more manuscripts were originally bound together, whether published in a single volume of *Qinghua daxue cang Zhanguo zhujian* or not, they are kept together.

Individual volumes of this series are the work of the individual author credited on the title page, who is solely responsible for the contents. Nevertheless, all authors would like to express their gratitude to colleagues at Tsinghua University's Research and Conservation Center for Unearthed Texts, who have been most helpful in sharing their scholarship with us, and also to the authors of the other volumes in the series, who have graciously read and criticized the volumes in draft.

Volumes begin with two General Prefaces by the general editors, followed by a Preface by the author of the individual volume. This is followed in turn by an introductory chapter or chapters discussing general questions concerning the manuscript or manuscripts included in the volume. Each individual manuscript is presented in separate chapters, with the following contents:

A. An introduction that discusses codicological features of the manuscript in question: material features of the manuscript, including its calligraphy and relevant paratextual features.
B. A slip-by-slip transcription and annotated translation. These transcriptions and translations are presented in four registers:
   1. Images of the individual graphs on a single bamboo slip, presented horizontally. These have been scanned from high-resolution photographs of the slips, with the background removed, and hand-processed to produce a black-and-white image. These have been prepared for the volumes by colleagues at the Research and Conservation Center for Unearthed Texts of Tsinghua University, to whom we express our heartfelt gratitude for the clarity brought about by this process.
   2. Strict or literal transcriptions (generally called *yanshi liding* 嚴式隸定 in Chinese) of the individual graphs, in which each individual component is rendered into its *kaishu* 楷書 equivalent, generally in the same position within the character. In almost all cases, these transcriptions follow those given in *Qinghua daxue*

cang Zhanguo zhujian. This transcription includes only punctuation that is explicit on the manuscript. Other conventions in it are as follows:

a) ☐ indicates a single missing graph

b) ☒ indicates an indeterminate number of missing graphs

c) punctuation seen on the manuscript is reflected with formal symbols

   (1) duplication marks, whether indicative of the standard ligature (*hewen hao* 合文號) or repetition (*chongwen hao* 重文號) marks, are given with a subscript equals sign (=)

   (2) heavy black squares or rectangles in the text, which seem to serve to indicate a break in the text or emphasis, are rendered formulaically as ■, ▃ or ▙ as appropriate

   (3) the 乙-shaped mark routinely used to mark the end of a section or end of a text is given as ↙

3. Interpretive transcriptions (generally called *kuanshi liding* 寬式隸定 or *podu* 破讀 in Chinese), in which a graph of the manuscript is rendered with a corresponding modern Chinese character (written in standard Chinese characters [*fantizi* 繁體字]). In addition, this transcription includes modern punctuation (according to standard Chinese punctuation) indicating the author's understanding of the grammar. At the end of this line of transcription is given the number of the slip, in Chinese characters inside subscript square brackets ($_{[\ -\ ]}$). Other conventions are as follows:

   a) ☐ indicates a single missing graph

   b) ☒ indicates an indeterminate number of missing graphs

c) [ ] indicates a missing graph or graphs that can be restored on the basis of context
d) , ; : ? ! are used as in English punctuation
e) 、 (called *dunhao* 頓號 in Chinese) separates items in lists
f) 。 represents a period (.)
g) " " indicates direct quotation (like quotation marks [" "] in English)

4. An annotated English translation. Note numbers are given to the English text whether the note concerns matters of transcription or of translation. At the end of this line of translation is given the number of the slip, in Arabic numerals inside subscript square brackets ($_{[1]}$). Some general comments concerning the translations seem warranted.

a) Every effort has been made to translate and not just to paraphrase the text, though without sacrificing intelligibility in English. Wording that is missing because of a break in the bamboo slip is indicated by two dots (..) for a single missing character (corresponding to □ in the Chinese transcription) or by three dots (…) for an indeterminate number of graphs (corresponding to ☒ in the Chinese transcription). Wording that is missing because of a break in the slip or that is otherwise illegible, but which can be restored on the basis of context is placed inside square brackets ([ ]). Wording that is added to make the meaning clear or to supply added information is placed inside parentheses (( )), though such additions are used only when essential.

b) The annotations are explanatory, but not exhaustive. In general, translations consistent with the explanation given in ***Qinghua daxue cang Zhanguo zhujian*** are not noted. Translations that differ and which draw on other scholarship, whether formally published or available on the internet, generally note either the earliest study to present the explanation or the most definitively argued study and explain why it has been adopted. Full bibliographic citations are provided at the first mention of any scholarship within a single chapter; thereafter, within that chapter citation is by author, an abbreviated title, and page number. For scholarship found on the internet, the url and date of posting, if available, is given; it is often not possible to provide page numbers for internet citations. Reconstructions of archaic pronunciation are generally given as in Axel Schuessler, ***Minimal Old Chinese and Later Han Chinese: A Companion to*** Grammata Serica Recensa (Honolulu: University of Hawai'i Press, 2009), with the addition of the rhyme group as typically given in Chinese scholarship.

C. The complete text, first in Chinese (according to the interpretive transcription) and then in English, presented in paragraph form to show the underlying structure of the text. These presentations include the slip numbers (₍₋₎ in the Chinese text, and [1] in the English text) so as to facilitate comparison with the annotated slip-by-slip transcription and translation. This is generally unannotated.

D. Any additional material that might bear on the understanding of the manuscript.

Preface and Acknowledgements

The manuscripts in this volume were first published in volumes 6 and 7 of the Tsinghua University Bamboo Manuscripts.[1] In light of the vast amount of scholarship engaging with these materials, the Research and Conservation Center for Unearthed Texts, Tsinghua University, decided to collate the various readings offered in Chinese language scholarship, and to publish updated editions and translations of the Tsinghua Manuscripts.[2] The translations in the present volume were prepared with consultation of the scholarship available up to July 2022, and I have been able to review a draft of the *Collated Interpretations* volume kindly shared with me by my colleague Wei Dong 魏棟.[3]

Not all scholarship on the materials has made it into the footnotes. Chinese language scholarship on manuscripts moves fast, often taking place on online fora and websites hosted by centers of manuscript study.[4] These

---

1 Li Xueqin 李學勤 ed.-in-chief, Qinghua daxue Chutu wenxian yanjiu yu baohu zhongxin 清華大學出土文獻研究與保護中心 ed., *Qinghua daxue cang Zhanguo zhujian (liu, qi)* 清華大學藏戰國竹簡（陸、柒）(Shanghai: Zhong-Xi shuju, 2016, 2017).
2 Huang Dekuan 黃德寬 ed.-in-chief, *Qinghua daxue cang Zhanguo zhujian jiaoshi* 清華大學藏戰國竹簡校釋 (Beijing: Shangwu yinshuguan, *forthcoming*).
3 Wei Dong 魏棟, Qinghua daxue cang Zhanguo zhujian *jiaoshi di liu ji*《清華大學藏戰國竹簡》校釋第六輯 (Beijing: Shangwu yinshuguan, *forthcoming*).
4 Especially the *Jianbo luntan* 簡帛論壇 forum, http://www.bsm.org.cn/forum/ and the websites of the centers of manuscript study at Fudan, Wuhan, and Tsinghua University, *Fudan daxue chutu wenxian yu guwenzi yanjiu zhongxin wangzhan* 復旦大學出土文獻與古文字研究中心網站, http://www.fdgwz.org.cn/; *Wuhan daxue jianbo yanjiu zhongxin wangzhan* 武漢大學簡帛研究中心網站, http://www.bsm.org.cn/; *Qinghua daxue chutu wenxian yanjiu yu baohu zhongxin wangzhan* 清華大學出土文獻研究與保護中心網站, https://www.ctwx.tsinghua.edu.cn/.

studies develop previous ideas and from them tend to emerge a consensus of what counts as a valid reading for a particular graph on the bamboo and what simply does not accord with standards of paleography, phonology, or language use for the Warring States period, as we understand them. As such, while I have consulted — as far as I am aware — the majority of scholarship on the materials, I have chosen to remain economical in my annotations and have not listed all opinions on the texts. For more complete — if slightly dated — overviews of the whole gamut of scholarship on the manuscripts and the texts they carry I highly recommend the reader to consult the master's thesis of Zhu Zhongheng's 朱忠恒,[5] and of course the *Collated Interpretations* by Wei Dong.

The texts contained in this volume are conventionally studied side by side with the *Zuo zhuan* 左傳 and the *Guo yu* 國語, if only because of the significant overlap in content. I have chosen not to make this my main approach — this line of inquiry, while highly valuable, is common enough in scholarship already. I have of course compared and contrasted the materials to these and other texts. Especially for the *Zuo zhuan*, the masterful translation by Durrant, Li, and Schaberg has been invaluable as a resource and I have quoted it whenever relevant.[6] But ultimately, the *Zuo zhuan* and the narratives discussed here are different texts altogether, and while fully aware of the cultural literacy that was certainly shared by the audience, I have tried to understand the texts as if they were relatively stand-alone narratives, if only to reveal their qualities as part of a recognizable form.

My focus in trying to understand these texts has therefore been the way they appear to us as narratives that tell a story about the past. As a result, my translations do (at least) two things that may not always sit well with readers accustomed to more rigid understandings of a particular function word or sentence structure. For one, I have chosen to translate rather literally many

---

5   Zhu Zhongheng 朱忠恒, "Qinghua daxue cang Zhanguo zhjian liu jishi" 清華大學藏戰國竹簡六集釋 (Wuhan University, MA Thesis, 2016).
6   Stephen Durrant, Li Wai-Yee, and David Schaberg (tr.), *Zuo Tradition / Zuo zhuan* 左傳: *Commentary on the "Spring and Autumn Annals,"* 3 vols. (Seattle: University of Washington Press, 2016), hereafter referred to as *Zuo Tradition*.

common appellations of Springs and Autumns characters that would normally be understood by convention. For example, in the *Zheng Wen Gong wen Tai Bo* 鄭文公問太伯, Bian fu 邊父 is translated as Sir Bian to preserve the paternal and hierarchic overtones in the honorific suffix *fu* 父.[7]

For the same reasons, Jian shu 蹇叔 in the *Zi Fan Zi Yu* 子犯子餘 is rendered Uncle Jian, in the general respectful *avuncular* sense without implying any actual familial relationship with Lord Mu of Qin. This use of the term is reinforced on slips 9 and 10 of the manuscript wherein *shu* 叔 is used in and of its own as a means of address twice in the space of two slips. The use of *bo* 伯 in Tai Bo "Grand Elder" reveals this same dynamic and while implying seniority does so discursively and not just within the context of the lineage.

I am of course aware that *shu* 叔 generally functions as "birth sequence indicator", in this case the seniority appellation "middleborn" within the lineage and that texts such as the *Zuo zhuan* make productive use of these distinctions.[8] My point here is that in the manuscript texts discussed in this volume, the baseline meaning of "middleborn" for *shu* 叔 or "oldest" *bo* 伯 is effectively wielded to evoke both the hierarchy *and* the closeness of the kin in the dialogue between ruler and advisor. Doing so enables a subtle restructuring of power relations. Not an advisor subservient to a lord but their proverbial "uncle" or "elder". The use of *zi* 子 in courtesy names such as Zi Fan 子犯 or Zi Yi 子儀 is rendered "Mr." here because it functions similarly to the "courteous prefix" in English,[9] without the problematic connotations to philosophers carried by the full-form "master".[10]

In general, the honorific *gong* 公 following the temple name of the ruler is rendered as the title "Lord," and *jun* 君, depending on the context

---

7 Axel Schuessler, *ABC Etymological Dictionary of Old Chinese* (Honolulu: University of Hawaii Press, 2006), 243.
8 See *Zuo Tradition*, XXXIII–XXXV, for instance.
9 *Oxford English Dictionary*, s.v. "Mr, n., sense 1.a", published September 2023, https://doi.org/10.1093/OED/9220885546.
10 I thank reviewer two for pointing me to Wolfgang Bauer, *Der chinesische Personenname* (Wiesbaden: Harrassowitz, 1959), 116–147, who notes the use of *zi* in courtesy names as a means of increasing their visibility as names.

and the mood as either "lord" without capitalization or "ruler." Self-deprecatory modes of address by these same rulers are taken literally, as they often highlight a particular aspect of the character, for example in the use of "the orphaned one" 孤 to highlight the fact that the ruler's father has just passed away and the lord is therefore in the need of assistance. The texts at hand make use of slight differentiations in the mode of address to convey a particular sense of the relationship between the characters of the narrative.

Especially when it comes to rhetorical questions, exclamations, and the frequent use of image-based language, I have tried to convey the drama inherent in the narratives as much as the grammatical form of the language. Where I have felt that I had to choose, while aware of the grammatical finesse in Chinese, I have prioritized conveying the *story* within the narrative. As noted by Chao Fulin 晁福林, when the *Zheng Wu Furen gui ruzi* 鄭武夫人規孺子 has the widow of Lord Wu reminiscence about her late husband's absence, for example, it makes sense to translate *shi* 室 in the sense of his private "chambers" rather than his royal "house" as it conveys the sense of a wife missing her husband:[11]

> 吾君陷於大難之中，處於衛三年，不見其邦，亦不見其室。
> My lord was trapped in great hardship, resided in Wei for three years and could not visit either his state or his chambers.

The texts are filled with such subtleties of meaning and I am afraid I have not given due justice to all of them, despite all the help I received in the preparation of this volume.

I have been fortunate to receive the help of a fantastic team of scholars brought together by Ed Shaughnessy for this project. Chris Foster, Yegor

---

11 Chao Fulin notes that the "chambers" here probably refer (metonymically) to Zheng Wu's wife; see Chao Fulin 晁福林, "Tan Qinghua jian *Zheng Wu Furen gui ruzi* de shiliao jiazhi" 談清華簡《鄭武夫人規孺子》的史料價值, *Qinghua daxue xuebao (zhexue shehui kexue ban)* 清華大學學報（哲學社會科學版）, 2017.3:128–129.

Grebnev, Ethan Harkness, David Lebovitz, Vincent Leung, Jens Østergaard Petersen, Maddalena Poli, Adam Schwartz, Ed Shaughnessy, Ondřej Škrabal, Newell Ann Van Auken, Zhang Hanmo, and Zhou Boqun have saved my readings from many mistakes and improved it in ways too numerous to elaborate. Meeting online on a weekly basis (with some hesitance we took a break for Christmas and such), I have learned a tremendous amount from the group's careful readings and spirited discussions.

I want to thank Zhang Bofan, Yang Qiyu, and Zhang Xinyu for their untiring assistance to the project, my colleagues at the Research and Conservation Center for Unearthed Texts, Tsinghua University for their help and support, Liang Fei, Li Yiqing, and the other editors at Tsinghua University Press for their invaluable assistance, and Paul Nicholas Vogt for the pleasant and instructive collaboration on the Shanghai Museum narratives that helped me form some of the ideas underlying the current study. I want to thank the two reviewers who provided kind and supportive feedback, helping me make sure I put my understanding of these materials in clear terms. Additionally, I received valuable comments on the *Zi Fan Zi Yu* and the **Jin Wen Gong ru yu Jin* from Antje Richter and the anonymous referees at *JAOS* in the preparation of a study on the manuscripts' use of punctuation.[12] Any errors and idiosyncrasies remaining are of course my own.

Last but certainly not least, I thank my family for bearing with my work, which in toddler speak apparently mostly consists of a lot of "blah blah blah."

The writing of this volume has received generous support from the "Western Dissemination and Research of Chinese Unearthed Texts" 中國出土文獻的西方傳播與研究 (G1817) project funded by the "Paleography and Chinese Civilization Inheritance and Development Program" 古文字與中華文明傳承發展工程, and a grant from the Beijing Municipal Foreign High Level Talent Support Plan 北京市外籍高層次人才資助計劃 (J202132).

---

12 Rens Krijgsman, "Punctuation and Text Division in Two Early Narratives: The Tsinghua University **Jin Wen Gong ru yu Jin* 晉文公入於晉 and *Zi Fan Zi Yu* 子犯子餘 manuscripts," *Journal of the American Oriental Society* 143.1 (2023): 109–124.

Introduction to Volume Six

This volume gathers seven Warring States-period manuscripts with stories about Springs and Autumns period affairs from Zheng 鄭, Qin 秦, Jin 晉, and Chu 楚. Originally published in volumes 6 and 7 of the Tsinghua Manuscripts, these were brought together in the *Collated Interpretations* (*Jiaoshi* 校釋) and the present volume because of their topical and material proximity.[1] The sequence chosen reflects the chronological order and geographical division amongst the texts, and where relevant, the similarity of the writing support:

1. **Zheng Wu Furen gui ruzi* 鄭武夫人規孺子 (Zheng, events ca. 744 BCE)
2. **Zheng Wen Gong wen Tai Bo* A 鄭文公問太伯(甲) (Zheng, events ca. 672 BCE)
3. **Zheng Wen Gong wen Tai Bo* B 鄭文公問太伯(乙) (same as above)
4. *Zi Fan Zi Yu* 子犯子餘 (Qin, Jin, events ca. 637–636 BCE)
5. **Jin Wen Gong ru yu Jin* 晉文公入於晉 (Qin, Jin, events ca. 636–628 BCE)
6. *Zi Yi 子儀 (Qin, events ca. 621 BCE)
7. *Zhao Jianzi 趙簡子 (Jin, events ca. 500? BCE)

The events narrated in these texts span well over two and a half centuries,

---

1 Wei Dong, Qinghua daxue cang Zhanguo zhujian *jiaoshi di liu ji*.

involving well-known figures from Zheng, Qin, and Jin, as well as Chu history. The majority of these narratives present dialogues between famous rulers of the period and a varied cast of interlocutors, including foreign emissaries, ministers, generals, elders, and mothers. Except for the outlier *Jin Wen Gong ru yu Jin* — likely a companion piece to the *Zi Fan Zi Yu* — which is a monologue, the texts are all dialogues that feature the rulers in an inferior position to their interlocutors. These rulers are either looking for goodwill or they receive advice — solicited or unsolicited — from their often more experienced counterparts. While the texts themselves do not have counterparts in received literature, this power dynamic between ruler and minister is familiar from the larger body of literature on the Springs and Autumns.[2] In terms of style, this type of text has been compared especially to texts such as the *Guo yu*, and other unearthed texts such as the narratives on Springs and Autumns Chu from the Shanghai Museum manuscripts, and, of course, the *Zuo Zhuan*.[3]

This volume is divided into two parts. The first part introduces the texts and studies their narrative form. I focus on the narrative structure of the texts, the types of narration and dialogue, the way the story's characters are represented, and the use of image-based language. The second half of the study presents the texts line by line, followed by a presentation of the full text in Chinese and English.

1. Manuscripts and Affiliation

Broadly speaking, the slips of the manuscripts in this volume are of two lengths.[4] The *Zi Yi and the *Zhao Jianzi feature shorter slips, at

---

2   See especially David Schaberg, "Playing at Critique: Indirect Remonstrance and the Formation of *Shi* Identity," in Martin Kern, ed., *Text and Ritual in Early China* (Seattle: University of Washington Press, 2005), 194–225, and Yuri Pines, "From Teachers to Subjects: Ministers Speaking to the Rulers from Yan Ying 晏嬰 to Li Si 李斯," in Garret Olberding, ed., *Facing the Monarch: Modes of Advice in the Early Chinese Court* (Cambridge: Harvard University Asia Center 2013), 69–99.
3   See for instance Chen Wei 陳偉, *Xin chu Chujian yandu* 新出楚簡研讀 (Wuhan: Wuhan daxue, 2010) 203–214, 238–241, and Li Ling 李零, *Jianbo gushu yu xueshu yuanliu* 簡帛古書與學術源流 (Beijing: Sanlian, 2004), 202 ff.
4   Measurements are necessarily tentative; I here present merely a rough average maximum

around 41.6–41.8 cm in length (maximum values) and 0.6 cm in width. The other manuscripts feature slips around 45 cm in length and 0.5–0.6 cm in width. Of the latter group, at least the *Zheng Wu Furen gui ruzi*, *Jin Wen Gong ru yu Jin, Zi Fan Zi Yu*, and *Zheng Wen Gong wen Tai Bo* manuscripts feature verso-lines carved on the back of the slips.[5] Among the manuscripts, only the *Zi Fan Zi Yu* comes with a title written on the back of the first slip.[6] All manuscripts are bound with three threads. Obvious similarities aside, the present state of the evidence does not allow us to make a firm assessment as to whether some of the manuscripts formed a larger, multi-text manuscript or not.[7] Similarities in the material carrier may equally have been due to production habits associated with a specific workshop,[8] and need not necessarily reflect that the texts were bound together to form a single manuscript.

Nevertheless, given that the Shanghai Museum manuscripts contain evidence of multi-text manuscripts with multiple historical narratives from the Springs and Autumns, it is possible that some of these manuscripts were originally bound together.[9] Especially the *Zi Fan Zi Yu* and *Jin Wen Gong ru yu Jin* would have formed a likely couple, given the presence of a title on the former and the historical progression between the events narrated in both texts.[10]

---

slip length. The slips shrink (unevenly) during the process of conservation, and, while working from the same images, the editors and Li Songru 李松儒 arrive at different measurements.

5   For their use in the ordering of these texts, see for example Jia Lianxiang 賈連翔, "Qinghua jian *Zheng Wu Furen gui ruzi* pian de zai bianlian yu fuyuan" 清華簡《鄭武夫人規孺子》篇的再編連與復原, *Wenxian* 文獻 2018.3: 54–59.

6   For an overview of the regularities in material characteristics of the Tsinghua manuscripts and how these can be used to infer scribal habits, see Xiao Yunxiao, "Mediating between Loss and Order: Reflections on the Paratexts of the Tsinghua Manuscripts," *Bamboo and Silk* 6.2 (2023): 186–237.

7   See Rens Krijgsman and Paul Nicholas Vogt, "The One Text in the Many: Separate and Composite Readings of an Early Chinese Historical Manuscript," *Bulletin of the School of Oriental and African Studies* 82.3 (2019): 473–492.

8   See Krijgsman, "Punctuation and Text Division in Two Early Narratives."

9   See for example, Xiao Yunxiao 肖芸曉, "Shilun Qinghua zhushu Yi Yin san pian de guanlian" 試論清華竹書伊尹三篇的關聯, *Jianbo* 簡帛 8 (2013): 471–476.

10 With those considerations in mind, some likely pairings may be: the *Zi Yi* and *Zhao*

Table 1: Basic manuscript data[11]

#	MS	Length	Width	Binds	Verso-Lines
1	*Zheng Wu Furen gui ruzi 鄭武夫人規孺子	~45	0.6	3	Yes
2	*Zheng Wen Gong Wen Tai Bo A 鄭文公問太伯 A	~45	0.6	3	Yes
3	*Zheng Wen Gong wen Tai Bo B 鄭文公問太伯 B	~45	0.6	3	Yes
4	Zi Fan Zi Yu 子犯子餘	~45	0.5	3	Yes
5	*Jin Wen Gong ru yu Jin 晋文公入於晋	~45	0.5	3	Yes
6	*Zhao Jianzi 趙簡子	~41.6	0.6	3	Not visible
7	*Zi Yi 子儀	~41.7	0.6	3	Not visible

Li Songru 李松儒 has argued that the *Zi Yi manuscript shares the same handwriting with the Zi Fan Zi Yu, *Jin Wen Gong ru yu Jin, *Zhao Jianzi, and *Yue Gong qi Shi 越公其事 from volume 7, and the *Zheng Wu Furen gui ruzi, *Zheng Wen Gong wen Tai Bo A and B from volume 6, and finally, parts of the *Huang Men from volume 1 of the Tsinghua manuscripts.[12] In general, the similarities between the writing of these manuscripts are quite apparent, and it seems likely that the materials came out of a single workshop, and possibly were written by a single scribe.[13]

It could be argued that Li Songru's analysis is not decisive because it is based mostly on stylistic criteria, and focuses less on structural qualities

---

Jianzi; the *Zheng Wen Gong wen Tai Bo A and/or B, and the *Zheng Wu Furen gui ruzi.

11 The data is drawn from the source publications and Li Songru 李松儒, "Qinghua qi Zi Fan Zi Yu yu Zhao Jianzi deng pian ziji yanjiu" 清華七《子犯子餘》與《趙簡子》等篇字迹研究, Chutu wenxian 出土文獻 15 (2019): 177–192; she also provides data on the relative spacing of the binds. Length and width in cm.

12 See Li Songru, "Qinghua qi Zi Fan Zi Yu yu Zhao Jianzi deng pian ziji yanjiu," 177–192, and references to earlier work therein. Shi Zhenying 史楨英, "Ye shuo Qinghua daxue cang Zhanguo zhujian (qi) shouxie wenti 也說《清華大學藏戰國竹簡（七）》寫手問題, Wuhan daxue jianbo zhongxin wangzhan, June 15, 2018, http://www.bsm.org.cn/?chujian/7899.html argues that at least for vol. 7, there are two scribes, basing herself on visual and statistical criteria, accordance to patterns of variation etc.

13 This assessment is shared by the editors, and this in part informed the current grouping of manuscripts. More materials associated with this scribe are forthcoming in future publications. See also Xiao, "Mediating Between Loss and Order."

of the graphs.[14] Nevertheless, given the variation introduced through errors of form visible throughout the manuscripts,[15] and the fact that variation in structure in the *Zheng Wen Gong wen Tai Bo* A and B stemmed from the scribe faithfully copying the structural features of the writing on the base-manuscripts, it seems fair to say that variation in structure is likewise not necessarily a determining criterion to distinguish hands in this batch of manuscripts and that stylistic criteria are therefore a useful aid in establishing scribal hand.

2. Approach

The texts in this volume are commonly studied alongside, and in comparison with, the *Zuo zhuan*, *Guo yu*, and other collections of narratives on the Springs and Autumns period.[16] The *Collated Interpretations* by Wei Dong, includes a wide range of references to these texts, inviting the reader to draw parallels and look for (dis-) similarities.[17] Much of the scholarship has focused on the historical import of the texts, and how they provide information previously unknown from, or in contradiction to, the transmitted and increasingly growing unearthed record of narratives about the Springs and Autumns.[18] In the analyses that follow, I will adopt a different perspective and instead analyze the literary structure and narrative devices of the texts.

These texts spoke to a Warring States audience, and conveyed a partic-

---

14 See Matthias Richter, "Tentative Criteria for Discerning Individual Hands in the Guodian Manuscripts," in Xing Wen 邢文 ed., *Rethinking Confucianism: Selected Papers from the Third International Conference on Excavated Chinese Manuscripts, Mount Holyoke College, April 2004* 儒學的再思考：第三屆國際簡帛研討會論文集 (San Antonio: Trinity University, 2006), 132–147, for an early critique of only relying on stylistic criteria in determining scribal hands.

15 See for example Shi Xiaoli 石小力, "Qinghua jian di liu ji zhong de e zi yanjiu" 清華簡第六輯中的訛字研究, *Chutu wenxian* 出土文獻 2016.2: 190–197.

16 The literature is vast; a good example is Chen Wei 陳偉, "Zheng Bo ke Duan 'qianzhuan' de lishi xushi" 鄭伯克段"前傳"的歷史敘事, *Zhongguo shehui kexue bao* 中國社會科學報, 30 May, 2016.

17 Wei Dong, Qinghua daxue cang Zhanguo zhujian *jiaoshi di liu ji*.

18 Li Xueqin 李學勤, "Youguan Chunqiu shishi de Qinghua jian wuzhong zongshu" 有關春秋史事的清華簡五種綜述, *Wenwu* 文物 2016.3: 79–83.

ular reading of the past to its audience. As stories, they filled gaps in other contemporary renditions of the past. These narratives present a characterization of the figures that inhabited the past, probing into their motivations and rhetorical skill, and, to an extent, their inner workings. By analyzing these texts as stories about Springs and Autumns' Zheng, Qin, Jin, and Chu, I make no claim about their historicity or factuality relative to other materials, or, whether contemporaries read them as fiction.[19] Instead, I discuss how these texts drew on narrative technique and devices to make for a compelling reception experience. The value of these texts to a Warring States audience, I suggest, did not just reside in the narratives' ability to contextualize past events, but also in their ability to transport their audiences and *make present* the past.[20]

In the following study, I draw on the toolkit of narratology. The study of narrative has gained renewed traction in our approach to the ancient world, especially in Classics, owing to the application of this toolkit to materials ranging from Homeric epic to classical historiography.[21] While narratives from classical Greece, Rome, Egypt, and Sumer, for instance, displayed markedly different concerns in their texts, reading them as narrative has provided us with a range of theoretical and methodological insights useful to the study of early Chinese texts, in particular the historiographical materials

---

19 A classic statement of this problem can be found in Hayden White, *The Content of the Form: Narrative Discourse and Historical Representation* (Baltimore: Johns Hopkins University Press, 1990).

20 See here the excellent discussion by Jonas Grethlein, *Experience and Teleology in Ancient Historiography: 'Futures Past' from Herodotus to Augustine* (Cambridge: Cambridge University Press, 2013), 1–26.

21 Irene de Jong, *Narratology and Classics: A Practical Guide* (Oxford: Oxford University Press, 2014), this study also provides a conveniently structured introduction to some of the key concepts drawing on the work of narratologists such as Mieke Bal, *Narratology: Introduction to the Theory of Narrative, Third Edition* (Toronto: University of Toronto Press, 2009); Gerard Genette, Jane E. Lewin trans., *Narrative Discourse: An Essay in Method* (Ithaca: Cornell University Press, 1980); Irene de Jong, René Nünlist, and Angus Bowie eds., *Narrators, Narratees, and Narratives in Ancient Greek Literature* (Leiden: Brill, 2004), esp. part 2, pp. 101–211; and Jonas Grethlein and Antonios Rengakos eds., *Narratology and Interpretation: The Content of Narrative Form in Ancient Literature* (Berlin: Walter de Gruyter, 2009), esp. part 5, pp. 451–571.

that concern us here.[22] Through comparison, the familiar becomes problematic, allowing us to see writing about the past in a new light.

Within early China studies, there is likewise a tradition of analyzing narrative technique, often focusing on transmitted texts, particularly the *Zuo zhuan*.[23] But the unearthed materials are not the *Zuo*. While the *Zuo* is a vast collection of complexly interwoven narratives, most of the narratives covered in this study stood on their own. At most, some of these texts may have shared a manuscript carrier, but there is no attempt to connect these texts through references or common events.[24] Nevertheless, the analysis below shows that these narratives shared a number of formal characteristics and themes. Do these unearthed narratives form a set or even genre of their own? What varieties do they reveal? Do they reveal similar concerns, share habits of using literary devices, and perhaps even assume a common audience? These are some of the questions that this study is concerned with.

Without the *Zuo zhuan*'s interpretive framework and paratextual encapsulation mediating the reader's engagement with the text,[25] texts and their stories behave and are read differently. In the unearthed narratives, there is no going back and forth between stories within a larger collection, no prophecy or signs inserted early on or flashbacks revealing the origins of events,[26]

---

22 For example, Yang Lei, *Narrative Devices in the Shiji: Retelling the Past* (Albany: State University of New York Press, 2024), and the work by Xia Dekao 夏德靠, for instance, his *Guo yu xushi yanjiu*《國語》敘事研究 (Beijing: Zhishi chanquan, 2015).

23 In recent years, see especially Wai Yee Li, *The Readability of the Past in Early Chinese Historiography* (Cambridge: Harvard University Asia Center, 2007), and David Schaberg, *A Patterned Past: Form and Thought in Early Chinese Historiography* (Cambridge: Harvard University Asia Center, 2002). For early incisive enquiries into the form of narration, see Ronald Egan, "Narratives in Tso Chuan," *Harvard Journal of Asiatic Studies* 37.2 (1977): 323–352. For an intellectual historical analysis, see Yuri Pines, *Foundations of Confucian Thought: Intellectual Life in the Chunqiu Period* (Honolulu: University of Hawaii Press, 2002).

24 Unlike the Shanghai Museum Springs and Autumns narratives, see Krijgsman and Vogt, "The One Text in the Many."

25 Genette, Gérard, Jane E. Lewin trans., *Paratexts: Thresholds of Interpretation* (Cambridge: Cambridge University Press, 1997).

26 The one exception is perhaps the *Zi Yi* which repeatedly looks back and alludes to events in the past. Note that some of the Shanghai manuscripts allow for such readings, often providing echoes between back-to-back narratives and rendering certain acts as, for example, signifying a future downfall; see Krijgsman and Vogt, "The One Text in the Many."

there are no unifying paratextual features such as the *junzi* 君子 comments or a *Chunqiu* 春秋 *Springs and Autumns* frame of reference heading units of text. The stories, in general, feature a comparatively limited range of interlocutors and the description of these characters does not hinge on earlier narratives introduced in preceding stories. It is tempting, therefore, to introduce such an interpretive framework by reading the materials through and against the *Zuo*. But this is likely not how a recipient encountered the narratives. And while we cannot know for sure whether the texts gathered in this volume were at some point read together, I will show that while they have their differences, they certainly also share a range of commonalities in their mode of narration that allows us to read the stories together.

That is not to say that the materials included in this volume operated in a vacuum. Narratives about the Springs and Autumns period functioned within a broader horizon of expectations and touched upon the same basic framework of the past.[27] Indeed, that is exactly why we must ask how these short narratives managed to edge out a niche within Warring States historiographical discourse at large.[28] More often than not, the texts cover events,

---

27 As I show below, a variety of context specific arguments are made in the individual texts that do not ascribe to a restricted set of identifiable valuations, a common motif that has been discerned within the *Zuo*. The stories discussed here may draw from similar motifs; see for instance, the Lord Wen of Jin stories' predilection with heaven's agency and accordance with ritual propriety (see Li, *The Readability of the Past*, ch. 4), but they are not the mainstay.

28 It should be clear by now that I treat the majority of unearthed manuscripts as having enjoyed a meaningful life before internment. Evidence of deliberate destruction of manuscripts (a particularly salient example is the deliberate damaging of several slips in the Shanghai Museum *Kongzi Shilun 孔子詩論) and genres that may have been particularly meaningful to the dead (think of the *Gao Di Shu* 告地書) aside, we have no reason to assume that the dead were supposed to enjoy other materials than the living, or, that the funeral economy (see Guo Jue, "Western Han Funerary Relocation Documents and the Making of the Dead in Early Imperial China," *Bamboo and Silk* 2.2 (2019): 141–273) went out of its way to produce fundamentally different historiographical narratives catering to the dead and their new home in the grave. For an exploration of that possibility, see Yuri Pines, "History as a Guide to the Netherworld: Rethinking the *Chunqiu shiyu*," *Journal of Chinese Philosophy* 31 (2003): 101–126. For an evaluation of the arguments on reading buried texts as, among others, grave goods, see the discussion in Enno Giele, "Using Early Chinese Manuscripts as Historical Source Materials," *Monumenta Serica* 51 (2003): 409–438.

(re-)imagined or not, that preceded or followed famous episodes of Springs and Autumns history.²⁹ One striking aspect is the lack of overlap and explicit intertextuality between the *Zuo* and the manuscripts in the concrete narration of events despite the fact that many of the unearthed narratives seem to tell the story left untold in these other traditions. Whether the unearthed narratives were engaging with accounts in the process of crystallization, that had ended up or would end up in collections such as the *Zuo*, or were simply responding to commonplaces in the collective memory of the Warring States, cannot be said for certain.³⁰

Even if we assume that texts close in form to the narratives in the *Zuo* (let alone the *Zuo zhuan* text as a whole) were widely distributed during the Warring States, the existence of shorter individual narratives and sets of narratives in the unearthed records should alert us that the past was received in other ways as well.³¹ Recent discoveries, if anything, have alerted us to the vast variety of forms of historiography. These include chronological and topical anecdotes collections, lists, and essays.³² The preservation bias and selection criteria

---

29 See Chen Wei, "Zheng Bo ke Duan 'qian zhuan' de lishi xushi"
30 The lack of concrete intertextual referencing seems to favor the latter position, but the engagement with exactly those scenes not narrated in texts such as the *Zuo* seems to support some form of the former position.
31 For a discussion of the formation and spread of the *Zuo*, but with limited reference to the unearthed record, see Durrant, Li, and Schaberg, *Zuo Tradition*, introduction, esp. XXXVIII-LIX. For a discussion on the diversity of unearthed historiography, see Yuri Pines, *Zhou History Unearthed: The Bamboo Manuscript Xinian and Early Chinese Historiography* (New York: Columbia University Press, 2020), esp. chapter 3.
32 Examples include, but are not limited to, the Tsinghua University manuscript's **Xinian* 繋年; see Newell Ann van Auken, forthcoming in this series, Olivia Milburn, "The *Xinian*: An Ancient Historical Text from the Qinghua University Collection of Bamboo Books," *Early China* 39 (2016): 53–109, and, Pines, *Zhou History Unearthed*; the **Chu ju* 楚居, Chris Foster, forthcoming in this series; the **Chunqiu Shiyu* 春秋事語, Pines, "History as a Guide to the Netherworld"; the narratives from the Shanghai Museum manuscripts, in particular the **Zhaowang huishi — Zhaowang yu Gong zhi Zhui* 昭王毀室 · 昭王與龔之脽, **Pingwang wen Zhengshou* 平王問鄭壽, **Pingwang yu Wangzi Mu* 平王與王子木, and the *Zhuangwang ji Cheng* 莊王既成, see Krijgsman and Vogt, "The One Text in the Many"; If we include materials not covering the Springs and Autumns period, the picture is complicated even further; see, for example, the Shanghai Museum *Rongchengshi* 容成氏; see Rens Krijgsman, "Elision and Narration: Remembering and Forgetting in Some Recent Unearthed Historiographical Manuscripts," in Albert Galvany, ed., *The Craft of Oblivion: Aspects of Forgetting and Memory in Ancient China*

these materials reflect should serve as a counterpoint to the biases inherent in the processes of selection that informed the transmitted materials.³³

Operating in broadly the same literary ecosphere, the narratives in this volume provided additional layers of meaning, contextualization, and characterization to the motivations, causes, and influences of events prominent in the historical memory of the Warring States literary elite. Some, such as the *Zheng Wu Furen gui ruzi* and the *Zi Fan Zi Yu*, explore the moral or psychological drives of famous rulers from the past. Others, such as the *Zheng Wen Gong wen Tai Bo* and *Zhao Jianzi*, note the reasons for the success and failures of former rulers in lists of short vignettes. The *Jin Wen Gong ru yu Jin*, is one of the few narratives here that focus on the successes of the ruler. And finally, the *Zi Yi* poetically explores the background of a potential alliance between Qin and Chu. Beyond examining these narratives for what they tell us about what happened in the past, they allow us to look into the techniques and devices used in telling their stories. Possibly, this in turn reveals some of the expectations a Warring States audience had about the narration of the past. Within the stable framework of historical events, these narratives explored new motivations, explanations, and philosophical underpinnings, all the while catering to their audience in their use of narrative form.

(Honolulu: University of Hawaii Press, 2023), 49–69.

33 For a discussion on Chu mortuary culture as a background to recent manuscript finds, see Lothar von Falkenhausen, "Social Ranking in Chu Tombs: The Mortuary Background of the Warring States Manuscript Finds," *Monumenta Serica* 51 (2003): 439–526. For a discussion on the distribution of the Daybook manuscript finds, but bearing on the issue of manuscript distribution and significance more broadly, see Alain Thote, "Daybooks in Archaeological Context," in *Books of Fate and Popular Culture in Early China: The Daybook Manuscripts of the Warring States, Qin, and Han*, ed. Donald Harper and Marc Kalinowski (Leiden: Brill, 2017), 11–56. For recent archaeological finds corroborating the spread of these types of texts, see for instance the *Wuwang Fuchai qi shi fa Yue* 吳王夫差起師伐越 excavated from the Zaolinpu paper factory Warring States tomb site in Jingzhou 荊州, Hubei. For a discussion, see Zhao Xiaobin 趙曉斌, "Jingzhou zaozhi jian *Wuwang Fuchai qi shi fa Yue* yu Qinghua jian *Yue Gong qi shi*" 荊州棗紙簡《吳王夫差起師伐越》與清華簡《越公其事》, paper presented at the conference "Qinghua Zhanguo Chujian guoji xueshu yantaohui" 清華戰國楚簡國際學術研討會, Tsinghua University, Beijing, November 19, 2021, and Chris Foster's volume in this series.

Chapter One
Narratives about the Past

In this chapter I discuss the basic form of narration characterizing the texts in this volume. These narratives contain a narrative frame and dialogue. On the primary level of the frame, the narrator situates the text in time and space. In addition, the narrator establishes relations between the characters of the narrative and labels the genre and illocutionary force of the speech in the dialogues, as admonitions, for instance. The frame thus provides a reading key that tells the audience how to situate and interpret the claims made within the dialogue along a set of discursive power relations.

With the roles and types of speech established, the next part in the narrative structure features a dialogue component that revolves around the search for and granting of knowledge beneficial to the rule of the lord. In most of the narratives, the advisor possesses this knowledge and the ruler seeks it out. The narratives predominantly feature a simple dialogic back and forth along this structure but some are almost monological. Those examples with higher narrative complexity feature a narrator that makes active use of detailed scene changes and a deeper understanding of the inner workings of the characters to increase the audience's expectations and heighten the dynamism and drama of the story. The voice of the narrator, while appearing neutral, is not just matter-of-factly relating the events of the narrative, but actively shapes the way the audience relates with the characters and judges their actions.

In the following, I give two examples of how the unearthed narratives covered in this study differ from the rendition of the same events in the *Zuo zhuan* to show the influence of the mode of narration on how we perceive the story.

For example, the *Zi Fan Zi Yu* manuscript version tells the story of the final part of Chong'er's 重耳 exile from his native Jin. After having been at times hosted and denied safe haven by a range of states, we find Chong'er residing in Qin just before he returns to Jin. In this rendition of the story, Chong'er's travels are only alluded to and not given particular importance. Instead, it highlights particular elements in the structure of events by focusing on the importance of Chong'er's advisors and by emphasizing the lord's moral uprightness and hesitance. But other versions are possible. When we look at the narrative in the *Zuo*, as noted by Wai-Yee Li, Chong'er's peregrinations are told in retrospect so as to highlight cause and effect, following a logic that departs from the *Zuo*'s more regular sense of contingency.[1] The *Zuo* rendition of this series of events (i.e., Chong'er is in Qin and about to go back to Jin) presents a story of "recompense" (*bao* 報) about all the states that supported or denied help to Chong'er in his peregrinations.[2] This element is not present in the *Zi Fan Zi Yu*'s rendition.

The manuscript instead gives much more agency and voice to the lord's followers who subtly talk back or correct their royal interlocutors. Accordingly, the *Zuo*'s focus on interstate power-dynamics can be contrasted to the *Zi Fan Zi Yu*'s back and forth between ruler and advisors in their competition over the power of discourse. Their different ways of telling the narrative thus make for a different reading experience, produce different arguments from historical precedent, and focus on different power relations.

Another example of how different narratives provide vastly different readings and emphases on features of the past can be found in the **Zheng Wu Furen gui ruzi* manuscript. The narrative is set after the death of Lord Wu of Zheng; his widow Lady Wu admonishes their son and heir to wait

---

1 Li, *The Readability of the Past*, 85
2 For an analysis, see Maria Khayutina, "Die Geschichte der Irrfahrt des Prinzen Chong'er und ihre Botschaft," in *Kritik im alten und modernen China: Jahrbuch der Deutschen Vereinigung für Chinastudien* 2, ed. Heiner Roetz (Wiesbaden: Harrassowitz, 2006), 20–47.

and learn from the ministers and high officials before taking command as the ruler. The story then develops around the son's initial silence and the resulting frustration of the ministers, before ending on a dramatic cry of a son not living up to his father's expectations. In the *Zuo* rendition, Lady Wu has a different role. She is presented as a femme fatale who in a story of political maneuvering schemes to have her younger son, Gongshu Duan 共叔段, placed in power instead.[3] Reading the *Zheng Wu Furen gui ruzi* with the *Zuo zhuan* account in mind would have a reader focus on the mother's advice with suspicion,[4] but this would be misleading. The manuscript's narrative is not interested in developing any potential suspicion and on the whole has a rather neutral presentation of Lady Wu.[5] It focuses on the struggles of the young lord to meet the expectations of his late father and his officials and therefore advances a decidedly more psychological reading of Lord Wen of Zheng's rise to power.

These different narrations of the same historical set of events therefore amount to different stories altogether. Their differences reside not just in a particular ordering of events or choice of central theme. They involve choices in the role division of narration and dialogue, the focalization (i.e., the viewpoint and access to information) of narrators and characters, and the use of language and images to color a particular presentation of the events. Taken together, these aspects reveal the particular reading of an event the narratives wanted to present, whether about the moral underpinnings of Chong'er's actions, or the advice of a mother faced with a son not entirely ready to follow into the footsteps of his father. These narratives explore the motivations and drama that drove historical characters and events to provide an intimate and vivid view into the past.

---

3 Compare the famous rendition in *Zuo*, Yin 1.
4 See, for example, Chao Fulin, "Tan Qinghua jian *Zheng Wu furen gui ruzi* de shiliao jiazhi," 127.
5 The narrative even appears to take explicit distance from this reading by noting on slips 6 and 7 that, "This old wife will also not dare to tell tales about brothers and relatives by marriage to disturb the governance of the high officials."

1.1 Basic Narrative Form

Narration refers to the act of telling a story, which can occur on a number of levels. The narratives included in this volume tend to develop a basic structure which in archetypical (often monological) form was used at least from early bronze inscriptions and the *shu* 書 "*writings*" onwards.[6] They open with a short frame introducing the dialogue or monologue. At this primary level of narration, an all-knowing but uninvolved, narrator describes the situation and reports the dialogue.[7] This same narrator then introduces a speaker, a character narrator. These character narrators, operate on a secondary level of narration and introduce the main problem of the story, before introducing other interlocutor(s). These in turn may present the solution, or deepen the problem for another character to resolve.

Many of these narratives only feature a short opening frame and introduction of characters ("X said"). In more complex narratives, the switches between characters are presented as a scene change, and involve more extensive narration, describing how one character left and another enters, and sometimes indicating the mood or setting of the dialogue. While it is tempting to equate the narrator with an author figure, for example, a court scribe from Zheng or a storyteller from Jin, this should be avoided.[8] For one thing, an author may hold different ideas from their narrators, but we will also see that the narrator and the characters (arguably rendered by the same author)

---

6   Compare texts such as the "Luo gao" 洛誥 and "Kang gao" 康誥 in the *Shang shu* 尚書. Note that in those texts the interlocutors to the king are often only indirectly present. Likewise, some of the devices in use in these texts date back to the lineage narratives included as early as the *Shi Qiang* Pan 史墻盤; for instance, see David M. Sena, "Arraying the Ancestors in Ancient China: Narratives of Lineage History in the 'Scribe Qiang' and 'Qiu' Bronzes," *Asia Major* 25.1 (2012): 63–81.

7   See de Jong, *Narrators and Narratees*, and, Irene de Jong, *Narrators and Focalizers: The Presentation of the Story in the Iliad* (London: Bloomsbury Academic, 2004 [1987]), for discussions concerning the various roles and levels of involvement of the narrator. The narrator in bronze inscriptions (donor) and in the *Shang shu* (royalty or scribe) tends to be at least indirectly involved or at least present in the context of narration whereas the texts in this volume tend to have an uninvolved narrator looking back in time.

8   Compare for instance, Egan, "Narratives in Tso Chuan," *passim*, in a discussion of the role of the narrator in the *Zuo*. For an enlightening discussion on narrators and focalization in the *Iliad*, see de Jong, *Narrators and Focalizers*.

exhibit subtle differences of perspective.[9]

Each of these narrators, be they characters talking about one another or the primary narrator relating the story as a whole, manifests a certain perspective or focalization.[10] By providing such coloring and perspective to the events and the inner workings of the characters, focalization reveals the relation between characters, and between the narrator and characters. Characters are presented by the narrative as having access to different levels of knowledge and discursive power. In the texts studied here, the fundamental story dynamic revolves around the clever manipulation of this access and how it is instrumental to good rule.

Especially within the dialogues, the narratives rely heavily on image-based language, including simile, metaphor, allusion, and language meant to evoke a visual experience. The use of image-based language brings the story alive on a linguistic and experiential level, helping the audience commit to the world created within the space of the narrative, all the while reveling in the character's artistry and skill in decoding, resisting, or accepting the images.

1.2 Frame

A representative example of how an opening frame is structured can be found in the *Zheng Wen Gong wen Tai Bo A:

> 子人成子既死，大伯當邑。大伯有疾，文公往問之。君若曰：……
>
> After Ziren Chengzi had passed away, Grand Elder was in charge of the city. Grand Elder had an illness, and Lord Wen

---

9 The audience of the text and the narratee addressed by the narrator within the text can be distinguished in the same way, see for example de Jong, *Narrators and Narratees*. This distinction does not impact the argument here and as such I refer to the text's audience more broadly.
10 Bal, *Narratology*, 8: "A choice is made from among the various 'points of view' from which the elements can be presented. The resulting *focalization*, the relation between 'who perceives' and what is perceived, 'colors' the story with subjectivity."

went and asked him about it. The ruler said to the effect: ...

The narrator is all-knowing and looks back from a privileged vantage point in history at the events that follow. The audience of the text is supposed to understand references to the characters without any formal introduction. Ziren Chengzi, Grand Elder, and Lord Wen are mentioned without further specification. Of figures from the Springs and Autumns period alone, there are numerous lords carrying the posthumous title "Lord Wen." Many of the designations in these narratives eschew proper names: Tai Bo, or "Grand Elder" is a periphrastic denomination. Such descriptive circumlocutions (more on this below) present a character's role and place in the hierarchy of the narrative.[11]

Important to the narrative here is not to introduce the historical background of the characters, but rather to establish their roles and relations. Grand Elder is presented as a wizened advisor, and we therefore expect him to present admonitions to the ruler, Lord Wen, who is faced with a problem resulting from the death of Ziren Chengzi. They are type-characters that adhere to a common form and we will encounter several of these characters throughout the texts.

The frames tend to use a recurring set of function words to structure the narrative. In the example cited above, the aspect marker *ji* 既 "after" is used to mark the event that, once passed, anchors and provides the background context of the story. By comparison, in other narratives, *xi* 昔 "In days of yore," functions as a marker of a story from the past. Finally, *wen* 問 "ask" in the frame introduces the central question that opens the dialogue and will lead towards the central conundrum of the text. In many of the texts, a character "hears" (*wen* 聞), such as a precedent or a piece of wisdom, which provides the solution to the conundrum, or, presents a deep-

---

11 See for instance de Jong, *Narratology and Classics: A Practical Guide*, 182. Compare e.g., "young child" 孺子, or, "the one unable to cultivate" 不穀. They indicate a particular role and coloring of the characters in the narrative, both in the address of others and in self-representation.

ening of the first question towards a more profound understanding of the problem.

The example from *Zheng Wen Gong wen Tai Bo* is interesting for its introduction of the dialogue, *jun ruo yue* 君若曰 "The ruler said to the effect." This structure echoes the *wang ruo yue* 王若曰 "The king said to the effect" formula often seen in the *Shang shu* and as such marks the speech as a form of paraphrase with a hint of royal gravitas. While recognizable, it is not commonly used in historiographical narratives set in the Springs and Autumns. Its occurrence here is both a conceit to traditional forms all the while showing a trace of the narrator's involvement in the phrasing of the text. The narrator, in marking the illocutionary force and type of speech of the character, suggests how the characters in the story should understand everything that follows.

Finally, this frame takes up another common element: illness as a pretext. The drama bestows a sense of immediacy and necessity to the story and places it within a larger group of deathbed narratives.[12] As the story proceeds, after Lord Wen's question, the lion's share of the narrative focuses on the long and final answer, effectively a monologue, by the Grand Elder. The primary narrator does not return anymore. The frame and opening question appear to have been a mere vehicle for the main focus of the text, i.e., Grand Elder's arguments on how to rule.

The use of such narrative framing as a pretext for philosophical argument is employed quite commonly. The *Zhao Jianzi*, for example, frames the narrative in the context of the court, where the newly appointed general Zhao Jianzi receives a remonstrance from his elder, Fan Xianzi:

趙簡子既受命將軍。在朝，范獻子進諫，曰：……

---

12 Yegor Grebnev, "The *Yi Zhoushu* and the *Shangshu*: The Case of Texts with Speeches," in Martin Kern and Dirk Meyer eds., *Origins of Chinese Political Philosophy: Studies in the Thought and Composition of the* Shangshu (Leiden: Brill, 2017), 249–280, and Paul Nicholas Vogt, "Towards a Metavocabulary of Early Chinese Deathbed Texts," paper presented at *The International Conference on the Tsinghua Bamboo Manuscripts* 清華簡國際研討會, Hong Kong and Macao, 26–28 October 2017.

> Zhao Jianzi had just been made a general. When he was at court, Fan Xianzi offered a remonstrance, saying: …

The narrator indicates that what follows is supposed to be understood as a remonstrance: Fan Xianzi cautions Zhao Jianzi to take responsibility for his own actions and show proper behavior. The narrator follows up on this by noting that, seemingly out of the blue, "Zhao Jianzi asked Cheng Zhuan, saying" 趙簡子問於成鱄曰. By virtue of bringing these two seemingly unrelated scenes together, Cheng Zhuan's advice is presented as an answer to Fan Xianzi's admonishment and presented as the main ideological thrust of the narrative.

In short, these dialogues expand on a basic structure where a question (or problem) is specified or redirected before it is finally resolved. Compared to the speech genre markers specifying illocutionary force (*ruo yue* 若曰, *jin jian yue* 進諫曰) in the opening frame,[13] the dialogues that follow in these two texts do not tend to mark how something is said. We can assume that the speech within the dialogue that ensues follows naturally from the opening question and should be understood in the same sense, as a remonstrance for example. As we will see below, however, the reader of the text also has other clues available so that they can generate an image of the relationships between the characters of the story.

1.3 Scene Changes and Complexity

Some of the narratives are more complex and introduce a number of scene changes to structure the narrative and events. Take the **Zheng Wu Furen gui ruzi*, for instance. In this story, the heir of Lord Wu of Zheng is admonished by his mother, Lady Wu. He is cautioned not to interfere in government until after the mourning period, causing unrest among his

---

13 Bakhtin has theorized on how speech genres used in day-to-day language are primary to the literary production of stories for instance. See Mikhail M. Bakhtin, Vern W. McGee trans., "The Problem of Speech Genres," in *Speech Genres and Other Late Essays* (Austin: University of Texas Press, 2010), 60–102.

ministers. Sir Bian, the senior high official and a benevolent uncle figure like Grand Elder, is sent to inquire, and the tension is finally resolved in the heir's fatalistic answer to these queries.

The opening frame sets the scene at the wake of Lord Wu of Zheng:

鄭武公卒，既殯，武夫人規孺子，曰：……
Lord Wu of Zheng died, and after his coffin had been placed in a temporary grave, the wife of Lord Wu admonished her young child, saying: …

In the speech marked as an "admonition" (*gui* 規), the mother of the future ruler introduces the central problem of this narrative. The ruler-to-be is both young and inexperienced, and will have problems securing his rule. Indeed, the heir is periphrastically introduced as *ruzi* 孺子 ("young child" cognate with and certainly evocative of the image of a babe at his mother's breast, *ruzi* 乳子).[14] In her monologue, the wife of Lord Wu, who is not given a proper name by the narrator but merely a role, also suggests a solution: the heir is to remain silent and uninvolved in the affairs of governance until the mourning period has passed. Later on, Sir Bian seems to challenge this solution by noting the restlessness of the ministers. The remainder of the narrative (eliding the dialogue for ease of reference) develops the burial context of the opening frame to introduce two changes in scene:

> The young child bowed, and then they wailed together. From that moment up to the date of burial, the young child did not dare to have any knowledge of it (i.e., the affairs of government), and left it to the high officials and the hundred functionaries. Everyone was afraid, and each respectfully carried out their

---

14 See Schuessler, *ABC Etymological Dictionary of Old Chinese*, 445. Compare also the argument in Liao Mingchun 廖名春, "*Shangshu* 'ruzi' kao ji qita" 尚書"孺子"考及其他, *Wenxian* 文獻 2019.5: 76–89, which provides a paleographical analysis to argue that the word means the same as "heir" *sizi* 嗣子.

affairs. Sir Bian admonished the high officials, saying: …

It was the Minor Auspicious sacrifice, and the high officials gathered to plan. They then sent Sir Bian to the lord, to say: …

The lord replied to Sir Bian, saying: …

Many historiographical narratives merely feature a simple alternation of the speaker, sometimes noting a scene change in passing. Time structure in these narratives is commonly highlighted with a limited set of connectives, especially *nai* 乃 "then," which generally marks the temporal movement into a new event within a scene, and *yue* 曰 "saying," to indicate the start of the speech.

The **Zheng Wu Furen gui ruzi* is slightly more complex. The scenes are all events within the sequence of the burial ritual. The frame starts with a burial in a temporary grave, *si* 肂. The admonition of the young child in the first scene ends when he wails together with his mother, *lin* 臨. Then, after an ellipsis,[15] the narrative comes to the time of the actual burial, *zang* 葬, the setting for scene two. The final scene is placed at the Minor Auspicious Sacrifice, *xiao xiang* 小祥.[16]

What is more, the primary narrator is aware of the emotional state of the characters, noting that "everyone was afraid and each respectfully carried out their affairs" and describes the action that triggers a change of speaker, "the high officials gathered to plan. They then sent Sir Bian to the lord, to say … " While certainly not a major plot twist, these short descriptions show a rare use of the gaze of the primary narrator into the complexities of the characters and their motives. The majority of these narratives do not have the narrator revealing the inner states of the characters. Instead, a simple reporting of speech is much more common. Compared to the phrase, "Zhao Jianzi asked Cheng Zhuan, saying" quoted above, for example, the

---

15 Using *yi zhi* 以至 "up to" to gloss over details not germane to the plot and progress to the next scene.
16 For these terms and their ritual significance, see Li Shoukui 李守奎, "*Zheng Wu Furen gui ruzi* zhong de sangli yongyu yu xiangguan de lizhi wenti" 《鄭武夫人規孺子》中的喪禮用語與相關的禮制問題, *Zhongguo shi yanjiu* 中國史研究 2016.1: 11–18.

involvement of the narrator in the *Ruzi* stands out. Most of the narratives discussed here include simple dialogues, and sometimes rather monologic responses by the interlocutors, and leave it at that.

Comparable narrative complexity can be found in the *Zi Fan Zi Yu*. As I have noted in earlier work, the narrative provides background drama and detail to Qin's support of Prince Chong'er in his bid for power in Jin.[17] Especially the dialogue portion of the text stands out through its frequent reversal of reader's expectations and witty subversion of the authority of the ruler by the advisors. While changes in scene have some minimal narration, the frequent and longer dialogues stand out in particular. Here I just present the narrative introductions of the dialogues, eliding any speech content:

> [Prince Chong'] Er went from Chu and took to Qin on his heels and resided there for three years ▬ . The lord of Qin thereupon summoned Mr. Fan and asked him ▬ , saying: …
> Mr. Fan replied, saying: …
> After a while the lord then summoned Mr. Yu and asked him, saying: …
> Mr. Yu replied, saying: …
> The lord then summoned Mr. Fan and Mr. Yu, saying: …
> Thereupon he bestowed upon each of them a sword belt and upper and lower garments, and praised them. Then he sent them back ▬ .
> The lord then asked Uncle Jian, saying: …
> Uncle Jian replied, saying: …
> The lord then asked Uncle Jian, saying: …
> Uncle Jian replied, saying: …
> Prince Chong'er asked Uncle Jian, saying: …

---

17 For a detailed description of the narrative and its use of punctuation to guide a particular reception, see Krijgsman, "Punctuation and Text Division in Two Early Narratives."

Uncle Jian replied, saying: …

In these dialogues, the advisor figures repeatedly correct and chide the ruler. This empowerment of the advisor in the dialogue, contrasts with the ostensible authority granted to Lord Mu of Qin in the frame. Where Lord Wen of Zheng mentioned above "went and asked him (Grand Elder) about it" 文公往問之, Lord Mu of Qin "summons" (*zhao* 召) Chong'er's advisors. At the ending of the first scene, Lord Mu "bestows" (*ci* 賜) the advisors with gifts before "sending them off" (*shi* 使). These are acts belonging to the superior, but this ostensible power of the office does not lead the lord's interlocutors into submission. Instead, they chide him on a rare tertiary level of narration, placing words in the ruler's mouth by presenting hypothetical indirect speech; e.g., "If this is what milord would call … " 主如此謂. The primary narrator does not appear aware of any emotional complexity or motivations. Instead, the richness of the narrative is focalized by the advisors within the dialogue, "If he has the fortune to gain an advantage, he does not enjoy it on his own —, and wants everyone to share in it." The power dynamic between advisor and ruler that plays out between the characters mimics the different access to discursive power by the primary narrator and the character narrators.

As with the *Ruzi, the structure of the narrative provides more than a mere indication of the progression of events through time, it adds a layer of narrative expectations, heightens drama, and sharpens contrasts.

1.4 The Narrator Intrudes

Compared to the shorter narrative frames in the stories discussed previously, some texts take much more liberty. Their narrators provide rich descriptions of the setting to the point that it gains a prescriptive, involved, or even ideological dimension. By lacing the description of the setting with seemingly innocuous descriptions of character and motivation, the primary narrator appears to influence the audience's reception of events by coloring the actions and characters.

The *Jin Wen Gong ru yu Jin is revealing in being rather non-dialogic.

In effect, the narrative consists of a frame followed by a series of commands of Lord Wen of Jin, fresh in power, and closes with a list of achievements.[18] The "elders of the state" 屬邦耆老 receive their commands mutely and collectively, and they are not given a voice. The narrator looks back in time to report the words of the ruler and list his victories and achievements, providing a 'summary' of the reign of Lord Wen in a voice that brooks no opposition. The opening frame, while incomplete, hints at the bias of the narrator:

> 晋文公自秦入於晋，端冕□□□□□□□□ [王]母，
> 毋察於好臧偏娸，皆見。明日朝屬邦耆老，命曰:
> When Lord Wen of Jin entered Jin from Qin, he put on his purple robe and hat of office, ... [grand]mother, he refrained from distinguishing between the good and excellent, and the partial and lowly. They were all granted an audience.
> The following day he held court with the elders of the state, and he commanded:

In describing Lord Wen as not distinguishing amongst courtiers, granting each and all an audience, the stock description of the lord in command putting on the apparel of his office is transformed into a prescriptive statement of ideal rule. Following the commands at court, the "inventions" 作 motif, a formula attributing historical firsts to famous rulers, is introduced to describe improvements to the army.[19] "As a result of (these reviews) he (accomplished) great success," the narrator notes, following up with a list of victories to buttress this judgement.

Other narratives, such as the *Zi Yi, are more subtle. This complex narrative is dialogically sophisticated, featuring metaphor and simile encap-

---

18 As a form, this is much more akin to the *Shang shu*'s indirect presentation of interlocutors.
19 This formula calls to mind similar narratives about sage kings and mythic rulers of antiquity; see, for example, Michael Puett, *The Ambivalence of Creation: Debates Concerning Innovation and Artifice in Early China* (Stanford: Stanford University Press, 2002).

sulated in coded song. Nevertheless, the opening frame presents a reading key causing the audience to judge the protagonist-ruler favorably.[20] Roughly three slips are devoted to the frame narrative of narration, detailing the fears and desires of the lord, describing idealized practices of governance, and the preparation and gathering undertaken by the lord and his three counselors to increase the army beyond its original size. Lord Mu uses this display of military might to assure the Chu emissary Mr. Yi that an alliance with Qin against Jin would be favorable to both:

既敗於殽，恐民之大病，移易故職。欲民所安，其亶不更。公益及三謀輔之，靡土不食，耄幼在公。陰者思陽，陽者思陰，民恒不實，乃毀常各務。降上品之，辨官相代，乃有見功。公及三謀慶而賞之。乃券册秦邦之羨餘，自鼉月至于秋至備焉。聚及七年，車逸於舊數三百，徒逸于舊典六百，以視楚子儀於杏會。公曰：…

Having been defeated at Xiao, (Lord Mu of Qin) feared that the people would be greatly distressed, and would move and alter their former occupations. He wanted what would pacify the people, and that their trust would not change. The Lord increasingly joined with the three counselors to support them; there was no area that was not fed, and the elderly and infants were taken care of at public expense. (But) those in the shade desired the sun, and those in the sun desired shade, the people were continuously restless, and this ruined the regularity of everyone's duties. (Lord Mu and his counselors) demoted superiors and evaluated them, and they differentiated officials to replace them, then they achieved results. The Lord joined with the three counsellors to laud and reward them. Then they

---

20 It is unclear why the *gong* 公, Lord Mu of Qin, is not specifically identified in the text but only elliptically through reference to the battle at Xiao. Perhaps the narrative originated from Qin. Local narratives tended to refer to their own lord by honorific only. This would also explain the ideological slant of the text.

registered the manpower and surplus of the Qin state, and they completed (the register) from the Month of the Silkworm (i.e., the height of spring) up to the Height of Autumn. They gathered (manpower and surplus) up to the 7th year (after the battle), and chariots exceeded previous numbers by three hundred, and troops exceeded the previous registers by six hundred. They showed them to Mr. Yi of Chu during the meeting at Xing. The lord said: ...

In the dialogues that follow, no reference is made to military might and instead the focus shifts to literary artistry in carefully crafted songs riddled with figurative language. Just as in the *Zi Fan Zi Yu*, the primary and secondary levels of narration, i.e., the primary narrator and the character narrators, operate in two different registers. Where the former is prescriptive and guides the audience, the latter is encoded, and invites the audience to engage in a playful teasing out of intentions.[21] Even in the final lines of the dialogue, where Lord Mu asks what Mr. Yi will tell his ruler, he receives no straight answer but three metaphors instead. Perhaps the clear prescriptive tone of the frame, '(our) Lord Mu was a good ruler despite his loss at Xiao,' is a strategy to mitigate the poetic vagueness of the message on the secondary level of narration.

1.5 Summary

The way a story is narrated, is crucial to how the contents are presented to the audience. In this chapter I have discussed the structure of these narratives. All narratives contain narrative frames that bracket and present the monologue or dialogue(s) that follow. This opening frame, together with simple and more complex scene changes, is the primary level of narration wherein the primary narrator tells the story. The narrator, even in simpler narratives, steers the reception of the story by marking the type of speech

---

21 Compare the compelling analysis in Schaberg, "Playing at Critique."

or by singling out attributes, feelings, and details of the characters. Through such focalization, the dramatis personae are placed in a certain perspective, guiding the way the audience judges their words and actions. Some of the narratives discussed here are narrated with more complexity than others, and a lot of the actual drama of the story is reserved for the dialogues, to which we turn now.

Chapter Two
Dialogue Dynamics

One of the main themes present across the texts in this volume is the question of gaining access to knowledge. In the dialogues, that make up the lion's share of these narratives, rulers and advisors are presented as type characters competing over a stake in discursive power. Except for the monologic outlier, *Jin Wen Gong ru yu Jin*, in each of the narratives, discursive power and knowledge are reserved for advisor figures. In order to hear the advisor's wise words, the ruler has to ask the right question. Authority rests with the advisors while the rulers are presented as questioning, asking, and in general, slightly lacking in ability. One of the techniques used is periphrasis, wherein short descriptive utterances by characters in self-reference. These designations characterize the role of the speaker and reinforce the power dynamic between advisor and ruler in these stories.

While the term dialogue suggests a spirited back and forth between multiple characters, often the narratives merely include a simple question and answer between the lord(s) and their advisor(s). In effect, some of this dialogue is rather monologic in character. The *Zheng Wen Gong wen Tai Bo* has Grand Elder answer a single question with a disproportionately long answer, and the *Ruzi* starts with an admonition taking up over half of the text. The *Zhao Jianzi*, while featuring a switch of interlocutor, has the text end on a long answer that admits no response. This monologic character of some of the speeches brings the *Shang shu* or the longer expositions of the *Zuo* to mind; indeed, a large portion of many of the texts revolve around the advisors 'preaching' to their lords.¹ When not presented in narration, the words of the wise advisor are the ideal vehicle for ideology and argument, and present the main 'payload' of these narratives. Several genres use this basic device to bring their argument across, and the trope of the wise advisor 'instructing' their liege is especially common for Warring States texts about proper rule.²

In the following, I examine three aspects of the dialogue portions of the texts. First, I briefly note the relative proportions and divisions of discursive power allotted to the characters, and their various roles and voices within the texts. Second, I analyze the recurring trope of the ruler seeking access to knowledge and being challenged by an advisor. In other words, who gets to question (*wen* 問), and who has access to knowledge (*wen* 聞)? Third, I look into the use of periphrastic denominations (the use of descriptive forms of address) as a means of characterization.

2.1 Character and Role: Who Gets to Say What?

The rulers,³ young or in their prime, encounter a variety of interlocutors. In general, these characters are varieties of the 'advisor' type. Those advisors given a voice in the dialogues include the senior figure Grand Elder in the *Zheng Wen Gong wen Tai Bo*; the *Ruzi* has the heir's mother, and Sir Bian occurs as spokesperson for the high-officials; Zhao Jianzi hears out the older general Fan Xianzi and high official Cheng Zhuan; finally, the *Zi Fan Zi Yu* has its two eponymous advisors and Lord Mu of Qin's Uncle Jian. Whether solicited or not, these various advisors tell the ruler what

---

1 For comparisons between *Shu*, *Zuo*, and *Guo yu* historiography, see David Schaberg, "Foundations of Chinese Historiography: Literary Representation in *Zuo zhuan* and *Guoyu*," (PhD Dissertation, Harvard University, 1995).
2 See David Schaberg, "Remonstrance in Eastern Zhou Historiography," *Early China* 17 (1997): 133–179, and his "Playing at Critique," Pines, "From Teachers to Subjects," and Yuri Pines, "Friends or Foes: Changing Concepts of Ruler-Minister Relations and the Notion of Loyalty in Pre-Imperial China," *Monumenta Serica* 50 (2002): 35–74. For an early study on the topic, see Edward L. Shaughnessy, "The Duke of Zhou's Retirement in the East and the Beginnings of the Ministerial-Monarch Debate in Chinese Political Philosophy," *Early China* 18 (1993): 41–72.
3 Note that Zhao Jianzi ended up as Chancellor (*qing* 卿) of Jin.

to do, and depending on their particular role, age, and status, they either "admonish" (*gui* 規), "speak" (*yan* 言), "remonstrate" (*jian* 諫), or "reprimand" (*zhe* 謫). Their most common task is to provide their knowledge/what they have heard (*wen* 聞) in response to the ruler's questions (*wen* 問). This form will be discussed below.

Some of the advisors are only obliquely mentioned and do not get a voice of their own. Lord Wen of Jin professes to rely on the elders of the state in the restoration of the various aspects of governance (由二三大夫以修……) but they only mutely receive commands. The *Zheng Wen Gong wen Tai Bo* has Grand Elder list a number of advisors that the ruler should listen to: Uncle Kong, Yi of Yi, Shi of Qulu, Du of Yumi, and Sir Zhan, but none of these are given a voice of their own. Finally, Mr. Yi the foreign emissary is not an advisor at all. Nevertheless, in his task of relaying Lord Mu of Qin's wish for an alliance with Chu, he likewise operates as a helper more generally.[4]

Except for the *Jin Wen Gong ru yu Jin*, all the rulers are on the receiving end of discursive power. In general, the last word is reserved for the advisors and the ruler is not shown to have wielded the advice to success. Whereas the *Jin Wen Gong ru yu Jin* ends the narrative on a list of victories and achievements of Lord Wen, the *Zheng Wen Gong wen Tai Bo* instead presents the glories of former rulers as opposed to the "young and weak" Lord Wen of Zheng. The *Zhao Jianzi*, in turn, has Cheng Zhuan's list of successes and failures of former Jin rulers end the narrative, and the *Ruzi* reads as a tragic outcry of the young ruler's inability to match his father, the former Lord Wu. This is reinforced when his mother (and later, the advisors) constantly extol the virtues of the father at the expense of the young heir. Here the future ruler does get the last word, but its defeatism is telling of the power dynamic:

---

[4] Compare Vladimir Propp's discussion of character types: Vladimir Propp, trans. Laurence Scott, *Morphology of the Folktale* (Austin: University of Texas Press, 1968), esp. chs. 3 and 6.

今二三大夫畜孤而作焉，豈孤其足爲勉，抑亡如吾先君之憂何？

"Now you high officials have taken care of me, the orphaned one, and have taken charge; is it not the case that even if the orphaned one is considered exerting himself enough, this would still not be up to my former lord's concern?"[5]

The *Zi Yi has the lion's share of its narrative allotted to Lord Mu of Qin, with only one-fifth of it relating to the words of Mr. Yi. Lord Mu and his policies are described in a favorable light. He is presented in the role of host, and he frequently asks rhetorical questions followed by narration or song. Despite all that, at the end of the narrative he asks, "Sir Yi, when you return, what will you say?" The narrator does not reveal any anxiety on Lord Mu's part, but the questioning embedded in many of the coded exchanges — "The elders had a saying that went: 'Do not harbor a grudge against those who committed an offense'" and Mr. Yi's thrice repeated "That is what I will say when I return" — closing the narrative, suggests that despite taking up the majority of the narrative, Lord Mu of Qin does not get the final say.

2.2 The Question Left Unanswered

The question "what will you say" reveals a pattern shared across the texts. Over and over again the rulers ask (wen 問) their advisors for knowledge (wen 聞). While at first sight more neutral, this question-and-answer dynamic is likewise skewed towards the advisor figures. They hold power

---

[5] By comparison, the editors (p. 108, n.51–52) understand this passage as a polite nod to the high official's loyalty to the former lord; in their understanding the passage would roughly translate as follows:

"This line reads you high officials have respected the will and actions of me, the orphaned one; this may be enough for me, the orphaned one, but can it let our former lord be without worry."
"此句是說諸大夫能遵順孺子的意志行事，足以勉勵孺子自己，但仍然不能使已故的先君無憂。"

over knowledge in the form of historical precedent, sayings, and figurative language. Grand Elder is straightforward about this dynamic:

> 君之無問也，則亦無聞也。君之無出也，則亦無入也。戒之哉，君！吾若聞夫殷邦，湯爲語而紂亦爲語。
>
> If you do not ask, then you will also not hear (i.e., have knowledge). If you do not give out, you will also not receive. Be warned, lord! When I hear of the state of Yin, Tang is talked about but Zhòu is talked about as well.

The ruler ought to take heed and consult with his advisor, or he may end up like Zhòu 紂, the vilified last ruler of the Shang (Yin) dynasty. Varieties of this formula, where the advisor is presented as the gatekeeper to knowledge, abound in the texts. The *Zi Fan Zi Yu* has Uncle Jian chastise the Lord of Qin and prince Chong'er for asking for something they are unequipped to handle or already know:

> 公乃問於蹇叔曰："叔，昔之舊聖哲人之敷政令刑罰，使眾若使一人，不穀余敢問其道奚如。猷叔是聞遺老之言，必當語我哉。寧孤是勿能用？譬若從雉然，吾當觀其風▬。"
>
> The lord then asked Uncle Jian, saying: "Uncle, when in times of yore the old sages and wise men promulgated their edicts and punishments, they employed the masses as if employing a single person. I, the one unable to cultivate, I dare to ask what their way was? Supposing that you have heard sayings of the elders, then you really ought to tell them to me! Or do you think that I the orphaned one alone would not be able to use them? Think of it rather as if I were chasing a pheasant, I should want to observe its habits ▬."
>
> 蹇叔答曰："凡君之所問莫可聞▬。""昔者 [……] 用 '凡君所問莫可聞▬。'"

62

Uncle Jian replied, saying: "Of all that you my lord ask, nothing could be heard ▬ . "In times of yore, […] That is why I said, 'All that you my lord ask of, cannot be heard ▬ .'"

The Lord of Qin's question "Or do you think that I the orphaned one alone could not be able to use them?" is answered first dismissively by Uncle Jian in an otherwise unattested denial of knowledge: "Of all that you my lord ask, nothing could be heard" 凡君之所問莫可聞, before entering into a vivid description of the rulers of the past. The point is that one cannot simply hear of these things and instead should experience these rulers in order to really know their way of rule. Uncle Jian's narration of the past stands synecdochical for the text as a whole: it is creating such a presence in literature. The text, like the advisor, gives us privileged access to a hidden facet of the past. Chong'er, in turn, receives a list of precedents, but is criticized for asking what he already knows:

蹇叔答曰："如欲起邦，則大甲與盤庚、文王、武王，如欲亡邦，則桀及紂、厲王、幽王，亦備在公子之心已，奚勞問焉▬？"

Uncle Jian replied, saying: "If one wants to start a state, then follow Da Jia and Pan Geng, Kings Wen and Wu; If one wants to lose a state, then follow Jie and Zhòu, Kings Li and You. This too is all already present in your heart, why belabor me in asking about it ▬ ?"

The contrast between the two rulers makes it clear that (as history would prove) Chong'er would end up the more famous and successful ruler. It probably did not help that Lord Mu was known for having a large following of advisors buried along with him after what was otherwise a rather successful rule.⁶ But both were chastised for asking the wrong question. This is a common motif in the narratives.

In the *Zhao Jianzi*, Cheng Zhuan is asked why the Lord of Qi lost power to the Chen clan. While Cheng Zhuan professes not to have heard of the reasons 臣不得聞其所由, he suggests a different line of questioning to the lord: "But the gains and losses of the past, they all come about for a reason ▂" 抑昔之得之與失之，皆有由也▂. After Zhao Jianzi changes his question, "Can I hear the manners of how it came about?" 其所由禮可聞也, the elder high official Cheng Zhuan responds with a long monologic answer relating a range of historical precedents and philosophical musings on "frugality" (*jian* 儉) and "excess" (*chi* 侈). Just as Lord Mu of Qin asked the wrong question in the *Zi Fan Zi Yu*, knowledge is only bestowed by Cheng Zhuan when a proper, more insightful question is asked.

In the *Zheng Wu Furen gui ruzi*, the young heir is told that being "a young child, you ought not to know of the governance of the state, but leave it to the high officials instead." 孺子汝毋知邦政，屬之大夫, and that he, the "young child, you respect the high officials, and take your lessons from them" 孺子汝恭大夫，且以教焉. By contrast, his father actively commanded knowledge or could "send people to *learn* of the (affairs of the) state from afar" 使人遙聞於邦. Access to knowledge is denied to the heir, underscored by periphrastically repeating again and again that he is a mere "young child."

This motif is of course not limited to these narratives and may be related to shifts in the power dynamic between ruler and advisor more generally.⁷ Here, however, it seems to be the fundamental point of conten-

---

6   After failing to curb Jin twice, Qin expanded westward instead: "Lord Mu of Qin became Hegemon of the Western Rong" 秦穆公霸西戎. Lord Wen of Jin would be known as the Hegemon 霸 of Huaxia proper. On the burying of Lord Mu's advisors, see *Zuo* Wen 6, Durrant, Li, and Schaberg, *Zuo Tradition*, 491: "Renhao, the Liege of Qin, died. They took Yanxi, Zhonghang, and Qianhu, three sons of the Ziche lineage, and buried them with him. All were good men of Qin. The inhabitants of the capital grieved over them and composed in their honor the ode 'The Oriole.'" 秦伯任好卒，以子車氏三子奄息、仲行、鍼虎為殉，皆秦之良也，國人哀之，為之賦《黃鳥》。

7   See Pines, "Friends or Foes."

tion—in a willing suspension of disbelief, the dramatic discursive command over the ruler keeps the narrative lively and entertaining, all the while presenting a literary reality longed for but probably not materialized for the audience.[8] For all the characterization of the current ruler as young, weak, and in need of advice, once we read between the lines, one cannot help but wonder whether the texts at some level do not reflect anxieties in the self-representation of the advisory class. For at the end of the day, and in contradistinction to many philosophical texts from the period,[9] the historical precedent mentioned in the narratives is all about successful *rulers* and completely elides their advisors. Despite all their knowledge and attempts at guiding rulers, the ruler could demand that the advisor be buried alongside him, and the advisor only held power over discourse set in the past.

2.3 Periphrasis

Periphrasis is used by characters to define the status and role of the other interlocutors and operates as a salient form of focalization in these narratives. Drawing from a range of potential appellations and modes of address, the selection reveals a particular persona a character wants to project, or a characterization of their interlocutors. A ruler may refer to himself with polite self-deprecation, *bu gu* 不穀 "I<the one who does not cultivate", *gu* 孤 "I<the orphaned one," or, instead choose a seemingly more neutral but in comparison more personal form of self-address, *wu* 吾 or *yu* 余, "I." Periphrasis is not semantically neutral. "The one unable to cultivate" suggests a lack of basic ability and "the orphaned one" focuses on the ruler being alone (at the top) or as being left without parental guidance.[10] The lat-

---

8   Schaberg, "Playing at Critique," esp. 217.
9   Sarah Allan, *The Heir and the Sage: Dynastic Legend in Early China* (San Francisco: Chinese Materials Center, 1981).
10 The majority of studies on this topic are a response to Xia Lu 夏渌, "Gu, gua ren, bu gu xinquan" 孤，寡人，不穀新詮, *Zhongguo yuwen* 中國語文 1983.4, 288, who argued against the whole of the commentarial tradition in stating that these terms are not self-deprecatory. For an overview and a reading close to my own, see Chen Yawen 陳雅雯 and Wang Lingjuan 王玲娟, "'bu gu' xintan" "不穀"新探, *Heihe xueyuan xuebao* 黑河學院學報 2019.12: 154–157. I do understand them as self-deprecatory but do not opt to read in the extended and moralistic sense of "not excellent" 不善 or "person lacking

ter appears more revealing of personal identity, but likely equally reflects a cultivated persona. A passage from the *Zi Fan Zi Yu* plays on these different modes of self-address:

> 不穀余敢問其道奚如。猷叔是問遺老之言，必當語我哉。寧孤是勿能用？譬若從雉然，吾當觀其風▅。
>
> I, the one unable to cultivate, I dare to ask what their way was? Supposing that you have heard sayings of the elders, then you really ought to tell them to me![11] Or do you think that I the orphaned one alone would not be able to use them? Think of it rather as if I were chasing a pheasant, I should want to observe its habits ▅.

In a rare turn of phrase, "unable to cultivate" 不穀 modifies *yu* 余 "I,"[12] possibly to further stress the self-deprecatory aspect, and it is quickly followed by a request for knowledge. In the almost whining repetition of the question, *wo* 我 "me" (or perhaps in the sense of the royal plural) is used. The assumption that the ruler *alone* could not apply or understand the knowledge asked for is highlighted through *gu* 孤 "orphaned one" before switching to a more personal *wu* 吾 "I," suggesting a *personal* willingness and effort on account of the ruler.

This alternation between periphrasis and regular pronouns is not just to provide variety; these choices highlight specific aspects of characterization and set the tone of the conversation. In a society where status and hierarchy

---

in virtue" 少德之人 advanced by the commentarial tradition but instead choose to highlight the more literal, and therefore evocative, meaning of the terms.

11 This whole section is much more informal, suggesting a more intimate relationship between lord Mu and his close advisor.

12 The use of *bu gu* 不穀 is hardly ever followed by a personal pronoun such as *yu* 余. In the earliest use of the term, however, see e.g. *Shi jing* 詩經 "Xiao pan" 小弁, it is still constructed as a predicate, 民莫不穀，我獨于罹. Possibly, the use of the personal pronoun in the construction of the *Zi Fan Zi Yu* highlights the self-deprecation. Indeed, in what follows, Lord Mu further positions himself as a learning subject to Uncle Jian. See for a vocative use, "Young child, you" 孺子，汝, discussed below.

were paramount the audience of the text would have been intimately sensitive to such shifts of role and self-representation.[13] Other examples, such as the ending of the *Zheng Wu Furen gui ruzi* draw on them for dramatic effect:

> 今二三大夫畜孤而作焉，豈孤其足爲勉，抑無如吾先君之憂何？
>
> Now you high officials have taken care of me, the orphaned one, and have taken charge; is it not the case that even if the orphaned one is considered exerting himself enough, this would still not be up to my former lord's concern?

The use of *gu* 孤, literally in the sense of "orphan," evokes not just an image of the high officials stepping in as substitute fathers to take care of the young ruler, but builds on the narrative's continued suggestion of the son not measuring up to the father. Even as an orphan, his late father's plans and worries are effectively still in command. This contrast makes for a tragic finale. Rather than promising a resolution to the conundrum 'ought not the young heir take charge?' the narrative ends on an outcry of incomparability to *my* former ruler and father.

Periphrasis often turns to metonymy to describe the agent indirectly. In the *Zi Yi*, we encounter the Chu emissary Zi Yi in a cryptic response to Lord Mu of Qin's overtures to an alliance between the two states:

> 子儀曰：「君欲乞丹方，諸任君不瞻彼沮漳之川開而不闔，抑虜夷之楷也。」
>
> Mr. Yi said: "If you want to request (an alliance) with the

---

13 For a call to take seriously differences in modes of self-address and the use of personal pronouns, see Christoph Harbsmeier, "*Xunzi* and the Problem of Impersonal First Person Pronouns," *Early China* 22 (1997): 181–220, esp. 195ff. For a discussion of the use of modes of address in historical judgment within a hierarchical framework, see Newell Ann Van Auken, *Spring and Autumn Historiography: Form and Hierarchy in Ancient Chinese Annals* (New York: Columbia University Press, 2023).

Cinnabar region (i.e., the south, i.e., Chu), the rulers do not look highly upon the Ju and Zhang plain (i.e., the border area between Qin and Chu) being open and not closed off (to each other), yet it is the model for this captured barbarian (i.e., me).

Cinnabar stands for the south as the plains stand for the connection between Qin and Chu, and the use of "captured barbarian" takes a jab at Qin as a hostage-taker of Mr. Yi in the past all the while self-deprecatingly referring to the people of Chu as barbarians. Mr. Yi's use of this juxtaposition shows how Chu can be forgiving, seeking cooperation despite earlier slights.

As is clear in these examples of self-address, the regular use of periphrasis to describe interlocutors (e.g., "Young child, you" 孺子, 汝; "elders of the state" 屬邦耆老) is a powerful tool in characterization. Far from rote formulae, these locutions provide a colored window into the role and perception of characters within the story. And in examples such as the *Jin Wen Gong ru yu Jin*'s use of "elders of the state," these descriptions are often the only clue towards visualizing the characters that the audience receives.

2.4 Summary

The main portion of the narratives is allocated to dialogue. Admittedly, some of these dialogues merely feature a single question and one long monological answer. Even when there is no dialogue, the speech of the characters is presented as directed at a named audience, effectively rendering them mute participants in the dialogue. The majority of the texts feature, often elderly, advisor figures instructing or admonishing the ruler. While actual power may rest with the liege, discursive power in these texts is allocated to the advisor figures. Whether asked or not, they provide candid advice and notify the ruler of his shortcomings. The ruler hardly gets the final say and often merely serves as a vehicle that introduces the central problem of the text, the main drive of the narrative then focuses on resolving that problem, often relying heavily on historical precedent and wise sayings. The ruler has to ask for the knowledge that will help him solve these issues, but is often told to rephrase the question. Once the proper question is asked, knowledge is bestowed by the advisors and the problem is resolved, although that resolution is not always specified. The use of periphrastic denominations and pronouns accentuates the role and status of the characters. The ruler is presented as in need of instruction or paternal guidance, and playful self-reference (e.g., "this captured barbarian") can highlight and defuse tensions within the narrative. In the deployment of the form, then, the dialogues tend to be skewed in favor of the advisors. They present the main challenge to the ruler and get to end the dialogue in a statement, rather than a question. One of the ways in which the advisors master discursive power over the ruler is through the clever manipulation of images, we will turn to this in the following chapter.

Chapter Three
Image-based Language

Image-based language is a broad category spanning forms of language that conjures up an image or speaks figuratively of one thing through another. In scholarship on early China, two major lines of study are visible. By far the largest body of scholarship is concerned with metaphor and theories of meaning.[1] In particular, conceptual metaphor theory has been used and criticized.[2] In the study of literature, the discussion has predominantly

---

1 Discussions on the meaning and use of particular schema and metaphors abound. These tend to be focused on philosophical materials; see for example: Carine Defoort, "Heavy and Light Body Parts: The Weighing Metaphor in Early Chinese Dialogues." *Early China* 38 (2015): 55–77; Griet Vankeerberghen, "Choosing Balance: Weighing (*quan* 權) as a Metaphor for Action in Early Chinese Texts," *Early China* 30 (2005–2006): 47–89; John S. Major, "Tool Metaphors in the *Huainanzi* and Other Texts," in Sarah Queen and Michael Puett eds., *The* Huainanzi *and Textual Production in Early China* (Leiden: Brill, 2014), 153–198.

2 George Lakoff and Mark Johnson, *Metaphors We Live By* (Chicago: Chicago University Press, 1980). The earliest use of this theory in sinological circles is in Sarah Allan, *The Way of Water and Sprouts of Virtue* (Albany: State University of New York Press, 1997). In recent years, the most ardent advocate of the theory is Edward G. Slingerland, *Effortless Action: Wu-wei as Conceptual Metaphor and Spiritual Ideal in Early China* (Oxford: Oxford University Press, 2003). For critiques see Jane Geaney, "Self as Container? Metaphors We Lose by in Understanding Early Chinese Texts," *Antiquorum Philosophia* 5 (2012): 11–30; Stefano Gandolfo, "Metaphors of Metaphors: Reflections on the Use of Conceptual Metaphor Theory in Premodern Chinese Texts." *Dao* 18.3 (2019): 323–345. See also Martin S. Ekstrom, "Does the Metaphor Translate?" in Ming Dong Gu and Rainer Shulte eds., *Translating China for Western Readers: Reflective, Critical, and Practical Essays* (Albany: State University of New York Press, 2014), 45–70, for pointed remarks against essentializing theories of metaphor.

Alternatively, Tobias Zuern, "Overgrown Courtyards and Tilled Fields: Image-Based Debates on Governance and Body Politics in the *Mengzi, Zhuangzi,* and *Huainanzi*," *Early China* 41 (2018): 297–332, and Zhou Boqun, "Subtle and Dangerous: The Crossbow Trigger Metaphor in Early China," *Early China* 44 (2021): 465–492, Zhou Boqun, "Mechanical Metaphors in Early Chinese Thought" (PhD dissertation, University of Chicago, 2019), have adopted Hans Blumberg's theory of metaphorology.

focused on poetics and seldom departs from the "Major Preface" *Daxu* 大序 of the *Shijing* 詩經.³

Many of the philosophical texts at the heart of these debates rely on narrative form. Nevertheless, the primary concern of scholarship has been with understanding the philosophical meaning of a particular metaphor or image, rather than exploring questions of literary form, aesthetics, and reception. The study of image-based language in narrative texts is less forthcoming, which is surprising given that the stories are littered with image-based language more generally.⁴

Beyond Sinology, the study of the ancient world has focused on image-based language more broadly.⁵ Jonathan Ready, for example, has examined the use of (series of) similes in the *Iliad* as a form of linguistic competition between the character-heroes of the story, the one outdoing the other as if at a public performance.⁶ As a model of interpretation, it complements earlier discussions on the decoding of signs in texts such as the *Zuo*,⁷ by

---

3   See especially, Pauline Yu, *The Reading of Imagery in the Chinese Poetic Tradition* (Princeton: Princeton University Press, 1987).
4   Major, "Tool Metaphors," 183, notes how in his tallying of tool metaphors these were (almost) surprisingly absent from historiographical narratives such as the *Zhanguo ce*. He speculates (188) this may point to a rather unedited inclusion of earlier source materials that did not yet tend to avail themselves of this metaphor scheme.
5   See for example the early collection of studies in Murray Mindlin, M. J. Geller, and J. Wansbrough eds., *Figurative Language in the Ancient Near East* (London: School of Oriental and African Studies, 1987). These studies cover everything from names for deities to talk of tradesmen, and speak towards the widespread and common use of figurative language beyond the realm of literature. For use beyond meaning, see especially the contribution by Talmon, pp. 108–109: "But it should be stressed that being carriers of ideas and concentrated expressions of concepts, in no way diminishes the artistic value, i.e., the aesthetic essence of biblical motifs, literary patterns and figurative language." For the particularly vibrant discussion in biblical studies, see, among others, Andrea Weiss, *Figurative Language in Biblical Prose Narrative: Metaphor in the Book of Samuel* (Leiden: Brill, 2006).
6   Jonathan L. Ready, *Character, Narrator, and Simile in the Iliad* (Cambridge: Cambridge University Press, 2011), esp. introduction and ch. 2. Ready notes (4): "the poet constructs similes in the narrator-text such that they contribute to his rendition of his characters as competitors for narrative attention," (5): "to exhibit his distinctive degree of linguistic competence"; and (8): "In other scenes, the poet makes a character explicitly attempt to incorporate, resist, or better the previous figurative effort of his interlocutor."
7   See e.g., Li, *The Readability of the Past*, esp. ch. 3.

suggesting a closer link between performance in the text and the audience as recipients of the encounters between interlocutors. Here, cases such as the *Zi Yi and the Zi Fan Zi Yu spring to mind.

The power of images to engage an audience and to transport them into the literary world created by the texts is noted by the biblical literature scholar Shemaryahu Talmon writing about motifs. His analysis, I think, describes one of the main reasons for the extensive use of imagery in early Chinese narrative texts:

> "In its literary setting ... a motif constitutes a concentrated expression of the essence which inheres in the original situation. The biblical writers make use of motifs with the express purpose of providing their audience with tools designed to bring about a reactualisation of the intrinsic sentiments and reactions shared by the individuals or groups who had experienced the original situation. They are recaptured in the motif as in a literary capsule.
>
> A motif stands for the essential meaning of a situation or an event, not for the facts themselves. It is not intended to bring to the mind of the listener or reader only the memory of the original situation or to effect a mere reiteration of the sentiments that it had evoked in those who were immersed in it. Rather it is meant to produce in the author's audience an intensified identification with the sensations to which the original participants in the event had been subjected."[8]

In what follows, I therefore do not wish to enter the debate on the fundamental epistemological concerns of metaphor or the validity of conceptual metaphor theory, nor do I see a need to explain every single metaphor or

---

8   Shemaryahu Talmon, "Har and Midbār: An Antithetical Pair of Biblical Motifs," in Mindlin, et al. eds., *Figurative Language in the Ancient near East*, 109.

image in the texts. Rather, and following along with comparative reflections on image-based uses of language, I wish to understand the role of image-based language in narrative historiography. In light of the persuasive and dialogic aspect of image-based language,[9] I want to examine what images were meant to do not just within a narrative but also with its audiences.[10]

---

9   Gandolfo, "Metaphors of Metaphors," 330, notes that the root understanding of many terms covering image-based language is involved with the act of persuasion; he summarizes: "To provide a 'metaphor' is to explain and to explain is to provide a 'metaphor.'" His use of metaphor covers image-based language more broadly, including *pi* 譬 "comparison" and *yu* 喻 "explanation," and a discussion on the familiar triad of *fu* 賦 "exposition," *bi* 比 "metaphor—simile—analogy," *xing* 興 "evocation." (331–332). Both Gandolfo, "Metaphors of Metaphors,"334, and Ekstrom, "Does the Metaphor Translate," 53 place a lot of weight on a crucial passage from the "Shanshuo" 善說 chapter of the *Shuo yuan* 說苑, discussing the fundamental necessity of comparison, here in Ekstrom's translation:

> A retainer said to King Liang, "When Master Hui discusses governmental affairs he likes to use comparisons [*pi* 譬]. If you forbid him to do so, he won't be able to speak." The king said, "Agreed." At the audience the following day, the king told Master Hui, "When you, sir, discuss governmental affairs, I would like you simply to speak directly [*zhi yan* 直言], without comparisons." Master Hui said, "Suppose there is a fellow who does not know what a *tan* is, and he said, 'What does a *tan* look like?' and we reply, 'A *tan* is like [*ru* 如] a *tan*,' would he then understand [*yu* 諭]?" The king said, "Not yet." "But if we changed our reply, saying, 'A *tan* is like a bow but with a bamboo string,' would he then understand?" "Possibly." Master Hui said, "Well, the intellectual always uses what is known to explain what is unknown, and so makes other people know it. Now you say, 'Don't use comparisons' — This is impossible." The king said, "Very well."
> 客謂梁王曰："惠子之言事也善譬，王使無譬，則不能言矣。"王曰："諾。"明日見，謂惠子曰："願先生言事則直言耳，無譬也。"惠子曰："今有人於此而不知彈者，曰：'彈之狀若何？' 應曰：'彈之狀如彈。' 則諭乎？"王曰："未諭也。""於是更應曰：'彈之狀如弓而以竹為弦。' 則知乎？"王曰："可知矣。"惠子曰："夫說者固以其所知，諭其所不知，而使人知之。今王曰無譬則不可矣。"王曰："善。"

For an early discussion of this passage, see Henri Maspero, "Notes sur la logique de Mo-tseu et de son école," *T'oung Pao*, Second Series, Vol. 25, No. 1/2 (1927): 32–33.
    Despite the emergence of discussions on the critical vocabulary in texts from the early Empires, and fully aware of ontological concerns, I have in my analysis chosen to use the standard critical idiom (simile, metaphor, analogy etc.) in use across modern fields and disciplines, if only for ease of comparison. For a discussion of the different epistemological and ontological bases for the terms that emerged out of early Chinese poetry commentary and the modern vocabulary stemming ultimately from the Greek classical tradition, see Yu, *The Reading of Imagery in the Chinese Poetical Tradition*, ch. 1.

10 For an early awareness of a deliberate effort to engage the audience in the *Zuo*, see Egan, "Narratives in *Tso Chuan*," 324–326.

First the vocabulary. Image, simile, analogy, and allusion are often marked to draw attention to their existence.[11] These discourse makers, such as "like," "as if," etc. notify the audience that what follows needs to be understood in non-literal, figurative ways. Certain genre settings, such as song, poetry, and persuasive contexts, almost automatically assume such a layered understanding of language and do not tend to mark the devices. In the texts discussed here, a limited set of terms is used to draw attention especially to similes and analogies:

- *ruo* 若 "as if"
- *ru* 如 "like, as if"
- *pi ru* 譬如 "can be likened to"

These discourse markers are all used to indicate forms of the simile, the latter, *pi ru*, possibly extending into full analogy. In brief, the very definition of simile revolves around its marking. It suggests a *likeness* but not an identity. Metaphor eschews discourse markers and instead often draws on syntactic structures suggesting identity between the vehicle and the tenor.

But the use of imagery in the texts under discussion is not limited to these common forms; indeed, the use of periphrasis and metonymy in the narratives is itself a form of imagery. Likewise, following Talmon, the use of images in these texts is not limited to a range of rhetorical devices showing off linguistic prowess in the layering of meaning (as with Jonathan Ready). They are employed to conjure up the contours, if not the narrative flesh and bone, of historical events, inviting an audience back in time to become (vicarious) participants and intimately experience the past. The narrative's power to transport its audiences across time and place did not merely function to gain a deeper understanding of the events of the past, it also served

---

11 Camilla Di Biase-Dyson and Markus Egg, *Drawing Attention to Metaphor: Case Studies Across Time Periods, Cultures and Modalities* (Amsterdam: John Benjamins, 2020), see especially the introduction and Di Biase-Dyson's contribution on Ancient Egyptian attention-drawing strategies and markers therein.

3.1 Heightened Distance: The Marked Simile

The wife of Lord Wu's admonition in the *Zheng Wu Furen gui ruzi* opens with a eulogistic description of the extent of Lord Wu's involvement in the government of the state despite taking refuge in Wei. During these 'three years of hardship' the lord is described as being in close contact with his ministers who took care of the state in his absence, "participating in (the affairs) of Zheng from Wei, they were as if huddling ear to ear and scheming" 自衛與鄭，若卑耳而謀 (5–6). The use of "as if" 若 here is to underline the lord's effort and his ministers' loyalty despite their distance.

This attention drawing through the use of discourse markers is echoed in the opening lines of the *Zheng Wen Gong wen Tai Bo*:

> 君若曰："伯父，不穀幼弱，閔喪吾君，譬若鷄雛，伯父寔被覆不穀，以能與就次▬。今天爲不惠，又援然與不穀爭伯父所，天不豫伯父，……"

> The ruler said to the effect: "Sir Bo, I, the one unable to cultivate, am young and weak, I mourn the loss of my lord. I can be likened to a chick and Sir Bo verily sheltered me, the one unable to cultivate, so that I could enter the mourning shack ▬. Now, heaven is not kind, and as if pulling, is contesting with me over Sir Bo's place. Heaven is not letting Sir Bo be comfortable … "

Lord Wen can be *likened* to a chick but Grand Elder *verily* 寔 sheltered him

---

12 See Hans Robert Jauss, trans. Elizabeth Benzinger, "Literary History as a Challenge to Literary Theory," *New Literary History* 2.1 (1970): 7–37. I would suggest that the power of images is instrumental in bridging this gap. The concept of *xing* 興 "to evoke," is suggestive of this dynamic between text and reader, in that it conveys the act of bringing an image to the mind's eye of the audience.

before Lord Wen could metonymically "enter the mourning shack" 就次 and start his ritual mourning period. Heaven's agency, in turn, is personified, unkind and fighting *as if pulling*.[13] Where Aristotle was noted for downplaying the literary craft of the simile compared to metaphor,[14] it seems that in these texts, the distance generated in the likening between vehicle and tenor, is instead productively used to increase the contrast between image and reality. Heaven and Lord Wen are represented figuratively. By comparison, Grand Elder's unadorned presentation casts him as stable and reliable, even in light of his illness, and underscores his role as advisor to the young lord.

But Grand Elder, in his own voice, does not eschew the figurative. He brackets his advice to the lord with an opening and closing analogy on the roles of minister and lord:

太伯曰："君，老臣□□□□毋言而不當。古之人有言曰：'爲臣而不諫，譬若饋而不式。'"

Grand Elder said, "Lord, your old servant .. .. if I were not to speak it would be improper. The people of old had a saying, 'Serving as minister and not remonstrating, can be likened to serving food without an alternative.'"

[followed by main body of the advice, littered with descriptions

---

13 Here it is noteworthy that the *Zheng Wen Gong wen Tai Bo B has *qing* 請 "request" instead of *zhong* 爭 "contest-fight." While near homophones, *tsheŋʔ and *tsrên respectively, the writing is nevertheless vastly different. Given that the same scribe closely copied the different versions following minute visual distinctions on the respective source manuscripts, it seems unlikely that this particular scribe introduced the variance by ear and the variation likely originated earlier in the formation of the texts. More to the point, I think, is that it suggests that at some point in the transmission of the text(s) *before* these two manuscript renditions, at least one of the copyists seems to have made an interpretation based on the sound of the word and decided that it was more appropriate for heaven to either "contest" or "invite" a person such as Tai Bo. For a lucid discussion on the copyist see Edward L. Shaughnessy, "The Tsinghua Manuscript *Zheng Wen Gong wen Tai Bo* and the Question of the Production of Manuscripts in Early China," *Bamboo and Silk* 3.1 (2020): 54–73.
14 Aristotle, *Poetics* 1407A, "Similes are metaphors needing an explanatory word," quoted from David Hills, "Metaphor," *The Stanford Encyclopedia of Philosophy* (Fall 2017 Edition), Edward N. Zalta (ed.), https://plato.stanford.edu/archives/fall2017/entries/metaphor/, accessed June 21, 2022.

of previous lords of Zheng]

君如是之不能戁，則譬若疾之亡醫。
My lord's inability to make an effort is to the extent that it can be likened to not having a doctor when you are ill.

Using contrasting analogies, Grand Elder likens ministers such as himself to a cook or host serving an alternative dish, and in the closing analogy, likens himself to a doctor if only implicitly. Given Grand Elder's illness, the lord's need of a doctor is ironic. It is telling that Grand Elder hedges the analogy about the minister in quotation whereas he is rather more direct with the characterization of the lord. He follows it up with commentary that the lord needs to ask for advice if he is to succeed. Similar to Jonathan Ready's notion of the competitive simile,[15] the two characters are presented in a bout of linguistic sparring, with the advisor obviously taking the discursive high ground. Grand Elder shows more command and is not passively subjected to analogy. The relative status of the subjects of the simile underscore this, animal versus cook (or even host), patient versus doctor.

The latter half of the *Zi Fan Zi Yu* likewise employs a rich tapestry of imagery. Whereas the first part of the text draws in the audience by the advisors' witty reversals of the ruler's words, this second part draws heavily on contrasting images to highlight power relations and the intellectual superiority of the advisors, all the while entertaining an audience likely composed to a large extent of self-identified — if not necessarily as successful — members of that class.[16]

公乃問於蹇叔曰："叔，昔之舊聖哲人之敷政令刑罰，使眾若使一人，不榖余敢問其道奚如。猷叔是聞遺老之言，必當語我哉。寧孤是勿能用？譬若從雉然，吾當觀

---

15 Ready, *Character, Narrator, and Simile in the Iliad.*
16 Compare Schaberg, "Playing at Critique," Pines, "From Teachers to Subjects."

其風▅。"

The lord then asked Uncle Jian, saying: "Uncle, when in times of yore the old sages and wise men promulgated their edicts and punishments, they employed the masses as if employing a single person. I, the one unable to cultivate, I dare to ask what their way was? Supposing that you have heard sayings of the elders, then you really ought to tell them to me! Or do you think that I the solitary one alone would not be able to use them? Think of it rather as if I were chasing a pheasant, I should want to observe its habits ▅."

The rule of the wise old sages, metonymically represented through edicts and punishments, is summarized in a simile wherein the rule over the masses is likened to the rule over a single person, in turn a metaphor for expedient rule. The analogy that follows sets up a vivid answer from Uncle Jian. Lord Mu of Qin likens himself to a hunter, a strong and confident but probably not a very apt image when the object of the chase stands for the old sages,[17] all the while claiming to carefully examine their habits. Uncle Jian's response contains two powerful images of water:

蹇叔答曰："凡君之所問莫可聞▅。""昔者成湯以神事山川，以德和民。四方夷莫後與人，面見湯，若濡雨方奔之而鹿膺焉，用果念政九州而命君之。後世就紂之身，殺三無辜，為炮為烙，殺梅之女，為拳桔三百。殷邦之君子，無小大，無遠邇，見紂若大岸將顛崩，方走去之，懼不死刑以及于厥身，邦乃遂亡▅。"

Uncle Jian replied, saying: "Of all that you my lord ask, nothing could be heard ▅." "In times of yore, Cheng Tang served

---

17 It is of course possible that there is precedent for this use as the *Huainan zi* 淮南子, "Lanming xun" 覽冥訓 chapter notes a version purportedly from the (lost?) *Documents of Zhou*: "As to the *Documents of Zhou*, it says: "If you cannot catch the hidden pheasant, then you need to follow its habits" 夫《周書》曰："掩雉不得，更順其風". He Ning 何寧 ann., *Huainan zi jishi* 淮南子集釋 (Beijing: Zhonghua shuju, 1998), 498.

the mountains and rivers with his spirit, and harmonized the people with his power. Of the peoples of the four directions, none wanted to be (placed) later than the others. When they saw Tang head-on, it was like a nourishing rain; they promptly rushed onward and deer-like responded to it. Thus, in the end they longed for his governance, and the Nine Regions diligently took him as their ruler. In later generations when we come to the person of Zhòu, he murdered the three innocents, and roasted and burned people. He murdered the daughters of Mei, and shackled over three hundred. The lords of the state of Yin, whether big or small, far or close, whenever they saw Zhòu it was like seeing a tall dike about to collapse, and they promptly ran off and left him. They feared that even if they were not killed, corporal punishment would be inflicted upon their bodies. The state was then consequently lost ▬ ."

The water imagery is rendered in an opposing pair, Tang is likened to a nourishing rain drawing in people whereas Zhòu, like a collapsing dike, unleashed a destructive flood of violence.[18] While the actions of these rulers could be construed as an answer to Lord Mu's question about their habits, Uncle Jian starts his reply with a dismissal: "Of all that you my lord ask, nothing could be heard." Perhaps the reason for this dismissal is encapsulated in the images. One had to be there to *see* Tang or Zhòu *head-on* 面見 and experience their presence. The power of the simile here is in conveying that image vividly to Lord Mu, and by extension the audience, allowing them a glimpse of what it was like to stand in fear or awe of these powerful rulers.

The *Zi Yi*, while predominantly drawing on metaphor, also has a vivid analogy to describe the need to work together:

公曰："儀父，以不穀之修遠於君，何爭而不好，譬之如

---

18 On this schema, see Allan, *Water and the Sprouts of Virtue*.

兩犬沿河，啜而䫞，豈畏不足，心則不察？……"

Lord (Mu) said: "Sir Yi, I, the one unable to cultivate, am so far from you oh lord, why fight and not have good relations? Liken it to two dogs following along the river, they bare their teeth at each other while drinking. How could we fear there is not enough, and not examine our hearts? ……"

The strength of the analogy is in the power of its image, the bared teeth of the dogs competing over water is evocative and violent. This show of power contrasts strongly with the ridiculous idea that the water would ever run out. By implication, Qin and Chu ought not to stoop to the same level but should cooperate instead. The use of rivers metonymically standing for the states throughout the text supports this strong web of identification.

The images discussed above tend to be easily visualized and can be related to by a broad audience; their vivacity is involved. They draw out a clear contrast between image and reality. The power of the simile lies in this distance, heightening the shortcomings of the ruler or the absurdity of a situation. They are often used in contradistinction with claims made by the ruler figure. As a result, the manipulation of images reflects the discursive mastery of the advisor figures; at the same time, it allows the audience to vicariously partake in a power dynamic skewed towards literary achievement over the concerns of realpolitik.

3.2 Metaphorical and Allusive Use of Images

In the preceding discussion of the simile, I have noted that the device is clearly indicated with discourse markers. Similarly, the tenor (the subject being compared) and the vehicle (the image) are easily identifiable. With the following examples of metaphor, the dynamic is slightly different. Instead of discourse markers, genre such as song or diplomatic discourse, gives a clue as to how to read the metaphorical statements. Because of the prevalence of allusion in those contexts, the tenor and its relation to the vehicle is not always clear. The tenor is described in general, often metonymic or deictic terms, and it is therefore not always clear which particular historical events or figures are alluded to. This uncertainty creates an interpretive space in which the characters of the story, and by extension, the text's perceived author and implied reader, engage in an interpretive tug of war. Who gets to decide the meaning of an encounter, and, which character entraps the other in a carefully crafted metaphor? The use of metaphor in these texts uses the interpretive ability to echo the general power dynamic between ruler and advisor.

The *Zheng Wen Gong wen Tai Bo* contains a rather straightforward metaphor, describing Lords Zhao and Li as penned up rats not able to share a hole, referring to the back-to-back succession struggles characterizing their intermittent reigns:

> 世及吾先君邵公、厲公，抑天也，其抑人也▄？爲是牢鼠不能同穴，朝夕鬥鬩，亦不逸斬伐。
>
> Reaching the age of our former rulers, Lord Zhao and Lord Li, was it heaven or was it because of man ▄ ? Because these penned up rats could not share a hole, day and night they fought and quarreled, yet did not run away from campaigning.[19]

Nevertheless, given the paucity of evidence for campaigns during this period, the last sentence is not unproblematic.[20] Likely, the campaigns alluded to are to be read in contrast to the quarrels of the metaphorical rats, to suggest that despite the struggles within, these lords did not diminish their military footprint abroad. Given that this is the final historical prece-

---

19 Yu Houkai 尉侯凱, "Du Qinghua jian liu zhaji" 讀清華簡六札記（五則）, *Chutu wenxian* 出土文獻 10 (2017): 124–129, notes two later instances of this image in the *Shi ji* and the *Liang shu* 梁書.
20 According to Wang Ning 王寧, "Qinghua jian liu *Zheng Wen Gong wen Tai Bo* Jia ben shiwen jiaodu" 清華簡六《鄭文公問太伯》（甲本）釋文校讀, *Fudan daxue chutu wenxian yu guwenzi yanjiu zhongxin wangzhan* 復旦大學出土文獻與古文字研究中心網站, May 30, 2016, http://www.fdgwz.org.cn/web/show/2809, the campaigning mentioned refers to Lord Li's assistance of the Zhou monarch. It would thus carry significance in terms of his status as protector of the realm.

dent recounted before a contrast is drawn to the heir's young age and weakness, it might suggest that a proper Zheng ruler, even at his darkest hour, still manages to uphold the tasks of his office.

A more complex example of metaphorical language use can be found in the *Zheng Wu Furen gui ruzi*. The ministers are in fear because their ruler-to-be — listening to his mother's advice — does not speak. Sir Bian admonishes the ministers and asks them to delay the burial rite — perhaps to stall for time. After the Minor Auspicious sacrifice, the ministers send Sir Bian to reason with the heir, drawing on their rote engagement in ritual tasks as a metaphor for their anxiety and forced idleness:

邊父規大夫曰：「君拱而不言，加重於大夫，汝慎重君葬而久之於上三月。」小祥，大夫聚謀，乃使邊父於君，曰：「二三老臣，使禦寇也▂，布圖於君。昔吾先君使二三臣，抑早前後之以言，思群臣得執焉，[且] 毋交於死。今君定，拱而不言，二三臣事於邦，惶惶焉，如削錯器於選藏之中，毋措手止，殆於爲敗，胡寧君是有臣而爲褻嫚，豈既臣之獲罪，又辱吾先君，曰是其蓋臣也？」

Sir Bian admonished the high officials, saying: "Our Lord holds his hands to his chest and does not speak. He has put an important (task) on you high officials. If you treat the burial of your lord with care and importance, then draw it out to three months at the most." It was the Minor Auspicious sacrifice, and the high officials gathered to plan. They then sent Sir Bian to the lord, to say: "We old ministers, if you would employ us to repel bandits ▂, will present our plans to you, our lord. In the past, when our former lord employed us ministers, he would precede it by talking to us first and last, wishing the numerous ministers to have the means to execute it (their employment), [and] not meet up with death.

"Now the lord is settled, he holds his hands on his breast and does not speak. We ministers are anxious while serving the state. It is like placing vessels to accompany the burial during the night. We do not know where to put hands and feet. It will run into the danger of causing failure. How is this not a case of our lord having ministers and yet engaging with body servants and favored concubines? Is that not a case of having incriminated us ministers and also insulting our former lord, by saying 'These are his loyal ministers?'"

The ministers' engagement in the burial procedures is evocative on a number of levels. On the one hand, it suggests loyalty and care for the former ruler. Nevertheless, the ministers themselves draw up a contrast with the proper work of government that they would engage in if only they were properly instructed. While they are wasting their time on ritual procedures unnecessarily drawn out, the heir is engaged with his servants and concubines. What appears like ritual dedication is actually an "insult" to the former lord.

The *Zi Fan Zi Yu* turns to the common tool metaphor to describe the ruler's function in government:[21]

公乃問於謇叔曰："……民心信難成也哉▬？"
謇叔答曰："信難成▬，抑或易成也。凡民秉度端正僭忒，在上之人，上繩不失，斤亦不僭▬。"
The lord then asked Uncle Jian, saying: " … are the hearts and minds of the people really that hard to win over ▬ ?"
Uncle Jian replied, saying: "Yes, they are truly hard to win over ▬. Or they might be easy to win over. In general, whatever standard the people hold on to, whether straight or transgressive, comes down to the person on top. If the one on top does not lose the (correct hold of) the plumb line, the axe will also not transgress ▬ ."

---

21 For an overview and discussion, see Major, "Tool Metaphors in the *Huainanzi* and Other Texts."

The ruler above serves as the plumb line, suspended straight down to indicate the proper place to cut. The precision of the measuring tool is contrasted with the crude axe symbolizing the people. The implication is simple, if the ruler is straight and correct, so are his people. Compared to the figurative description of Tang and Zhòu that follows, the use of this common metaphor appears idiomatic and less vivid. When we compare it to the evocative metaphor of the penned-up rats before, unattested before texts of the early empires, this metaphor of rule had instead become lexicalized to the point that it lost its ability to truly captivate an audience.

The *Zi Yi appears much more successful in this regard. Lord Mu of Qin and Mr. Yi's interaction is laced throughout with metaphor. The whole exchange is shrouded in allusion, and brings to mind the carefully polished diplomatic encounters of the Zuo. After the opening frame, the dialogue begins with a compound metaphor on balancing power relations and working together:

> 公曰："儀父，不穀擩左，右絙，擩右，左絙，如權之有加，橈也。君及不穀專心戮力以左右諸侯，則何爲而不可？"
>
> The Lord said: "Sir Yi, if I, the one unable to cultivate, pull to the left, the right (string) draws taut, and if I pull to the right the left draws taut. It is as when the scales have something added, the balance is upset. If you sir, and I, the one unable to cultivate, focus our minds and join our strength to move the many lords left and right, then what could we not achieve?"

Lord Mu of Qin's goal throughout the text is to gauge Sir Yi's willingness to plead a case for cooperation between Qin and Chu. The use of metaphor, in a rare display of discursive acumen for a ruler in these texts, presents a careful dance of interpretation. In what is surely a test of each other's discursive strength, it further provides a means to tap the other's willingness to engage in a shared discourse as well, as if Lord Mu and Sir Yi are asking each other: "Do we understand one another?"

Their combined power to "move the many lords left and right" into a more favorable configuration is contrasted with the problem of doing it on one's own. The metaphor is clear in general import; i.e., manipulating one element (or lord) leads to a counter-reaction in another. Pulling left and right may refer to the steering of a chariot,[22] but it is not made concrete and may just be a more general metaphor of action and reaction. Indeed, it is further likened by analogy to the scales, itself a common metaphor for balancing power.[23] But whereas scales ought to be balanced to get a proper result, what is asked for is a further weighing down of the scales in order to tip the balance in Qin and Chu's favor.[24]

In the ritualized exchange of song that follows, Lord Mu avails himself of a hunting metaphor asking Mr. Yi to be his trustworthy messenger of cooperation:

乃命升琴歌於子儀，楚樂和之，曰："鳥飛兮適永，余何矰以就之？遠人兮離宿，君有尋言，余誰思于告之？強弓兮挽其絕也，矰追而及之；莫往兮何以實言？余畏其忒而不信，余誰思于協之。昔之獵兮余不與，今茲之獵余或不與，施之責兮而奮之職，任之不成，吾何以祭稷？"

Then he ordered Sheng Qin to sing to Mr. Yi, and harmonize it with Chu music. It went: "The bird flies, going further away. With what corded-arrow could I reach it? A person from far away, about to leave your lodge; my lord, I have words seeking an audience. Who will I think of to tell them? The bow is strong, and is drawn to its end; the corded-arrow pursues and reaches them; if you did not go, how could I place my words?

---

22 Charioteering is often metaphorically used to describe government; see Major, "Tool Metaphors in the *Huainanzi*," 180ff.
23 Vankeerberghen, "Choosing Balance," 47–89.
24 Zhou Boqun, "Mechanical Metaphors in Early Chinese Thought," 73, refers to this use of the weighing metaphor as "weight manipulation," often used in terms of gaining political or military advantage.

I am afraid that he will doubt them and not trust me. Who will I think of to mediate my words? In the hunts of the past, I did not participate. Now (if) in this hunt, I was not to participate, (would this not be) exercising my duties and exerting myself in my task, yet not seeing it to completion. How could I offer at the altar of grain?"

Mr. Yi, as corded-arrow, is asked to "mediate" (*xie* 協) the lord's desires and present them favorably to the Chu king. Given the poetic context, the metaphor is drawn out (much like the use of *xing* 興 "evocation" in traditional poetry commentary) with repeated reference to component elements (bow, hunt, offering etc.) It gains in aptitude because it is presented in the context of the archery ritual, indirectly asking Mr. Yi to conceive of the arrows he fires at the target as a symbol for delivering Lord Mu's message. When finally asked what he will say, Mr. Yi replies with three short metaphors:

子儀曰："臣觀於潿溰，見屬鸛踦濟，不終需鸛，臣其歸而言之；臣見二人仇競，一人至，辭於儺，獄乃成，臣其歸而言之；臣見遺者弗復，翌明而叛之，臣其歸而言之；公曰'君不尚荒隔，王之北沒，通之於鈠道'，豈於子孫若？臣其歸而言之▬。"

Mr. Yi said: "I, your minister, touring along the Wei and Shi rivers, saw a type of crane that wanted to cross over on one foot. It did not reach the end and had to wait for another (to do it together). That is what I will say when I return. I saw two people fighting. Another person arrived and adjudicated between the pair. The case was then solved. That is what I will say when I return. I saw someone giving something that was not given back. The next day they were betrayed. That is what I will say when I return. When you, milord, say: 'If you do not value desolate separation (between our states), and do not want the territories north of your king lost, and connected to the

Xiao corridor,' can we really leave that to our sons and grandsons? That is what I will say when I return ▬."

The reply consists of four answers in a layering of codes. The first is about cooperation. The Wei and Shi rivers stand metonymically for Qin and Chu. The crane standing on one leg evokes images of mythical birds that require a partner to cross over.²⁵ The second reply draws on the image of an adjudicator mediating a fight. It probably refers to the role of Chu in the conflict between Qin and Jin. The referent of the third metaphor is less clear, especially because 遺 can be read as either *wei* "to give" or *yi* "lost." Yang Mengsheng is probably correct in reading this in the context of Qin giving grain to Jin and being attacked in return.²⁶ It presents a powerful message about loyalty, suggesting that Chu should think twice about supporting a fickle Jin and should instead work together with trustworthy Qin. The last answer is less metaphoric and instead draws on a rhetorical question to convey a sense of urgency to the possible consequences if Qin and Chu were not to align.

Taken together, the use of metaphor in the *Zi Yi* evokes the linguistic acumen of diplomacy and shares in the *Zuo*'s predilection of exchanging coded messages through song.²⁷ In the context of the diplomatic meeting,

---

25 This is another enigmatic reference. According to the editors, it refers to the crane, often seen standing on one foot, or, with Zi Ju 子居, a *man* 鸞 bird which only has one foot, one wing, and one eye, and needs another to fly; see "Qinghua jian *Zi Yi* jiexi" 清華簡《子儀》解析, *Zhongguo Xianqin shi wangzhan* 中國先秦史網站 May 11, 2016, originally published at http://xianqin.byethost10.com/2016/05/11/333, now available at, https://www.academia.edu/41579284/%E6%B8%85%E5%8D%8E%E7%AE%80_%E5%AD%90%E4%BB%AA_%E8%A7%A3%E6%9E%90

26 Yang Mengsheng 楊蒙生, "Qinghua liu *Zi Yi* pian jianwen jiaodu ji" 清華六《子儀》篇簡文校讀記, *Qinghua daxue Chutu wenxian yanjiu yu baohu zhongxin wangzhan* 清華大學出土文獻研究與保護中心網站, April 16, 2016, https://www.ctwx.tsinghua.edu.cn/info/1081/2228.htm, Wang Ning 王寧, "Qinghua jian liu *Zi Yi* shiwen jiaodu" 清華簡六《子儀》釋文校讀, *Fudan daxue chutu wenxian yu guwenzi yanjiu zhongxin wangzhan* 復旦大學出土文獻與古文字研究中心網站, June 9, 2016, http://www.fdgwz.org.cn/Web/Show/2824, suggests it refers to an unclaimed lost object returned the next day, where the lost object supposedly refers to the states that Chu needed to bring into alignment against Jin.

27 David Schaberg, "Song and the Historical Imagination in Early China," *Harvard Journal of Asiatic Studies* 59.2 (1999): 305–361, and Zhang Suqing 張素卿, *Zuo zhuan cheng shi yanjiu*《左傳》稱詩研究 (Taipei: Guoli Taiwan daxue, 1991).

the metaphors are not necessarily in competition with each other, but certainly for the audience's attention. While they suggest a shared understanding of language and intent, they invite the audience to become a partner in the act of decoding. As a sub-genre within narrative historiography about the Springs and Autumns period, it has a recognizable form and horizon of expectations. One of the ways in which texts such as these could draw in their readers and generate a pleasant aesthetic experience is through the creative manipulation of image and metaphor.[28] While the genre and its rules of employment may be familiar, a particular rendering of a story can still stand out by the novelty of its images and the complexity of its encoded allusions. The stability of the form generates familiarity, allowing an audience to feel *as if present*, whereas the rich variety of imagery allows one to immerse in the experience, as if it were a new *encounter*.

3.3 Coloring with Words, the Language of War

Whereas the current ruler is presented in a subordinated position to the advisors, the rulers of the past are generally exalted as models of achievement. In the recounting of these precedents, the visual description of military achievement takes primacy of place. What the current ruler lacks in linguistic acumen, leadership experience, and command of cultural code (roughly mapping *wen* 文 "cultural attainment"), the former rulers excelled in military might, innovation, and determination (roughly, *wu* 武 "martial prowess").

In the **Zheng Wen Gong wen Tai Bo*, Grand Elder depicts a vivid image of Zheng's former ruler Lord Huan's achievements:

昔吾先君桓公後出自周，以車七乘，徒三十人，鼓其腹心，奮其股肱，以協仇偶，攝冑擐甲，攫戈盾以造勳。

---

28 Jauss notes the aesthetic gap between the horizon of expectations (i.e., genre rules and common plot structures established at the beginning of the narrative, and changes in the middle and end (horizon of change)), as a way of engaging and surprising the reader. See, Jauss, "Literary History as a Challenge to Literary Theory," 12–14.

Of yore, our former ruler, Lord Huan, moved last from Zhou, with seven chariots and thirty foot-soldiers. He drummed on their bellies and hearts, and let their arms and legs take wing, so as to join them in pairs.[29] They fastened their helmets and strapped on their armor, they seized their halberds and shields in order to reap glory.

Not recounting actual battles, the use of precedent focuses on the inspiring leadership of the lord. Turning a band of soldiers into an army that would end up laying the foundations for the state of Zheng is presented idiomatically. Lord Huan drummed them on and gave them wings, as the soldiers took their weapons. All of this presents an idealized and idiomatic image of war, but does not describe actual action. Avoiding descriptions of the horrors and violence of war is common enough in early Chinese historiographical narratives. The use of image-based language compensates for this lack of actual drama by dramatizing in visual terms the narration of war preparation.

The *Zhao Jianzi* evinces a similar strategy. The former ruler Lord Xiang of Jin's expeditions is rendered through the image of him donning his armor. His frugality is visualized in his unwillingness to don furs and spread a fan. After more concrete examples of frugality (integration of sacrifices), Lord Ping's largesse and waste are synecdochically represented through the grandeur of his palace and his clothing, among other things:

就吾先君襄公，親冒甲冑，以治河濟之間之亂▆。冬不裘，夏不張箑，不食濡肉，宮中六䆷并六祀，然則得輔相周室，兼霸諸侯。就吾先君平公，宮中三十里，馳馬四百駟，奢其衣裳，飽其飲食，宮中三臺，是乃侈已，然則失霸諸侯，不知周室之……儉之侈……侈之儉乎▆？

When we come to our former ruler Lord Xiang, he personally

---

29 An alternative translation reads *fuxin* 腹心 and *gugong* 股肱 as metaphors for the close confidants of the ruler. Given that they seem to refer to soldiers here, I have chosen to translate literally.

donned his armor, in order to subdue the unrest between the Yellow River and the Ji ▬. In the winter he did not don furs, and in the summer he did not spread a fan. He did not eat soft-boiled meats, the six stoves of the inner palace were integrated into the six sacrifices, and thus he managed to assist the governing of the Zhou royal house and stand as hegemon among the lords of the states. When we come to our former ruler Lord Ping, the inner palace grounds (grew to) thirty li, he had four-hundred teams of thoroughbred steeds, he was extravagant in his clothing, was satiated in food and drink, and the three platforms in the inner palace were used to indulge himself. Thus he lost the hegemony over the lords of the states, and did not know of the affairs of the Zhou royal house … an excess of frugality … or a frugality of excess ▬?

This passage contains concrete examples of expenditure that are easily visualized and clearly contrasted with regular norms. They are used to draw up an image of the achievements of these rulers instead of, say, a list of policy decisions. The images conjure up a known and relatable experience (everyone wears clothes and lives in a house) but extend it into the absurd (one normally wears furs in the winter, and probably did not have a 30 *li* residence). The distance to normal experience characterizes the rulers while it draws in the audience.

In the **Jin Wen Gong ru yu Jin*, Lord Wen's achievements as a ruler are rendered visually in his innovative deployment of flags and formations:

乃作為旗物：為升龍之旗，師以進；為降龍之旗，師以退▬。為左……為角龍之旗，師以戰；為交龍之旗，師以舍。[……]乃為三旗以成：至遠旗死，中旗刑，近旗罰。成之以挾于郊三。因以大作▬。元年克原▬，五年啟東道，克曹、五鹿，敗楚師於城濮▬，建衛，成宋，圍許，反鄭之陴▬，九年大得河東之諸侯▬。

Thereupon he instituted the use of flag insignia: with the flag of the rising dragon, the army would advance; with the flag of the descending dragon, the army would retreat ▬ . With the (flag of the …) left … With the flag of dragons (interlocking) horns, the troops would engage; with the flag of rising and falling dragons, the troops would desist; […] Thereupon, three flags were established to mark accomplishment: those (only) reaching the far flag were put to death; those reaching the middle flag were given corporal punishment; those reaching the near flag were fined. He completed it by having three caned in the outskirts of the city. As a result of (these reviews) he (accomplished) great success ▬ . In the first year he conquered Yuan ▬ . In the fifth year he opened the Eastern Road, conquering Cao and Wu Lu, and defeated the Chu armies at Chengpu ▬ . He set up Wei, pacified (the situation in) Song, besieged Xu, and overturned the parapet wall of Cheng ▬ . In the ninth year he greatly gained (the loyalty of) the lords east of the River ▬ .

The array of mythical and rare animals symbolizes the action of the troops and renders the act of warfare in simple visual terms. Eschewing actual violence and detailed narration, the raising of a flag with a recognizable image stands synecdochally for war and achievement. The closest thing to action appears in the final list of achievements, relating punishments inflicted on the soldiers and a short list of military victories.

While the victories take the form of a list, they alternate with visual descriptions of the type of battle, such as overturning parapet walls or a siege. This dynamic is seen in the *Zheng Wen Gong wen Tai Bo* as well:

戰於魚羅，吾[乃]獲函、訾，覆車襲介、克鄶，專斷如容社之處，亦吾先君之力也。世及吾先君武公，西城伊闕，北就鄔、劉，縈軛蔦、邘之國，魯、衛、蓼、蔡來見。世及吾先君莊公，乃東伐齊虇之戎爲徹，北城溫、原，遺陰喪次，東啟隤、樂，吾逐王於葛。

They battled in Yuluo, and we [then] gained Han and Zi. They covered their chariots, seized Jie and conquered Kuai. They solidified their hold on a place to accommodate our altars. That too was due to the efforts of our former ruler. Reaching the age of our former ruler, Lord Wu, in the west he scaled the walls of Yique, in the north he went to Wu and Liu, he entangled and yoked the states of Wei and Yu, and Lu, Wei, Liao, and Cai came to audience. Reaching the age of our former ruler, Lord Zhuang, (he) then attacked the Rong of Qihuan and made a path; in the north he scaled the walls of Wen and Yuan, gave away Yin, and lost his place, (but) opened Tui and Le in the east, and we chased the king up to Ge.

Whether "covering chariots," "entangling and yoking states," or "scaling walls," the choice of words in these truncated descriptions contain the kernel of a much larger story. Perhaps it was meant to evoke war stories anecdotally circulating in the realm — there must have been *some* form of narration of the grit and detail of war going around. The point is that these narratives did not give those details, and instead drew a picture of an idealized state of war just enough to characterize the rulers yet vivid enough to keep the audience engaged.

3.4 Summary

The use of image-based language is comparable with other forms of narrative historiography more broadly and the effects I have discussed above are of course not limited to the texts included in this volume. Nevertheless, despite their short length, these texts rely extensively on image-based language. It is one of their main ways of drawing in the audience and having them engage with the central concerns of the narrative. In summary, two dynamics can be observed. On the one hand the recognizability and vivacity of a well-chosen image has the power of a proverbial "thousand words" allowing the audience to transport itself across space and time and become participants in the events of the narrative. On the other hand, some examples feature a clear distance between image and reality, or, require extensive decoding on behalf of the audience before the image makes sense. It is this willingness to decode that again draws the audience closer in that it engages their intellect and plays on a sense of linguistic superiority to allow the audience to "one-up" the ruler along with the advisors. Finally, images are used to stand in as a token for another story. A flag or battle formation elides the battle at the same time that it evokes the more familiar aspects of war. Accordingly, precedents and anecdotes could be rendered short and effective, adding to and not disturbing the main flow of the narrative. Where in a philosophical text, a well-chosen image or metaphor allows one to understand a complex argument in a more innate and direct way, the audience of narrative historiography was likewise able to connect on more intimate terms with the events of the past through image-based language.

Chapter Four
Conclusion

In these chapters accompanying the translations, I have focused on analyzing the literary structure and devices of the texts. Drawing on narratological theory and the study of image-based language, I have highlighted common elements in the structure of narration, the presentation of characters and dialogue, and the use of language in these texts.

In general, the texts follow a simple structure composed of a narrative that frames a dialogue between a ruler and an advisory figure. Sometimes, this basic structure is expanded. The *Zi Fan Zi Yu* and *Zheng Wu Furen gui ruzi*, for example, introduce more complex scene changes and multiple interlocutors. In other texts, such as the *Jin Wen Gong ru yu Jin* and the *Zi Yi*, the opening frame is expanded to include a more active narrating voice, inscribing a certain reading on the events and characters of the text. As a rule, the advisors are presented in control, albeit discursively, of the dialogues. The advisors challenge the rulers and set them up to ask a more incisive question. They control the access to knowledge and a major focus of these texts is the inscription of power relations between characters, often, periphrastic descriptions are used instead of names and titles to indicate the relative status of the characters.

The clearest outlier to this form is the *Jin Wen Gong ru yu Jin*. That text presents the ruler firmly in command. Indeed, it effectively neuters the dialogue form altogether and it ends on a list of achievements of the present, rather than past rulers. Nevertheless, the *Jin Wen Gong ru yu Jin* text likewise contains its fair share of image-based language, a feature common to all these texts. Both the *Zhao Jianzi and *Zheng Wen Gong wen Tai Bo, for example, likewise contain lists of achievements of former rulers filled with imagery. In general, the texts productively use similes and metaphors to involve the audience and draw them over the threshold into the microcosm of the narrative.

All of these features taken individually are not unique, of course, and present common tools in narrative. Whether in the *Zuo* or within the span of a single anecdote, we can often find a similar use of language or narrative structure. Nevertheless, the narratives analyzed here, with the possible exception of the *Jin Wen Gong ru yu Jin*, share a regular combination of narrative features that suggest they form at least a subset or subgenre of narrative historiography. In the introduction I have already noted the difference between these stand-alone narratives and the larger and more complexly integrated narrative structure of the *Zuo*. Here, I want to illustrate the features of these narratives in comparison with a representative anecdote from the Shanghai Museum collection of Warring States bamboo manuscripts, titled the *Zhuangwang ji cheng* 莊王既成:

> 莊王既成無射，以問沈尹子莖曰："吾既果成無射以供春秋之嘗，以 [一] 待四鄰之賓，[吾]後之人，幾何保之？"沈尹固辭，王固問之，沈尹子莖 [二] 曰："四與五之間乎？"王曰："如四與五之間，載之傳車以上乎？繫四航以 [三] 逾乎？"沈尹子莖曰："四航以逾。" ┗ [四 a]
>
> When King Zhuang [of Chu] had completed [the bell(s) called] "Tireless" (*wuyi*), he asked Zijing, the Deputy of Shen, about it: "I have managed to complete the 'Tireless' for use in providing the *chang*-offerings in the spring and autumn and hosting the guests of the neighboring states. How many of those who come after me will protect it/them?" The Deputy of Shen firmly declined [to answer], and the King firmly asked again. Zijing, the Deputy of Shen, replied: "Between four and five?" "If [it will be] between four and five", said the King, "[will

they] load [it/ them] on a single cart and go up, or [will they] head downstream on four boats?" "Head downstream on four boats", said Zijing, Deputy of Shen.[1]

The anecdote opens with a frame noting that King Zhuang of Chu 楚莊王 had just completed the *wuyi* 無射 bells, metonymically standing for his future hegemony. In the ensuing dialogue with Zijing, the Deputy of Shen 沈尹子莖, he asks about the future protectors of the state. At first unwilling to answer, the Deputy of Shen then provides a cryptic "between four and five." King Zhuang apparently understands this foreshadowing of the tumultuous succession following his own demise and asks whether a cart will carry the bells up or whether boats carry them downriver. These are metaphorical references to Jin and Wu respectively. The Deputy of Shen's answer that it will be downriver ends the text. Indeed, Wu would defeat Chu and sack the capital during the reign of King Zhao.

From this short summary, it is clear that the anecdote appears very similar in form to the texts discussed in this volume. It features a short frame and the majority of the text is made up of a simple dialogue. Likewise, the central premise of the narrative (i.e., the problem) revolves around decoding the cryptic "between four and five" and the short text is filled with metonymy and metaphor. Nevertheless, the power dynamic is markedly different. While the interlocutor similarly does not give an answer straight away, the ruler here pressures him into answering the question. The ruler is presented as smart enough to decode the cryptic statement that follows. The ruler further asks a follow-up question without being prompted by his interlocutor and is answered clearly and directly. Unlike the rulers we have seen in the texts in this volume, the king is in command of the dialogue and the metaphorical answers of his interlocutor. The interlocutor does not present advice let alone admonishment; he merely answers.

---

1   The edition and translation are adapted from Krijgsman and Vogt, "The One Text in the Many," 481–482.

What is more, where the texts discussed here could all reasonably stand on their own and did not require an extensive awareness of Springs and Autumns period history, the anecdote requires a historical awareness to link the "between four and five" to the ambiguity in the succession of King Zhuang. The use of foreshadowing beyond the scope of the individual anecdote, imbues the characters of the anecdote with a foresight eschewed by the narratives discussed in this book but seen more often in the *Zuo*. Another similarity it shares with the *Zuo* is the text's use of full titles in denominating characters rather than periphrastic descriptions. The *Zhuangwang ji cheng* anecdote is much shorter. It stands at four bamboo slips totaling roughly 90 graphs of text. By comparison, that is about a third of the *Zhao Jianzi, one of the shortest texts included in this volume. Finally, the anecdote deals with a purely historiographical problem while the narratives discussed in this volume seek to explore the motivations or moral and philosophical underpinnings of the events of the past. The anecdote asks what is about to happen, the narratives explore why and how they happened as they did.

But do these differences amount to fundamentally different genres of historiography? That may be overstating the case. It is clear that the areas where the texts are the most similar in basic structure, they differ the most in their execution. In other words, they draw on the same features in narrative form but perform them in different ways. Perhaps, therefore, they are best understood as varieties or subgenres of a larger genre of narrative historiography.[2] In their variety, they met different needs of a Warring States audience. It goes without saying that the narration of the past served historiographic and didactic purposes. But as I hope to have shown, it also met experiential, aesthetic, and psychological needs in the audience. These needs went beyond historical fact and explored the underlying drive behind the great encounters and events of the past.

---

2 Compare also Dirk Meyer's discussion of the *Shu* in his *Documentation and Argument in Early China: The Shàngshū* 尚書 *(Venerated Documents) and the Shū Traditions* (Berlin: De Gruyter/Mouton, 2021).

Chapter Five
*Zheng Wu Furen Gui Ruzi 鄭武夫人規孺子 *Lady Wu of Zheng Admonished her Young Child

The Manuscript

The *Zheng Wu Furen gui ruzi* is composed of eighteen slips, and was originally tied together with three binding strings. The slips measure 45 cm in length and 0.6 cm in width. The text is written between the binding strings and it is possible that the manuscript was bound before writing. Nevertheless, especially on the bottom parts of slips 2 and 3 some smudging occurred to the graphs, possibly due to the movement of the binds. Other than a punctuation mark following *ye* 也 on slip 9, the significance of which is not quite clear, and the standard use of reduplication marks, the only punctuation is on the final slip of the manuscript. The text is closed with a thick, hook-shaped mark, after which the remainder of the slip is left blank. A single graph was supplemented, placed to the left and in between the adjacent graphs on slip 11. It is entirely possible that this correction happened in the process of copying and it need not have been a later correction.

On the verso side, lines are carved diagonally across the slips. Based on an analysis of the verso lines, Jia Lianxiang has shown that slips 1–13 and 14–18 were taken from two different sections of bamboo.[1] The first group of slips features a more standard downward oriented line on the back, carved from the middle left downwards to the bottom right. The second group, in turn, features two lines starting from the middle and moving grad-

---

1   Jia Lianxiang, "Qinghua jian *Zheng Wu Furen gui ruzi*" pian de zai bianlian yu fuyuan."

ually towards each other, approaching a sort of leftwards opening V shape ">" without meeting at the point.

As noted early on by Yu Houkai and Zi Ju, slip 9 was likely misplaced in the original ordering and needs to be placed between slips 13 and 14.[2] In the original report, there was speculation regarding a possible missing slip 15, but based on Jia's observations we now know that in fact several slips were taken out of the bundles that would furnish the manuscript before the text was written on the bamboo. Therefore, while there is likely no text missing, slips were removed in the production process. It is unclear whether damage to the slips or errors in the copying led to this choice.

In the current arrangement, the text can be reconstructed with a reasonable modicum of certainty. While many possibilities for variant readings and different interpretations remain, this is not due to the physical state of the manuscript. The script is clear and legible, and known from other manuscripts across the Tsinghua University collection.[3]

The Text

The text describes the period just after Lord Wu of Zheng (r. 770–744 BCE) passed away. Structured along the various steps of the burial rite, the narrative recounts the admonitions of his widow to his firstborn. Lady Wu instructs the young Lord Zhuang (r. 743–701 BCE) to refrain from any knowledge of government in the first three years, and to learn from the high officials. The high officials, becoming anxious after this prolonged silence, task Sir Bian 邊父 to ask the ruler for direction. The narrative ends with Lord Zhuang lamenting that he may never live up to his father.

The editors understand the text to have formed during the Springs and

---

2 Yu Houkai, "Du Qinghua jian liu zhaji (wu ze)," Zi Ju 子居, "Qinghua jian *Zheng Wu Furen gui ruzi* jiexi" 清華簡《鄭武夫人規孺子》解析, *Zhongguo xianqin shi wangzhan* 中國先秦史網站, June 26, 2016, original link expired, now available at https://www.academia.edu/41579308/%E6%B8%85%E5%8D%8E%E7%AE%80_%E9%83%91%E6%AD%A6%E5%A4%AB%E4%BA%BA%E8%A7%84%E5%AD%BA%E5%AD%90-%E8%A7%A3%E6%9E%90.

3 See the discussion in the introduction, section 1.1 "Manuscripts and affiliation."

Autumns period, and that the present manuscript is a Warring States copy. Presumably, this assumption rests on the idea that the text presents narrative detail not preserved in texts such as the *Zuo*. True, the *Zuo* opens with the famous flashback on the breech birth of the future Lord Zhuang, and the subsequent scheming by his mother Wu Jiang 武姜 to have his younger brother Gongshu Duan 共叔段 placed in power.[4] Yet it does not suggest that Lord Zhuang was completely inactive in the first three years of his reign. In the *Zuo* account, he merely waits for the right time to counter his younger brother. What is more, the present text does not seem directly concerned with this famous episode. Lord Wu of Zheng is present in spirit only. Likewise, there is no mention of Gongshu Duan.[5] Chen Wei has referred to the text as a "prequel" 前傳 to the *Zuo*'s famous "The Elder of Zheng Overcame Duan in Yan" 鄭伯克段於鄢 episode.[6] However, given that the *Zuo* episode contains narrative material that covers the period both before and after the events narrated in the present text, this label may not be very apt. Following this idea of a prequel, Li Shoukui has argued that the **Zheng Wu Furen gui ruzi* should be read as describing a veiled attempt by Lord Zhuang's mother to stave off his accession to the throne.[7]

While this is certainly a context evoked by the *Zuo*'s rendition of a *femme fatale* hellbent on scheming to have her favorite placed on the throne, the mother figure in this narrative is cast in the role of an advisor. She "admonishes" the young ruler, instructing him with reference to historical precedent and proper use of his ministers in a manner very similar to some of the other texts we encounter in this collection. That she suggests the young heir should wait and learn from the high officials for three years is also not out of the ordinary. Springs and Autumns lore is rife with stories of

---

4 See *Zuo* Yin 1.4, Durrant, Li, and Schaberg, *Zuo Tradition*, 9–13.
5 A possible exception would be the statement by Lady Wu that she will not meddle in government with talk of brothers and relatives.
6 Chen Wei, "Zheng Bo ke Duan 'qian zhuan' de lishi xushi."
7 Li Shoukui, "*Zheng Wu Furen gui ruzi* zhong de sangli yongyu yu xiangguan de lizhi wenti," esp. 12–16.

Chapter Five *Zheng Wu Furen Gui Ruzi* 鄭武夫人規孺子 *Lady Wu of Zheng Admonished her Young Child*

rulers waiting or told to wait for an opportune moment.[8]

The text at hand seems more concerned with comparing Lord Zhuang with his deceased father.[9] Lord Wu hangs as a specter over his son's every (in)action and Lord Zhuang is repeatedly compared unfavorably to his father by both the ministers and his mother. There is no closure in the narrative, and the reader is left unsure whether or not Lord Zhuang successfully convinces his ministers of his qualities, receives his deceased father's assistance from the netherworld, or manages to turn around his mute image. The text ends in Lord Zhuang's voice, noting:

> 今二三大夫畜孤而作焉，豈孤其足爲勉，抑無如吾先君之憂何？
>
> Now you high officials have taken care of me, the orphaned one, and have taken charge; is it not the case that even if the orphaned one is considered exerting himself enough, this would still not be up to my former lord's concern?

The narrative ends on a tragic, and rather Freudian, lament. Lord Zhuang is doomed to always operate under the shadow of his father, and may never prove himself worthy.

The level of narrative complexity and psychological depth revealed by this text make it very unlikely that it originated in the Springs and Autumns period. As noted earlier, this narrative is one of the few in this selection that has the narrator comment on the anxieties of the characters. I believe it is much more likely that the narrative presents a Warring States imagination or 'telling' of the inner motivations of the characters familiar from famous episodes in the cultural memory of the central states. There is no resolution in terms of the historical events underlying the account. Instead, the text

---

8   Compare for instance King Zhuang of Chu, who did not promulgate any edicts in the first three years of his reign.
9   For an insightful discussion on the various readings enabled by the *Zuo* episode, see Li, *The Readability of the Past*, 59–84.

delves into the details behind Lord Zhuang's apparent silence. While it is certainly possible, and perhaps even likely, that the composers of this text had something like the *Zuo* account in mind as a structuring context for their narrative, at the end of the day this is moot. The text aims to engage its audience on a level that goes beyond the understanding of history to explore tensions and struggles of a more fundamental human concern.

Zheng Wu Furen Gui Ruzi 鄭武夫人規孺子
Lady Wu of Zheng Admonished her Young Child

[ancient script line 1]

[ancient script line 2]

奠 武 公 夲 既 斃 武 夫 人 訳 乳= 曰 昔 虐 先 君 女 邦 廼 又
大 事 㢰 再 三 進 夫= 而 與 之 膚

鄭武公卒，既肂，武夫人規孺子，曰："昔吾先君如邦將有大事，必再三進大夫而與之偕 [一]

Lord Wu of Zheng died, and after his coffin had been placed in a temporary grave,[10] the wife of Lord Wu admonished her young child,[11] saying: "In the past, whenever the state faced major events, my former lord would, without fail, again and again call upon the high officials and together with them [1]

---

10 *Si* 肂 refers to the temporary display of the coffin in a shallow grave for the first three months before the actual burial in a deeper grave. See Li Shoukui, "*Zheng Wu furen gui ruzi* zhong de sangli yongyu yu xiangguan de lizhi wenti," 15–16. He notes the use of *lin* 臨 further on in the text (slip 11) to designate the wailing in front of the coffin/corpse.

11 *Ruzi* 孺子<乳子, heir apparent<young child<suckling babe refers to the future Lord Zhuang of Zheng 鄭莊公. At this point, the young heir would be around 13 years of age. See Zhu Zhongheng, "Qinghua daxue cang Zhanguo zhjian liu jishi," 5. On reading 訳 as *gui* 規 see Li Shoukui 李守奎, "Shi Chu jian zhong de 'gui' — jianshuo 'zhi' yi 'gui' zhi biaoyi chuwen" 釋楚簡中的"規"——兼說"支"亦"規"之表意初文, *Fudan xuebao (shehui kexue ban)* 復旦學報（社會科學版）2016.3: 80–86. While the *gui* functioned similarly to a compass (and, given its shape, possibly to a protractor), used in establishing a circle (and gradient), the relation between admonishment and woodworking implements is somewhat similar to the English usage of "square" or "rectify," which draw on the metaphor of the carpenter's square, or "straighten" which draws on the straight-edge.

𗈷𗈷𗈷𗈷𗈷𗈷𗈷𗈷𗈷𗈷𗈷𗈷𗈷𗈷𗈷𗈷𗈷𗈷𗈷𗈷𗈷𗈷𗈷𗈷𗈷𗈷𗈷𗈷𗈷

恩既旻恩乃爲之毀恩所臤者女繡之以龜筭古君與夫=戭女不相旻晉區=奠邦

圖。既得圖乃爲之毀,圖所賢者焉申之以龜筮,故君與大夫晏焉不相得惡。區區鄭邦[二]

draw up plans. When they came up with a plan, they set out to pick it apart, and the best parts of the plans would be subjected (to divination) with shell and milfoil,[12] and this is why my lord and his high officials were at ease with the process and did not displease one another. Our tiny state of Zheng, [2]

---

12 The punctuation of this line, and the interpretation of *hui* 毀 and 所賢者 is much debated. I follow the punctuation given by the editors, noting that *nai* 乃 functions structurally with *ji* 既. The reading of *hui* 毀 as "criticize" follows Chao Fulin, "Tan Qinghua jian Zheng Wu Furen gui ruzi de shiliao jiazhi," 126.

Chapter Five *Zheng Wu Furen Gui Ruzi* 鄭武夫人規孺子 *Lady Wu of Zheng Admonished her Young Child*

䏍虐君亡不溋亓志於虐君之君己也吏人姚餌於
邦₌亦無大繇䑑於萬民虐君函

望吾君，亡不逞其志於吾君之君己也。使人遙聞於邦，邦亦無大䌛賦於萬民。吾君
陷 [三]

looked in hope at our lord, none were unhappy at the prospect of being ruled by our lord.[13] He sent people to learn of the (affairs of the) state from afar, and (learned) that there were indeed no major corvee duties or taxes wrought upon its myriad people. My lord was trapped [3]

---

13 I follow Wang Tingbin 王挺斌, who suggests to read 溋 as 逞. See Qinghua daxue chutu wenxian dushu hui 清華大學出土文獻讀書會, "Qinghua liu zhengli baogao buzheng" 清華六整理報告補正, Qinghua daxue chutu wenxian yanjiu yu baohu zhongxin wang 清華大學出土文獻研究與保護中心網, April 16, 2016, https://www.ctwx.tsinghua.edu.cn/info/1081/2230.htm. Compare *Zuo* Zhao 25 "No one has ever fulfilled his ambitions while lacking the people's support." 無民而能逞其志者，未之有也. See Durrant, Li, and Schaberg, *Zuo Tradition*, 1635.

於 大 難 之 中 凥 於 㙛 三 年 不 見 亓 邦 亦 不 見 亓 室 女
母 又 良 臣 三 年 無 君 邦 豖 䜌 也

於大難之中，處於衛三年，不見其邦，亦不見其室。如毋有良臣，三年無君，邦家
亂巳。[四]

in great hardship, resided in Wei for three years and could not visit either his state or his chambers.[14] Were it not for our good ministers, those three years without a ruler, would have seen state and home[15] fall into disorder. [4]

---

14 This text is the first to mention Lord Wu of Zheng residing in Wei. Li Xueqin and Cheng Hao link it to the troubles under King Ping of Zhou moving the capital east, being welcomed by Lord Wu of Zheng among others. See Li Xueqin, "You guan Chunqiu shishi de Qinghua jian wu zhong zongshu," 79–80, and "Qinghua liu zhengli baogao buzheng." Chao Fulin notes that the "chambers" here probably refer (metonymically) to Zheng Wu's wife, see Chao Fulin, "Tan Qinghua jian *Zheng Wu furen gui ruzi* de shiliao jiazhi," 128–129.

15 *Bang jia* 邦家 likely echoes *bang* 邦 and *shi* 室 just before.

Chapter Five   *Zheng Wu Furen Gui Ruzi 鄭武夫人規孺子 *Lady Wu of Zheng Admonished her Young Child

[seal/bronze script characters]

自衛與奠若卑耳而㖣今是臣₌亓可不寶虐先君之
常心亓可不述今虐君既枼乳₌

自衛與鄭，若卑耳而謀。今是臣臣，其何不寶？吾先君之常心，其何不述？今吾君即世，孺子 [五]

Participating in (the affairs) of Zheng from Wei, they were as if huddling[16] ear to ear and scheming. Now the ministering of these ministers, how could it not be treasured? My former lord's constancy, how could it not be passed on? Now my lord has passed away, a young child, [5]

16 Wang Tingbing, in "Qinghua liu zhengli baogao buzheng," reads *bei* 卑 as *bi* 比, side-by-side. The editors read it as close *jin* 近. The word *bei* 卑 can mean "to bow down," the image being of two people huddling together, ear-to-ear, to connive a plan. The idea is that Lord Wu of Zheng could influence affairs in Zheng from Wei as if he were physically present.

卉 虫 訇 鮮 之 誈 上 大 夢 摆 厼 暗 勹 偢 含 圭 上 云 州 檆
上 外 卑 紥 又 訇 殳 夢 憿 厼 乎 敨

女母智邦正誈之夫=老婦亦牐丩攸宮中之正門檻
之外母敢又智女老婦亦不敢

汝毋知邦政，屬之大夫。老婦亦將糾修宮中之政，門檻之外毋敢有知焉。老婦亦不敢[六]

you[17] ought not to know of the governance of the state, but leave it to the high officials instead. This old wife will also (merely) inspect and maintain the governing of the inner palace, all that lies beyond the threshold I dare not know of.[18] This old wife will also not dare to [6]

---

17 Commentators are uncomfortable with *ru* 汝 as a mode of address. I follow the editors in reading it so, and note that whatever form of address may have been considered proper, many texts seem to have productively used these minute distinctions of hierarchy to convey a sense of intimacy, rather than shying away from these modes of address altogether. (cf. Li Shoukui, "*Zheng Wu furen gui ruzi* zhong de sangli yongyu yu xiangguan de lizhi wenti," 14ff). For this reason, I have also chosen to translate *ruzi* 孺子 as "young child" as opposed to "young heir," as it seems the power relation here draws on the mother-son relationship and emphasizes youth and, comparative, weakness.

I have translated *zhi* 知 literally as to 'know' of the affairs of government in order to maintain consistency across the various texts in this volume. Here, like the biblical 'knowing in the flesh,' it means more than common knowledge but implies active participation in the process of government.

18 As a notorious *femme fatale*, she is known to have actively contrived to establish her other, younger son Duan 段 to accede to the throne.

Chapter Five   *Zheng Wu Furen Gui Ruzi* 鄭武夫人規孺子 *Lady Wu of Zheng Admonished her Young Child

[bamboo slip characters]

以 姪 弟 昏 因 之 言 以 𡄹 夫₌ 之 正 乳₌ 亦 母 以 埶 豎 卑 御
勤 力 抉 駅 婟 妒 之 臣 躬 共 亓 鹿 色

以兄弟婚姻之言以亂大夫之政。孺子亦毋以褻豎、嬖御，勤力射馭，媚妒之臣躬恭
其顏色，[七]

tell tales about brothers and relatives by marriage to disturb the governance of the high officials.[19] Young child, you also ought not engage with body servants and favored concubines, or spend your energies on archery and charioteering;[20] obsequious and jealous servants comport themselves respectfully in their appearance, [7]

---

19 Li Xueqin reads this as related to Wu Jiang's background, coming from Shen 申. For the classic problem of the relatives of the royal consort forming a power at court see Andrew Eisenberg, *Kingship in Early Medieval China* (Leiden: Brill, 2008). Possibly, the use of 'brothers' hints at Gongshu Duan.

20 I do not agree with Zi Ju who reads *qin li* 勤力 and *she yu* 射馭 as servants, as there are no examples in pre-Qin literature to support this. For a good discussion on problems in earlier readings, see Shen Pei 沈培, "Qinghua jian *Zheng Wu furen gui ruzi* jiaodu wuze" 清華簡《鄭武夫人規孺子》校讀五則, *Hanzi Hanyu yanjiu* 漢字漢語研究, 2018.4: 38–55. I have chosen to read *yi* 以 as a full verb. Given that this text operates in an area not covered by other material it is hard to reconstruct the context. The *Chunqiu* provides a potential reference to Lord Zhuang's chariot antics, albeit much later in his reign; see Yin 3.6, Durrant, Li, and Schaberg, *Zuo Tradition*, 27: "The chariot of the Liege of Zheng tipped over into the Ji river" 鄭伯之車僨于濟. This event, while removed in time from the events of the narrative, may have been resonant enough in Zheng cultural memory that it was sourced for the behavior of the ruler in his youth. Alternatively, these should just be taken as standard behavior of bad heirs.

盅於亓考語以龖夫₌之正乳₌女共夫₌虗以教𡚇女及三戔幸果善之乳₌亓童旻良

掩於其巧語，以亂大夫之政。孺子，汝恭大夫，且以教焉。如及三歲，幸果善之，孺子其重得良 [八]

and hide behind their cunning words, to disrupt the governance of the high officials. Young child, you respect the high officials, and take your lessons from them. If after three years, you perchance end up excelling at it,[21] you, young child, will deeply gain the (support of) the good[22] [8]

21　Not interfering with the ministers and high officials, i.e., good governance.
22　Slip 9 has been moved between slips 13 and 14, following Jia Lianxiang, "Qinghua jian *Zheng Wu Furen gui ruzi*" pian de zai bianlian yu fuyuan.

Chapter Five *Zheng Wu Furen Gui Ruzi* 鄭武夫人規孺子 *Lady Wu of Zheng Admonished her Young Child*

臣三鄰以虖先君爲能敘女弗果善欪虖先君而孤
孺₌亓辠亦欿婁也邦人既聿𦖞之乳₌

臣，四鄰以吾先君爲能敘。如弗果善，死吾先君而孤孺子，其罪亦足數也。邦人既盡聞之，孺子 [+]

ministers, and the (states) neighboring us in the four directions will regard our former lord as being able to put his affairs in order.[23] If you do not end up excelling at it, they will consider our former lord well and truly dead[24] and abandon you, young child, those faults would be enough to cast blame. Once the people of the state have all heard it,[25] young child [10]

---

23 Shen Pei, "Qinghua jian Zheng Wu furen gui ruzi jiaodu wuze" transcribes as *xu* 敘 and reads it as *yu* 豫, "to prepare," indicating that Lord Wu excelled at managing his ministers, to the point they would keep up good governance even in his absence.

24 He Youzu 何有祖, "Du Qinghua jian liu zhaji (er ze)" 讀清華簡六札記（二則）, *Chutu wenxian* 出土文獻 10 (2017): 119–123, notes that the graph *zi* 欪 is a variant form of *si* 死. Shen Pei op. cit. develops this idea and suggests that the added *qian* 欠 signifies an emotional interpretation of the word (he compares *yu* 欲, *xin* 欣, *huan* 歡, etc.), noting that while obviously dead, the king has now died in spirit as well.

25 That the young child had entrusted government to the grandees and ministers.

或 延 告 虐 先 君 女 忍 乳=忐= 亦 猷 欤 虐 先 君 㔻 酒 相 乳=
以 定 奠 邦 之 社 稷 乳=拜 乃 膚 臨 自 是

或誕告吾先君，如忍孺子之志，亦猶足。吾先君必將相孺子，以定鄭邦之社稷。"孺子拜，乃皆臨。自是 [十一]

if you also greatly report to our former lord, and if he accepts the young child's intent, it will also[26] be enough. Our former lord will certainly support you the young child in stabilizing the altars of grain and soil of the Zheng state. The young child bowed, and then they wailed together. From that [11]

---

26 *Yi* 亦 was added in-between *zhi* 志= and *you* 猶, likely by the same scribe.

Chapter Five *Zheng Wu Furen Gui Ruzi* 鄭武夫人規孺子 *Lady Wu of Zheng Admonished her Young Child*

[ancient script line 1]

[ancient script line 2]

旮 以 至 㱇 日 乳₌ 母 敢 又 智 女 諲 之 夫₌ 及 百 執 事 人 虘
思 各 共 亓 事 䛑 父 訛 夫₌ 曰 君 共 而

幾以至葬日，孺子毋敢有知焉，屬之大夫及百執事，人皆懼，各恭其事。邊父規大夫曰："君拱而 [十二]

moment[27] up to the date of burial, the young child did not dare to have any knowledge of it (i.e., the affairs of government), and left it to the high officials and the hundred functionaries. Everyone was afraid, and each respectfully carried out their affairs. Sir Bian admonished the high officials, saying: "Our lord holds his hands to his chest and [12]

---

27 Reading *ji* 幾 follows "bulang" (nickname) on the *Jianbo luntan* forum thread "Qinghua liu *Zheng Wu Furen gui ruzi* chudu" 清華六《鄭武夫人規孺子》初讀, post 17, April 18, 2016, http://www.bsm.org.cn/forum/forum.php?mod=viewthread&tid=3345&extra=page%3D10&page=2. He refers to Qiu Xigui, 裘錫圭, "Shi Zhanguo Chujian zhong de 'ji' zi" 釋戰國楚簡中的"旮"字, *Qiu Xigui xueshu wenji—Jiandu boshu juan* 裘錫圭 學術文集：簡牘帛書卷, (Shanghai: Fudan daxue chubanshe, 2012), 456–464. Qiu notes that the graph ought to be transcribed as *ji* 幾 and should be understood as *qi* 期, instead of directly transcribing it as *qi* 期.

113

辛雪兒斬自夫中斬鼄丮爨亮鴌之自上三习少羕
寿界中乃身象父自月曰二三耂

不言加鼄於夫=女斬鼄君爨而舊之於上三月少羕
夫=聚𠭯乃吏𥱼父於君曰二三耂

不言，加重於大夫，汝慎重君葬而久之於上三月。"小祥，大夫聚謀，乃使邊父於君，曰："二三老[十三]

does not speak. He has put an important (task) on you high officials. If you treat the burial of your lord with care and importance, then draw it out to three months at the most."[28] It was the Minor Auspicious sacrifice,[29] and the high officials gathered to plan. They then sent Sir Bian to the lord, to say: "We old [13]

---

28 Following "Musilang" 暮四郎 (nickname) for the reading of *yu shang* 於上. See *Jianbo luntan* forum thread "Qinghua liu *Zheng Wu Furen gui ruzi* chudu," post 13, April 18, 2016, http://www.bsm.org.cn/forum/forum.php?mod=viewthread&tid=3345&extra=page%3D10&page=2.

29 According to Li Shoukui, the 'Minor Auspicious' sacrifice designates a break of ritual fasting after a year, Li Shoukui, "*Zheng Wu furen gui ruzi* zhong de sangli yongyu yu xiangguan de lizhi wenti," 17.

Chapter Five *Zheng Wu Furen Gui Ruzi* 鄭武夫人規孺子 *Lady Wu of Zheng Admonished her Young Child*

臣 叓 戠 寇 也▬ 尃 悤 於 君 昔 虐 先 君 叓 二 三 臣 归 杲
䖒 勺 之 以 言 思 羣 臣 旻 執 女 □

臣，使禦寇也▬，布圖於君。昔吾先君使二三臣，抑早前後之以言，思群臣得執焉，[且][九]

ministers, if you would employ us to repel bandits ▬,[30] will present our plans to you, our lord. In the past, when our former lord employed us ministers, he would precede it by talking to us first and last, wishing the numerous ministers to have the means to execute it (their employment),[31] [and][32] [9]

---

30 The use of "bandits" here possibly refers to cliques opposed to the heir.
31 See "Zizhu daoren" 紫竹道人 (nickname) on the *Jianbo luntan* forum thread "Qinghua liu *Zheng Wu Furen gui ruzi* chudu," post 38, April 26, 2016, http://www.bsm.org.cn/forum/forum.php?mod=viewthread&tid=3345&extra=page%3D10&page=4.
32 This graph probably writes *qie* 且; see Jia Lianxiang, "Qinghua jian *Zheng Wu Furen gui ruzi* zai bianlian yu fuyuan," 57.

丹文绚刉勹呂含鼄豖木㝵一三也叀勹羊䭞戉今
舎�勹巽賏之车虫止夵之勻勹

母交於死今君定䭞而不言二三臣吏於邦远=女=宵
昔器於巽賏之中母乍手止刮於

毋交於死。今君定，拱而不言，二三臣事於邦，惶惶焉，如宵錯器於選藏之中，毋措手止，殆於 [十四]

not meet up with death.[33] "Now the lord is settled, he holds his hands on his breast and does not speak. We ministers are anxious while serving the state. It is like placing vessels to accompany the burial during the night. We do not know where to put hands and feet.[34] It will run into the danger of[35] [14]

---

33 Following "Musilang"; see *Jianbo luntan* forum thread "Qinghua liu *Zheng Wu Furen gui ruzi* chudu," post 16, April 18, 2016, http://www.bsm.org.cn/forum/forum.php?mod=viewthread&tid=3345&extra=page%3D10&page=2.

34 This reading follows "Dongshanduo" 東山鐸 (nickname) and "Luoxiaohu" 羅小虎 (nickname); see *Jianbo luntan* forum thread "Qinghua liu *Zheng Wu Furen gui ruzi* chudu," post 37, April 24, 2016, http://www.bsm.org.cn/forum/forum.php?mod=viewthread&tid=3345&extra=page%3D10&page=4, and post 55, June 16, 2016, http://www.bsm.org.cn/forum/forum.php?mod=viewthread&tid=3345&extra=page%3D10&page=6. The ministers were earlier tasked by Sir Bian to concern themselves with the funeral preparations.

35 Slip 15 is likely not missing, as first assumed by the editors. See Jia Lianxiang, "Qinghua jian *Zheng Wu Furen gui ruzi*' pian de zai bianlian yu fuyuan," 58.

Chapter Five　*Zheng Wu Furen Gui Ruzi* 鄭武夫人規孺子　*Lady Wu of Zheng Admonished her Young Child*

爲敗者盍君是又臣而爲執辟幾既臣之膞皋或辱
虐先君曰是亓侓臣也君曾枲

爲敗，胡寧君是有臣而爲褻嬖？豈既臣之獲罪，又辱吾先君，曰是其藎臣也？"君答邊[十六]

causing failure. How is this not a case of our lord having ministers and yet engaging with body servants and favored concubines?[36] Is that not a case of having incriminated us ministers and also insulting our former lord, by saying 'These are his loyal ministers?'"[37] The lord replied to Sir Bian, [16]

36　Following Chen Wei, "Zheng Bo ke Duan 'qian zhuan' de lishi xushi."
37　The editors gloss *jin chen* 藎臣 as *jin chen* 進臣, or, "loyal" ministers. Ma Nan in "Qinghua liu zhengli baogao buzheng," suggests that it should be interpreted as the ministers remaining from the former ruler.

𠔽曰一三夫𠂤㝵中𥷁一三夫𩰫坒矛㡰䶒侭㞋亡
坒芳㡰䜌一三尹𡈼𠂤𧻚用屚𣪠𡈼

父 曰 二 三 夫= 不 尚 母 然 二 三 夫= 虐 先 君 斋= 仅 孫 也
虐 先 君 智 二 三 子 之 不 忎= 甬 屚 受 之

父曰：“二三大夫不當毋然，二三大夫皆吾先君之所付孫也。吾先君知二三子之不二心，用兼授之[十七]

saying: "You high officials are not proper and ought not to act like this. You high officials were all entrusted his successors by our former lord. Our former lord knew of your undivided hearts, and therefore bestowed the state on you together."[38] [17]

---

38 I follow Li Shoukui, "*Zheng Wu Furen gui ruzi* zhong de sangli yongyu yu xiangguan de lizhi wenti," 13.

Chapter Five *Zheng Wu Furen Gui Ruzi* 鄭武夫人規孺子 *Lady Wu of Zheng Admonished her Young Child*

〔甲骨文字〕

邦 不 是 肰 或 再 记 虐 先 君 於 大 難 之 中 今 二 三 夫=畜
孤 而 乍 女 幾 孤 亓 䟱 爲 勉 归 亡 女

邦。不是然，又稱起吾先君於大難之中？今二三大夫畜孤而作焉，豈孤其足爲勉，抑亡如 [十八]

If not so, who helped our former lord when he was amidst great hardship?[39] Now you high officials have taken care of me, the orphaned one, and have taken charge; is it not the case that even if the orphaned one is considered exerting himself enough, this would still not be up to [18]

---

39 The idea is to draw a parallel between his period of silence and the former ruler's three years of hardship.

虗先君之慐可

吾先君之憂何？"[十九]

my former lord's concern ?" [19]

鄭武夫人規孺子

鄭武公卒，既肂，武夫人規孺子，曰：

"昔吾先君如邦將有大事，必再三進大夫而與之偕[一]圖。既得圖乃爲之毀，圖所賢者焉申之以龜筮，故君與大夫晏焉不相得惡。區區鄭邦[二]望吾君，亡不遑其志於吾君之君己也。使人遙聞於邦，邦亦無大繇賦於萬民。吾君陷[三]於大難之中，處於衛三年，不見其邦，亦不見其室。如毋有良臣，三年無君，邦家亂已。[四]自衛與鄭，若卑耳而謀。今是臣臣，其何不寶？吾先君之常心，其何不述？今吾君即世，孺子[五]汝毋知邦政，屬之大夫。老婦亦將糾修宮中之政，門檻之外毋敢有知焉。老婦亦不敢[六]以兄弟婚姻之言以亂大夫之政。孺子亦毋以褻豎、嬖御，勤力射馭，媚妬之臣躬恭其顏色，[七]掩於其巧語，以亂大夫之政。孺子，汝恭大夫，且以教焉。如及三歲，幸果善之，孺子其重得良[八]臣，四鄰以吾先君爲能敘。如弗果善，死吾先君而孤孺子，其罪亦足數也。邦人既盡聞之，孺子[十]或誕告吾先君，如忍孺子之志，亦猶足。吾先君必將相孺子，以定鄭邦之社稷。"

孺子拜，乃皆臨。自是[十一]幾以至葬日，孺子毋敢有知焉，屬之大夫及百執事，人皆懼，各恭其事。邊父規大夫曰：

"君拱而[十二]不言，加重於大夫，汝慎重君葬而久之於上三月。"

小祥，大夫聚謀，乃使邊父於君，曰：

"二三老[十三]臣，使禦寇也，布圖於君。昔吾先君使二三臣，抑早前後之以言，思群臣得執焉，[且][九]毋交於死。今君定，拱而不言，二三臣事於邦，惶惶焉，如宵錯器於選藏之中，毋措手止，殆於[十四]爲敗，胡寧君是有臣而爲褻嬖？豈既臣之獲罪，又辱吾先君，曰是其蓋臣也？"

君答邊[十六]父曰：

"二三大夫不當毋然，二三大夫皆吾先君之所付孫也。吾先君知二三子之不二心，用兼授之[十七]邦。不是然，又稱起吾先君於大難之中？今二三大夫畜孤而作焉，豈孤其足爲勉，抑亡如[十八]吾先君之憂何？"[十九]

*Lady Wu of Zheng Admonished her Young Child

Lord Wu of Zheng died, and after his coffin had been placed in a temporary grave, the wife of Lord Wu admonished her young child, saying:

"In the past, whenever the state faced major events, my former lord would, without fail, again and again call upon the high officials and together with them [1] draw up plans. When they came up with a plan, they set out to pick it apart, and the best parts of the plans would be subjected (to divination) with shell and milfoil, and this is why my lord and his high officials were at ease with the process and did not displease one another. Our tiny state of Zheng, [2] looked in hope at our lord, none were unhappy at the prospect of being ruled by our lord. He sent people to learn of the (affairs of the) state from afar, and (learned) that there were indeed no major corvee duties or taxes wrought upon its myriad people. My lord was trapped [3] in great hardship, resided in Wei for three years and could not visit either his state or his chambers. Were it not for our good ministers, those three years without a ruler, would have seen state and home fall into disorder. [4] Participating in (the affairs) of Zheng from Wei, they were as if huddling ear to ear and scheming. Now the ministering of these ministers, how could it not be treasured? My former lord's constancy, how could it not be passed on? Now my lord has passed away, a young child, [5] you ought not to know of the governance of the state, but leave it to the high officials instead. This old wife will also (merely) inspect and maintain the governing of the inner palace, all that lies beyond the threshold I dare not know of. This old wife will also not dare to [6] tell tales about brothers and relatives by marriage to disturb the governance of the high officials. Young child, you also ought not engage with body servants and favored concubines, or spend your energies on archery and charioteering; obsequious and jealous servants comport themselves respectfully in their appearance, [7] and hide behind their cunning words, to disrupt the governance of the high officials. Young child, you

Chapter Five　*Zheng Wu Furen Gui Ruzi* 鄭武夫人規孺子　*Lady Wu of Zheng Admonished her Young Child*

respect the high officials, and take your lessons from them. If after three years, you perchance end up excelling at it, you, young child, will deeply gain the (support of) the good [8] ministers, and the (states) neighboring us in the four directions will regard our former lord as being able to put his affairs in order. If you do not end up excelling at it, they will consider our former lord well and truly dead and abandon you, young child, those faults would be enough to cast blame. Once the people of the state have all heard it, young child [10] if you also greatly report to our former lord, and if he accepts the young child's intent, it will also be enough. Our former lord will certainly support you the young child in stabilizing the altars of grain and soil of the Zheng state.

The young child bowed, and then they wailed together. From that [11] moment up to the date of burial, the young child did not dare to have any knowledge of it (i.e., the affairs of government), and left it to the high officials and the hundred functionaries. Everyone was afraid, and each respectfully carried out their affairs.

Sir Bian admonished the high officials, saying:

"Our lord holds his hands to his chest and [12] does not speak. He has put an important (task) on you high officials. If you treat the burial of your lord with care and importance, then draw it out to three months at the most."

It was the Minor Auspicious sacrifice, and the high officials gathered to plan. They then sent Sir Bian to the lord, to say:

"We old [13] ministers, if you would employ us to repel bandits▬, will present our plans to you, our lord. In the past, when our former lord employed us ministers, he would precede it by talking to us first and last, wishing the numerous ministers to have the means to execute it (their employment), [and] [9] not meet up with death.

"Now the lord is settled, he holds his hands on his breast and does not speak. We ministers are anxious while serving the state. It is like placing vessels to accompany the burial during the night. We do not know where to put hands and feet. It will run into the danger of [14] causing failure. How is this not a case of our lord having ministers and yet engaging with body servants and favored concubines? Is that not a case of having incriminated us ministers and also insulting our former lord, by saying 'These are his loyal ministers?'"

The lord replied to Sir Bian, [16] saying:

"You high officials are not proper and ought not to act like this. You high officials were all entrusted his successors by our former lord. Our former lord knew of your undivided hearts, and therefore bestowed the state on you together. [17] If not so, who helped our former lord when he was amidst great hardship? Now you high officials have taken care of me, the orphaned one, and have taken charge; is it not the case that even if the orphaned one is considered exerting himself enough, this would still not be up to [18] my former lord's concern ⌐ ?" [19]

Chapter Six
*Zheng Wen Gong Wen Tai Bo 鄭文公問太伯 A & B
*Lord Wen of Zheng Asks Grand Elder

The Manuscript

The *Zheng Wen Gong wen Tai Bo narratives come to us in two manuscripts, A and B. It is unclear whether or not these manuscripts made up one longer manuscript. Both manuscripts feature slips 45 cm in length and 0.6 in width, bound by three strings. Manuscript A has 14 extant slips to B's 12. Both manuscripts were significantly damaged, slip 3 has roughly two-thirds missing in A, and B lacks slip 3 completely, with slips 2 and 4 missing the entire top-half. The calligraphy is clear and legible and in the same scribal hand responsible for a large number of texts in this selection. Similar to the *Zheng Wu Furen gui ruzi, a number of corrections and a limited number of punctuation marks are present, and the texts are closed with a fat, hook-shaped punctuation mark after which the remainder of the last slip is left blank.

What sets the manuscripts apart is that the same scribe copied them from different *vorlagen*. While highly similar in terms of the texts they carry, the scribe meticulously and consistently copied the graphic structure of the graphs on the source manuscript. As discussed most comprehensively by Edward Shaughnessy,[1] this resulted in a regular alteration between forms in

---

1 Shaughnessy, "The Tsinghua Manuscript *Zheng Wen Gong wen Tai Bo and the Question of the Production of Manuscripts in Early China." The observation was first made in the source publication by Ma Nan 馬楠, the editor responsible for these manuscripts,

the two manuscripts. The most salient example is the choice of placing the *yi* 邑 "city" signific on the left of graphs in A and on the right in B. The differences are predominantly graphical, featuring two ways of writing the same word. In a limited number of cases, such as the use of *zheng* 争 "contest" on slip 2 in A and *qing* 請 "request" in B, there are obvious consequences for the understanding of the text but these do not change the plot or the overall import of the narrative significantly.

The Text

The narrative is relatively easy to understand, and much of the discussion in the scholarship has focused on geographical details from the campaigns listed in the text.[2] The text features a dialogue between Lord Wen of Zheng 鄭文公 (r. 672–628 BCE) and a certain Grand Elder. The latter cannot be identified with certainty. He succeeds Ziren Chengzi 子人成子 whom the editors cautiously identify as Ziren Yu 子人語. In any case, both must have been powerful figures among the ruling elite, given that they held charge of the city, presumably because Lord Wen was still in mourning over his recently deceased father.

"Grand Elder" or Tai Bo, acts as a substitute father figure of sorts, easing the transition into rule for Lord Wen, in ways similar to Sir Bian in the *Zheng Wu Furen gui ruzi*. His illness that prompts the dialogue also hints at this role. Many deathbed narratives, such as the Tsinghua University *Bao xun* 保訓 *Treasured Instructions*,[3] feature dying fathers or paternal uncles instructing the young heir.[4] In this role as a paternal-advisory figure, Grand

---

and developed in Ma Nan, "Qinghua jian *Zheng Wen Gong wen Tai Bo* yu Zhengguo zaoqi shishi" 清華簡《鄭文公問太伯》與鄭國早期史事, *Wenwu* 文物 2016.3: 86.

2 See, for example, Liu Guang 劉光, "Qinghua jian *Zheng Wen Gong wen Tai Bo* suo jian Zhengguo chunian shishi yanjiu" 清華簡六《鄭文公問太伯》所見鄭國初年史事研究, *Dang'an yanjiu* 檔案研究 2016.6: 31–34.

3 See Edward L. Shaughnessy, vol. 1 in this series and Rens Krijgsman, "Cultural Memory and Excavated Anecdotes in 'Documentary' Narrative: Mediating Generic Tension in the *Baoxun* Manuscript," in Paul van Els and Sarah Queen eds., *Between History and Philosophy: Anecdotes in Early China* (New York: SUNY, 2017), 301–329.

4 Grebnev, "The *Yi Zhoushu* and the *Shangshu*: The Case of Texts with Speeches," and Vogt, "Towards a Metavocabulary of Early Chinese Deathbed Texts."

Chapter Six *Zheng Wen Gong Wen Tai Bo* 鄭文公問太伯 A & B *Lord Wen of Zheng Asks Grand Elder*

Elder takes on his prerogative to remonstrate (*jian* 諫) with the young ruler.

In effect, the remonstrance consists of a history lesson, listing the achievements and failures of the Lords of Zheng preceding Lord Wen, and closing on the note that whether or not one listens to remonstrance determines how one is spoken of by future generations. The history lesson itself is composed primarily of the military successes of Lords Huan, Wu, and Zhuang, and the failures and wasteful expenditure of Lords Zhao and Li. Grand Elder admonishes Lord Wen by noting that he cannot match the preceding lords in their military prowess. Instead, he resembles Lords Zhao and Li in having fallen under the influence of "that one from Chu," referring to Lord Wen's wife from the Mi clan 羋氏.

Other than the initial question, where Lord Wen asks Grand Elder for advice, the ruler does not get a voice and the remainder of the text is a long monologic answer by Grand Elder. As noted in the study above, the text is rife with image-based language and shares the basic structure of these texts wherein the ruler asks for wisdom from an advisor figure.

Zheng Wen Gong Wen Tai Bo A 鄭文公問太伯（甲本）
(*Lord Wen of Zheng Asks Grand Elder* A)

子人成子既死太白堂邑太白又疾夲公逹䎹之君
若曰白父不亭學弱忩甕

子人成子既死，太伯當邑。太伯有疾，文公往問之。君若曰："伯父，不穀幼弱，閔喪 [一]

After Ziren Chengzi[5] had passed away, Grand Elder[6] was in charge of the city. Grand Elder had an illness, and Lord Wen went and asked him about it. The ruler said to the effect: "Sir Bo, I, the one unable to cultivate, am young and weak,[7] I mourn the loss [1]

---

5 The editors note this may be Lord Wen of Zheng's uncle, Ziren Yu 子人語.
6 Li Xueqin, "Youguan Chunqiu shishi de Qinghua jian wu zhong zongshu," 80 suggests that Tai Bo is the oldest son of Ziren Chengzi, and may be an older nephew.
7 B writes 教 and 幽 instead of 亭 and 學 for *gu* 穀 and *you* 幼.

Chapter Six *Zheng Wen Gong Wen Tai Bo* 鄭文公問太伯 A & B *Lord Wen of Zheng Asks Grand Elder*

[bronze/seal script characters]

虐 君 皁 若 鷄 鶵 白 父 是 被 複 不 孛 以 能 與 遉 宓▬ 今
天 爲 不 惠 或 爰 肰 與 不 孛 争 白 父

吾君，譬若鷄雛，伯父寔被覆不穀，以能與就次▬。今天爲不惠，又援然與不穀争伯父[二]

of my lord. I can be likened to a chick and Sir Bo verily[8] sheltered me, the one unable to cultivate, so that I could enter the mourning shack ▬.[9] Now, heaven is not kind, and as if pulling, is contesting[10] with me over Sir Bo's place. [2]

---

8   I follow Zhu Zhongheng, "Qinghua daxue cang Zhanguo zhjian liu jishi," 68, in reading *shi* 寔 for *shi* 是.

9   The use of *yu* 與 is problematic. I understand *yu* 與 as *yu* 於 here, following Huadong Shifan daxue zhongwen xi chutu wenxian yanjiu gongzuo shi 華東師範大學中文系出土文獻研究工作室, "Du *Qinghua daxue cang Zhangguo zhujian (liu) Zheng Wen Gong wen Tai Bo* shu hou (yi) 讀《清華大學藏戰國竹簡（陸）·鄭文公問太伯》書後（一）, *Wuhan daxue jianbo yanjiu zhongxin wangzhan* 武漢大學研究簡帛中心網站, April 20, 2016, http://www.bsm.org.cn/?chujian/6685.html.

   I follow Shaughnessy, "The Tsinghua Manuscript *Zheng Wen Gong wen Tai Bo* and the Question of the Production of Manuscripts in Early China," 59 in reading *ci* 次 as a place of mourning. Manuscript B has *xi* 榳 instead, and it may perhaps refer to a wooden hut.

10 This reading follows Shi Xiaoli 石小力 in "Qinghua liu zhengli baogao buzheng." Note that whereas manuscript A has *zheng* 争 "struggle," B has *qing* 請 "request."

129

所，天不豫伯父，伯父而□□□□□□□□[不]穀。"太伯曰："君，老臣□□□□ [三]

Heaven is not letting Sir Bo be comfortable, Sir Bo you[11] .. .. [the one unable to][12] cultivate." Grand Elder said, "Lord, your old servant .. .. .. [3]

11 I read *er* 而 as the second person pronoun "you."
12 I tentatively supplement *bu* 不 here because of the repetition of *bu gu* 不穀 "the one unable to cultivate" throughout.

Chapter Six *Zheng Wen Gong Wen Tai Bo* 鄭文公問太伯 A & B *Lord Wen of Zheng Asks Grand Elder*

[Chu script characters]

母言而不䈞故之人又言曰爲臣而不諫卑若餽而
不䤈昔虐先君逗公逡出

毋言而不當。古之人有言曰：'爲臣而不諫，譬若餽而不式。' 昔吾先君桓公後出 [四]

if I were not to speak it would be improper. The people of old had a saying, 'Serving as minister and not remonstrating, can be likened to serving food without an alternative.'[13] Of yore, our former ruler, Lord Huan, moved last[14] from [4]

---

13 Reading *kui* 餽 follows Shi Xiaoli in "Qinghua liu zhengli baogao buzheng." For changing the transcription to 䤈 and reading as *er* 弍, see the arguments by Cheng Yan 程燕, "Qinghua liu kaoshi san ze" 清華六考釋三則, *Wuhan daxue jianbo yanjiu zhongxin wangzhan* 武漢大學簡帛研究中心網站, April 19, 2016, http://www.bsm.org.cn/?chujian/6683.html, Su Jianzhou 蘇建洲, "*Qinghua liu Zheng Wen Gong Wen Tai Bo* "kui er bu er" bushuo 《清華六・鄭文公問大伯》"餽而不二"補說, *Wuhan daxue jianbo yanjiu zhongxin wangzhan* 武漢大學簡帛研究中心網站, April 26, 2016, http://www.bsm.org.cn/?chujian/6693.html.

14 The editors note that the use of *hou* 後 "later" probably refers to the relatively late establishment of Zheng. Cheng Hao 程浩 in "Qinghua liu zhengli baogao buzheng," notes that this may refer to the movement outwards of Zheng after the state had been established within the Zhou royal territories.

自 𠭯 㠯 車 七 𥝦 徒 卅= 人 鼓 亓 腹 心 畬 亓 肕 抾 㠯 頿 於
𠬝 𠁁 䈞 㪯 𦁉 虢 㝛 戈 盾 㠯 娭

自周，以車七乘，徒三十人，鼓其腹心，奮其股肱，以協於仇偶，攝胄擐甲，攫戈盾以造 [五]

Zhou, with seven chariots and thirty foot-soldiers. He drummed on their bellies and hearts, and let their arms and legs take wing, so as to join them in pairs.[15] They fastened their helmets and strapped on their armor, they seized their halberds and shields in order to reap [5]

---

[15] By comparing the A (頿) and B (猒) versions, Xu Zaiguo 徐在國, "Qinghua liu *Zheng Wen Gong wen Tai Bo* zhaji yi ze" 清華六《鄭文公問太伯》札記一則, *Zhongguo wenzi xuebao* 中國文字學報 8 (2017): 122–124, argues that *ran* 肰 is likely the phonophore and not *ye* 頁, and suggests reading it as *quan* 勸. While the analysis of the phonophore may be correct, the loan analysis is not without problems, and as such I follow the editors' original suggestion of *xie* 協 for now.

Shi Xiaoli, "Qinghua liu zhengli baogao buzheng," suggests reading it as *qiu* 仇 or *qiu* 逑. It often pairs with *ou* 偶 to describe a pair of people or states.

Chapter Six   *Zheng Wen Gong Wen Tai Bo* 鄭文公問太伯 A & B *Lord Wen of Zheng Asks Grand Elder*

[seal/bamboo script line]

勛戰於魚羅虘□䑛陳阯輂車闌淼克鄶㝬=女容裨
之凥亦虘先君之力也枼

勛。戰於魚羅，吾[乃]獲函、訾，覆車襲介、克鄶，專斷如容社之處，亦吾先君之力也。世 [六]

glory. They battled in Yuluo,[16] and we [then] gained Han and Zi.[17] They covered their chariots, seized Jie and conquered Kuai.[18] They solidified their hold on a place to accommodate our altars.[19] That too was due to the efforts of our former ruler. Reaching the age [6]

---

16 There is a debate whether *yuluo* 魚羅 refers to a place, as is indicated by the grammar and all the places that follow, or a particular battle formation. The editors refer to *Zuo Huan* 5 to argue that it was a battle formation. See Durrant, Li, and Schaberg, *Zuo Tradition*, 93: "Gongzi Hu formed a counterforce on the right, Zhai Zhong formed an opposing force on the left. Yuan Fan and Gao Qumi led the army of the center to support the Lord of Zheng and formed a 'fish school formation' with twenty-five chariots in front, each followed by five chariots to close up gaps" 曼伯為右拒，祭仲足為左拒，原繁、高渠彌以中軍奉公，為魚麗之陳。先偏後伍，伍承彌縫. Durrant, Li, and Schaberg, *Zuo Tradition*, 92, n. 38 note the problems of this interpretation and refer to other interpretations. Even if it was a formation, it may have equally been named after a place.

17 There is a small break in the slip here, and the editors supplement *nai* 乃 based on version B. The historical geography is debated here; see, for instance, discussions in Yu Houkai, "Du Qinghua jian liu zhaji." I tentatively follow the editors. For a narrative predicated on the political geography behind Lord Huan of Zheng's move east, see the opening of the "Zheng yu" 鄭語 chapter of *Guo yu* 國語.

18 I follow the reading of Xu Zaiguo, "Qinghua liu *Zheng Wen Gong wen Tai Bo* zhaji yi ze." The parsing follows Yang Mengsheng 楊蒙生, "Du Qinghua liu *Zi Yi* biji wuze — fu *Zheng Wen Gong wen Tai Bo* yi ze" 讀清華六《子儀》筆記五則——附《鄭文公問太伯》筆記一則, *Qinghua daxue Chutu wenxian yanjiu yu baohu zhongxin wangzhan* 清華大學出土文獻研究與保護中心網站, April 16, 2016, https://www.ctwx.tsinghua.edu.cn/info/1081/2227.htm.

19 I follow the parsing and interpretation by Yang Mengsheng, "Du Qinghua liu *Zi Yi* biji wuze — fu *Zheng Wen Gong Wen Tai Bo* yi ze."

及 虐 先 君 武 公 西 瓾 泋 闕 北 邊 𨸏 餾 縈 厄 陘 竽 之 國
魯 衛 膠 䧘 坴 見 枽 及 虐 先

及吾先君武公，西城伊闕，北就鄔、劉，縈軛蔦、邢之國，魯、衛、蓼、蔡來見。世及吾先 [七]

of our former ruler, Lord Wu, in the west he scaled the walls of Yique,[20] in the north he went[21] to Wu and Liu, he entangled and yoked the states of Wei and Yu, and Lu, Wei, Liao, and Cai came to audience. Reaching the age of our former [7]

---

20 I follow Meng Yuelong 孟躍龍, "Qinghua jian 'Yi jian' ji 'Yi que' shuo" 清華簡"伊閑"即"伊闕"說, *Wuhan daxue jianbo yanjiu zhongxin wangzhan* 武漢大學簡帛研究中心網站, April 15, 2016, http://www.bsm.org.cn/?chujian/6679.html.

21 An alternative, more literal, reading for *jiu* 就 would be to 'take the high ground,' but this seems unlikely, and is unattested for military usage.

Chapter Six *Zheng Wen Gong Wen Tai Bo* 鄭文公問太伯 A & B *Lord Wen of Zheng Asks Grand Elder

君臧公乃東伐齊薩之戎爲斂北䩭陥原徫陰桑宋
東啟遺樂虐达王於鬲

君莊公，乃東伐齊薩之戎爲徹，北城温、原，遺陰喪次，東啟隤、樂，吾逐王於葛。[八]

ruler, Lord Zhuang, (he) then attacked the Rong of Qihuan and made a path;[22] in the north he scaled the walls of Wen and Yuan, he gave away Yin,[23] and lost his place,[24] (but) opened up Tui and Le in the east, and we chased the king up to Ge. [8]

---

22 I tentatively follow the reading of the editors here. In all likelihood, the choice for *che* 徹, understood by the editors as 'path,' over, say, *dao* 道 (as seen in *Ziyi* for instance), may have indicated 'removal' of the Rong problem or is best understood in terms of preparing the space for cultivation; see for example, *Shi jing* "Gong Liu" 公劉: "Breaking open the fields to grow crops" 徹田爲糧.

23 According to the editors' first suggestion, this refers to the ford at Pingyin 平陰津. I follow the editor's second suggestion and read it as *wei* 遺 "give away."

24 I follow Shi Xiaoli in "Qinghua liu zhengli baogao buzheng," in directly transcribing 桑 as *sang* 桑, instead of the editors' *e* 檀, read as *sang* 喪. Manuscript B has *shi* 事 "to serve" and not *ci* 次 "place."

葉及虐先君卲公剌公殹天也亓殹人也▁ 爲是牢
籔不能同穴朝夕戔戕亦不逸斬

世及吾先君卲公、厲公，抑天也，其抑人也▁？爲是牢鼠不能同穴，朝夕鬥鬩，亦不逸斬 [九]

Reaching the age of our former rulers, Lord Zhao and Lord Li, was it heaven or was it because of man ▁? Because these penned up rats could not share a hole,[25] day and night they fought and quarreled, yet did not run away from campaigning. [9]

---

25 Yu Houkai, "Du Qinghua jian liu zhaji," notes two later instances of this analogy in *Shi ji* and the *Liang shu* 梁書.

Chapter Six *Zheng Wen Gong Wen Tai Bo* 鄭文公問太伯 A & B *Lord Wen of Zheng Asks Grand Elder*

伐 今 及 虐 君 弱 學 而 䛐 長 不 能 莫 虐 先 君 之 武 徹 戕
玌 色 淫 䖒 桊 于 庚 䐉 皮 㗅 甬

伐。今及吾君，弱幼而嗣長，不能慕吾先君之武徹壯功，色淫媱于康，獲彼荊寵。[+]

Now we reach you, my lord, you are weak and young yet have succeeded to seniority.[26] You cannot imitate the martial pioneering and vast achievements[27] of our former rulers, and (through) skin and license,[28] you dally in leisure, and receive the affections of that one from Jing,[29] [10]

---

26 I follow Wang Ning, "Qinghua jian liu *Zheng Wen Gong Wen Tai Bo* Jia ben shiwen jiaodu."
27 The choice of words, *wu* 武 and *zhuang* 壯 are likely puns on the temple names of the most successful former rulers.
28 There are multiple readings possible. Shi Xiaoli in "Qinghua liu zhengli baogao buzheng," transcribes as *yin* 印 and reads as *yi* 抑, in order to form a grammatical contrast between the former rulers and the present one. He sees *fu* 孚 from version B as a case of similar form corruption. Others, such as the editors and Shaughnessy, "The Tsinghua Manuscript *Zheng Wen Gong wen Tai Bo* and the Question of the Production of Manuscripts in Early China," transcribe *fu* 孚 and read *fu* 浮 following manuscript B. I chose to transcribe and read directly as *se* 色 "skin" here as it is often linked with *yin* 淫 and conjures up the image of the wily and exotic wife.
29 This refers to his wife of the Mi clan 羋氏 from Chu.

敓大亓宫君而虩之不善找君女由皮孔雪逯之㠯
帀之㐁鹿皇之俞珎是四人

爲大其宫，君而狎之，不善哉。君如由彼孔叔、佚之夷、師之㐁鹿、堵之俞彌，是四人[十一]

so that she may enlarge her palace; and for you to be lord and draw close to her is not good indeed! If my lord were to follow those (such as) Uncle Kong, Yi of Yi, Shi of Qulu, Du of Yumi,[30] these four persons, [11]

---

30 Compare *Zuo* Xi 7.3, Durrant, Li, and Schaberg, *Zuo Tradition*, 286–287.

Chapter Six *Zheng Wen Gong Wen Tai Bo* 鄭文公問太伯 A & B *Lord Wen of Zheng Asks Grand Elder*

者方諫虖君於外茲贍父內謫於中君女是之不能
茅則卑若疾之亡瘍君之亡䤋也

者，方諫吾君於外，茲詹父內謫於中，君如是之不能戀，則譬若疾之亡醫。君之無問也，[十二]

while[31] they remonstrate my lord from the outside, Sir Zhan reprimands from the inside. My lord's inability to make an effort is to the extent that it can be likened to not having a doctor when you are ill. If you do not ask, [12]

---

31 I read *fang* 方 and *zi* 茲 as a temporal contrastive pair, "while" and "now."

則 亦 亡 䎽 也 君 之 亡 出 也 則 亦 亡 内 也 戒 之 㦲 君 虗
若 䎽 夫 䜴 邦 庚 爲 語 而 受 亦

則亦無聞也。君之無出也，則亦無入也。戒之哉，君！吾若聞夫殷邦，湯爲語而紂亦 [十三]

then you will also not hear. If you do not give out, you will also not receive. Be warned, lord! When I hear of the state of Yin, Tang is talked about but Zhòu is [13]

Chapter Six   *Zheng Wen Gong Wen Tai Bo* 鄭文公問太伯 A & B *Lord Wen of Zheng Asks Grand Elder*

𣍘 𧧻、

爲 語 ╱

爲語▬。"[十四]

talked about as well ▬ ."[14]

鄭文公問太伯（甲本）

子人成子既死，太伯當邑。太伯有疾，文公往問之。

君若曰："伯父，不穀幼弱，閔喪 [一] 吾君，譬若鷄雛，伯父寔被覆不穀，以能與就次▃。今天爲不惠，又援然與不穀争伯父 [二] 所，天不豫伯父，伯父而□□□□□□□□ [不] 穀。"

太伯曰："君，老臣□□□ [三] 毋言而不當。古之人有言曰：'爲臣而不諫，譬若饋而不式。'昔吾先君桓公後出 [四] 自周，以車七乘，徒三十人，鼓其腹心，奮其股肱，以協於仇偶，攝胄擐甲，攖戈盾以造 [五] 勳。戰於魚羅，吾 [乃] 獲函、訾，覆車襲介、克鄶，專斷如容社之處，亦吾先君之力也。世 [六] 及吾先君武公，西城伊闕，北就鄔、劉，縈軛蔦、邘之國，魯、衛、蓼、蔡來見。世及吾先 [七] 君莊公，乃東伐齊蘁之戎爲徹，北城温、原，遺陰喪次，東啟隤、樂，吾逐王於葛。 [八] 世及吾先君邵公、厲公，抑天也，其抑人也▃？爲是牢鼠不能同穴，朝夕鬥鬩，亦不逸斬 [九] 伐。今及吾君，弱幼而嗣長，不能慕吾先君之武徹壯功，色淫嫚于康，獲彼荆寵， [十] 爲大其宮，君而狃之，不善哉。君如由彼孔叔、佚之夷、師之佢鹿、堵之俞彌，是四人 [十一] 者，方諫吾君於外，茲詹父內謫於中，君如是之不能懋，則譬若疾之亡醫。君之無問也， [十二] 則亦無聞也。君之無出也，則亦無入也。戒之哉，君！吾若聞夫殷邦，湯爲語而紂亦 [十三] 爲語▃。" [十四]

Chapter Six *Zheng Wen Gong Wen Tai Bo* 鄭文公問太伯 A & B *Lord Wen of Zheng Asks Grand Elder*

*Lord Wen of Zheng Asks Grand Elder A

After Ziren Chengzi had passed away, Grand Elder was in charge of the city. Grand Elder had an illness, and Lord Wen went and asked him about it.

The ruler said to the effect: "Sir Bo, I, the one unable to cultivate, am young and weak, I mourn the loss [1] of my lord. I can be likened to a chick and Sir Bo verily sheltered me, the one unable to cultivate, so that I could enter the mourning shack ▬. Now, heaven is not kind, and as if pulling, is contesting with me over Sir Bo's place. [2] Heaven is not letting Sir Bo be comfortable, Sir Bo you .. .. [the one unable to] cultivate."

Grand Elder said, "Lord, your old servant .. .. [3] if I were not to speak it would be improper. The people of old had a saying, 'Serving as minister and not remonstrating, can be likened to serving food without an alternative.' Of yore, our former ruler, Lord Huan, moved last from [4] Zhou, with seven chariots and thirty foot-soldiers. He drummed on their bellies and hearts, and let their arms and legs take wing, so as to join them in pairs. They fastened their helmets and strapped on their armor, they seized their halberds and shields in order to reap [5] glory. They battled in Yuluo, and we [then] gained Han and Zi. They covered their chariots, seized Jie and conquered Kuai. They solidified their hold on a place to accommodate our altars. That too was due to the efforts of our former ruler. Reaching the age [6] of our former ruler, Lord Wu, in the west he scaled the walls of Yique, in the north he went to Wu and Liu, he entangled and yoked the states of Wei and Yu, and Lu, Wei, Liao, and Cai came to audience. Reaching the age of our former [7] ruler, Lord Zhuang, (he) then attacked the Rong of Qihuan and made a path; in the north he scaled the walls of Wen and Yuan, he gave away Yin, and lost his place, (but) opened up Tui and Le in the east, and we chased the king up to Ge. [8] Reaching the age of our former rulers, Lord Zhao and Lord Li, was it heaven or was it because of man ▬? Because these penned up rats could not share a hole, day and night they fought and

143

quarreled, yet did not run away from campaigning. [9] Now we reach you, my lord, you are weak and young yet have succeeded to seniority. You cannot imitate the martial pioneering and vast achievements of our former rulers, and (through) skin and license, you dally in leisure, and receive the affections of that one from Jing, [10] so that she may enlarge her palace; and for you to be lord and draw close to her is not good indeed! If my lord were to follow those (such as) Uncle Kong, Yi of Yi, Shi of Qulu, Du of Yumi, these four persons, [11] while they admonish my lord from the outside, Sir Zhan reprimands from the inside. My lord's inability to make an effort is to the extent that it can be likened to not having a doctor when you are ill. If you do not ask, [12] then you will also not hear. If you do not give out, you will also not receive. Be warned, lord! When I hear of the state of Yin, Tang is talked about but Zhòu is [13] talked about as well ▬." [14]

*Zheng Wen Gong wen Tai Bo B 鄭文公問太伯（乙本）
(*Lord Wen of Zheng Asks Grand Elder B)

Issues solved for A will not be footnoted again here, differences will be marked and reflected in translation.

[子]人 成 子 旣 死 太 白 噹 邑 太 白 又 疾 吝 公 逵 䎹 之 君
若 曰 白 父 不 敎 幽 弱 忢 尭 虐 君 卑

[子] 人成子旣死，太伯當邑。太伯有疾，文公往問之。君若曰："伯父，不穀幼弱，忢喪吾君，譬[一]

After [Zi]ren Chengzi had passed away, Grand Elder was in charge of the city. Grand Elder had an illness, and Lord Wen went and asked him about it. The ruler said to the effect: "Sir Bo, I, the one unable to cultivate, am young and weak,[32] I mourn the loss of my lord. I can be likened [1]

---

32 Manuscript A has 孛, 睪, instead of 敎, 幽.

☐ 辛 𢖻 戜 㥛 𢟪 𨛷 辛 歖 㝯 曰 以 𠩺 天 辛 豫 𠙴 曰

☐ 不 惠 或 爰 然 與 不 𣪠 請 白 父 所 天 不 豫 白₌父₌

☐不惠，或援然，與不穀請伯父，所天不豫伯父，伯父₍₂₎

… not kind, and as if pulling,³³ is requesting³⁴ Sir Bo's presence from me, if Heaven is not letting Sir Bo be comfortable,³⁵ Sir Bo ₍₂₎

☐ ₍三₎

☐ ₍3₎

---

33 Manuscript A has 肰 instead of 然.
34 Manuscript A has *zheng* 争 "contest" instead of *qing* 請 "request."
35 Because of the difference in wording here, I read this line differently from Manuscript A and understand *suo* 所 as a conditional marker instead of "place." Note that this interpretation was used by the editors in their reading of manuscript A. In manuscript A, the use of "contest" suggests that the reading "place" may be more apt. I do not doubt that at some point in the formation of the text a specific reading was intended, but given the potential for variation, I choose to preserve both alternatives here.

Chapter Six *Zheng Wen Gong Wen Tai Bo* 鄭文公問太伯 A & B *Lord Wen of Zheng Asks Grand Elder

☐ ▁ 〾〾車十〾〾〾〾〾〾〾〾〾〾〾

☐ [自] 周 以 車 七 䡅 徒 卅₌ 人 故 亓 腹 心 畚 亓 胋 抾

☐ [自] 周，以車七乘，徒三十人，鼓其腹心，奮其股肱，[四]

… from Zhou, with seven chariots and thirty foot-soldiers. He drummed on their bellies and hearts, and let their arms and legs[36] take wing, [4]

---

36 Manuscript A writes 胭 instead of 抾.

147

以 猷 於 攸 瓜 籢 韋 䙴 虩 允 戈 盾 以 娭 勛 戠 於 魚 羅 虜
乃 膢 陳 邮 輹 車 闌 淼 克 鄫 寴₌ 女 容 袿

以協於仇偶，攝冑擐甲，攖戈盾以造勛。戠於魚羅，吾乃獲函、訾，覆車襲介，克鄫，專斷如容社。[五]

so as to join[37] them in pairs. They fastened their helmets[38] and strapped on their armor, they seized their halberds and shields in order to reap glory. They battled in Yuluo, and we then gained Han and Zi.[39] They covered their chariots, seized Jie and conquered Kuai. They solidified their hold on a place to accommodate our altars. [5]

---

37 Manuscript A has 頯 instead of 猷.
38 The writing of 籢 has the bottom right *ji* 卂 component corrupted to *nü* 女.
39 The editor (Ma Nan) and Shaughnessy note the consistent different placement of significs between the two versions; note here the presence of the *yi* 邑 component on the right of 鄫, while A has it on the left.

Chapter Six *Zheng Wen Gong Wen Tai Bo* 鄭文公問太伯 A & B *Lord Wen of Zheng Asks Grand Elder

[Seal script characters, line 1]

[Seal script characters, line 2]

之尻亦虗先君之力也枼及虗先君武公西𧗁尹闕
北𠈇郍酃緐厄鄟筡之國魯衛鄝䣕

之處，亦吾先君之力也。世及吾先君武公，西城伊闕，北就邔、劉，緐軛蔦、邘之國，魯、衛、蓼、蔡。[六]

That too was due to the efforts of our former ruler. Reaching the age of our former ruler, Lord Wu, in the west he scaled the walls of Yique,[40] in the north he went[41] to Wu and Liu, he entangled and yoked the states of Wei and Yu, and Lu, Wei,[42] Liao, and Cai.[43] [6]

---

40 The editors note corruption of the *yin* 尹 component to *si* 四, Manuscript A has 𦥑.
41 The editors note A has 𠈇 instead of 𠈇, and that the bottom right component in B is corrupted to *gao* 高.
42 Manuscript A has 衞 instead of 衛.
43 The editors note that *cai* 蔡 here presents a corrupted form. Likewise, 䣕 should be 邘. They suggest this type of 'similar form corruption' (*e zi* 訛字) is similar to the use of *nü* 女 in 甈 noted above. Perhaps, given the consistent structural differences between manuscript A and B it is more productive to understand these cases of 'similar form corruption' as reflecting particular scribal habits that were in turn faithfully copied by the scribe responsible for the manuscript.

坴見枼及虐先君臧公乃東伐齊薵之戎爲啟北甗
邔原遺鄞櫘事東攺遺樂虐逐王於鄁

來見。世及吾先君莊公，乃東伐齊薵之戎爲徹，北城溫、原，遺陰喪事，東啟隤、樂，吾逐王於葛。[七]

came to audience. Reaching the age of our former ruler, Lord Zhuang, then attacked the Rong of Qihuan and made a path; in the north he scaled the walls of Wen and Yuan, he gave away Yin and lost his service,[44] (but) opened up Tui and Le in the east, and we chased[45] the king up to Ge. [7]

---

44 Manuscript A has *ci* 次 "place" instead of *shi* 事 "service."
45 Manuscript A has 达 instead of *zhu* 逐.

Chapter Six *Zheng Wen Gong Wen Tai Bo* 鄭文公問太伯 A & B *Lord Wen of Zheng Asks Grand Elder

葉 及 虗 先 君 邵 公 剌 公 殹 天 也 亓 殹 人 也 亓 爲 是 牢
䑕 不 能 同 穴 朝 夕 戬 戕 亦 不 愞 斬 伐 今

世及吾先君邵公、厲公，抑天也，抑人也？其爲是牢鼠不能同穴？朝夕鬥閟，亦不逸斬伐。今 [八]

Reaching the age of our former rulers, Lord Zhao and Lord Li,[46] was it heaven or was it because of man? Was it not[47] because these penned up rats could not share a hole? Day and night they fought and quarreled, yet did not run away from campaigning. Now [8]

---

46 The editors note that 剌 is corrupted to 刾 here.
47 The particle *qi* 其 is not present in Manuscript A. Here I read it as indicating a rhetorical question; possibly it ought to be read as *qi* 豈.

151

☐ 㝬絅幽亢稚长不能莫虐先君之武徹臧扗孚淫
㐱于康朕皮壡戠螸大亓宮君而

☐ 君弱幽而稚長不能莫虐先君之武徹臧扗孚淫
㐱于康朕皮壡戠螸大亓宮君而

[及吾]君，弱幽而滋長，不能慕吾先君之武徹壯功，浮淫媱于康，獲彼荊寵，爲大其宮，君而 [九]

[we reach you], my lord, you are weak and young yet have succeeded to seniority. You cannot imitate the martial pioneering and vast achievements of our former rulers, you are adrift in license and you dally in leisure,[48] and receive the affections of that one from Jing,[49] so that she may enlarge her palace; and for you to be lord and [9]

---

48 Manuscript A has 庚 instead of 康. Reading *fu* 浮 "adrift" for *fu* 孚 follows Shaughnessy, "The Tsinghua Manuscript *Zheng Wen Gong wen Tai Bo* and the Question of the Production of Manuscripts in Early China." In Manuscript A, it likely reads *se* 色 "skin."
49 The editors note a corruption of 螸 to 敨. A has *yong* 俑 instead of *yong* 螸.

Chapter Six   *Zheng Wen Gong Wen Tai Bo* 鄭文公問太伯 A & B   *Lord Wen of Zheng Asks Grand Elder*

虢之不善哉君女由皮孔吊逯之巨帀之佢鹿皇之俞瓕是四个者方諫塦君自外88贍父

虢之不善弋君女由皮孔吊逯之巨帀之佢鹿皇之俞瓕是四人者方諫虐君於外兹贍父

狎之，不善哉。君如由彼孔叔、佚之夷、師之佢鹿、堵之俞彌，是四人者，方諫吾君於外，兹詹父 [+]

draw close to her is not good indeed! If my lord were to follow those (such as) Uncle Kong, Yi of Yi, Shi of Qulu, Du of Yumi, these four persons, while they admonish my lord from the outside, Sir Zhan [10]

內 謫 於 中 君 女 是 之 不 能 茅 則 卑 若 疾 之 亡 瘖 君 之
亡 䎹 也 則 亦 亡 䎹 也 君 之 亡 出 ▅ 則 亦 亡 內 也

內謫於中，君如是之不能懋，則譬若疾之亡醫。君之無問也，則亦無聞也。君之無出 [也] ▅，則亦無入也。[十一]

reprimands from the inside. My lord's inability to make an effort is to the extent that it can be likened to not having a doctor when you are ill. If you do not ask, then you will also not hear. If you do not give out ▅, you will also not receive. [11]

Chapter Six   *Zheng Wen Gong Wen Tai Bo* 鄭文公問太伯 A & B *Lord Wen of Zheng Asks Grand Elder*

☐ 㠯 𠩺 𡥈 𥎦 夫 𨾔 邦 曰 湯 𣉻 語 㐡 受 亦 𣉻 語 ▪

☐ 君 虐 若 䎽 夫 𨾔 邦 曰 康 爲 語 而 受 亦 爲 語 ＿

[戒之哉，] 君。吾若聞夫殷邦曰湯爲語而紂亦爲語。" [十二]

[Be warned,] lord! When I hear spoken of the state of Yin,[50] Tang is talked about but Zhòu is talked about as well." [12]

---

[50] The editors suspect that 𨾔 was added later in a different hand. The *er* 而 that follows further on the slip is added later as well, I thank Zhang Bofan for pointing this out. Manuscript A writes 䁳 instead. Manuscript A does not include *yue* 曰 "speak."

鄭文公問太伯（乙本）

　　[子]人成子既死，太伯當邑。太伯有疾，文公往問之。
　　君若曰：“伯父，不穀幼弱，恣喪吾君，譬[一]……不惠，或援然，與不穀請伯父，所天不豫伯父，伯父[二]……[三]
　　……[自]周，以車七乘，徒三十人，鼓其腹心，奮其股肱，[四]以協於仇偶，攝冑擐甲，擭戈盾以造勛，戰於魚羅，吾乃獲函、訾、覆車襲介，克鄶，專斷如容社[五]之處，亦吾先君之力也。世及吾先君武公，西城伊闕，北就鄔、劉，縈軛蔦、邘之國，魯、衛、蓼、蔡[六]來見。世及吾先君莊公，乃東伐齊蘄之戎為徹，北城溫、原，遺陰喪事，東啟隤、樂，吾逐王於葛。[七]世及吾先君邵公、厲公，抑天也，抑人也？其為是牢鼠不能同穴？朝夕鬥鬩，亦不逸斬伐。今[八][及吾]君，弱幽而滋長，不能慕吾先君之武徹壯功，浮淫媱于康，獲彼荊寵，為大其宮，君而[九]狎之，不善哉。君如由彼孔叔、佚之夷、師之佢鹿、堵之俞彌，是四人者，方諫吾君於外，茲詹父[十]內謫於中，君如是之不能戀，則譬若疾之亡醫。君之無問也，則亦無聞也。君之無出[也]▃，則亦無入也。[十一][戒之哉，]君。吾若聞夫殷邦曰湯為語而紂亦為語。”[十二]

*Lord Wen of Zheng Asks Grand Elder B

After [Zi]ren Chengzi had passed away, Grand Elder was in charge of the city. Grand Elder had an illness, and Lord Wen went and asked him about it.

The ruler said to the effect: "Sir Bo, I, the one unable to cultivate, am young and weak, I mourn the loss of my lord. I can be likened [1] … not kind, and as if pulling, is requesting Sir Bo's presence from me, if Heaven is not letting Sir Bo be comfortable, Sir Bo … [3]

… from Zhou, with seven chariots and thirty foot-soldiers. He drummed on their bellies and hearts, and let their arms and legs take wing, [4] so as to join them in pairs. They fastened their helmets and strapped on their armor, they seized their halberds and shields in order to reap glory. They battled in Yuluo, and we [then] gained Han and Zi. They covered their chariots, seized Jie and conquered Kuai. They solidified their hold on a place to accommodate our altars. [5] That too was due to the efforts of our former ruler. Reaching the age of our former ruler, Lord Wu, in the west he scaled the walls of Yique, in the north he went to Wu and Liu, he entangled and yoked the states of Wei and Yu, and Lu, Wei, Liao, and Cai [6] came to audience. Reaching the age of our former ruler, Lord Zhuang, then attacked the Rong of Qihuan and made a path; in the north he scaled the walls of Wen and Yuan, he gave away Yin and lost his service, (but) opened up Tui and Le in the east, and we chased the king up to Ge. [7] Reaching the age of our former rulers, Lord Zhao and Lord Li, was it heaven or was it because of man? Was it not because these penned up rats could not share a hole? Day and night they fought and quarreled, yet did not run away from campaigning. Now [8] [we reach you], my lord, you are weak and young yet have succeeded to seniority. You cannot imitate the martial pioneering and vast achievements of our former rulers, you are adrift in license and you dally in leisure, and receive the affections of that one from Jing, so that she may enlarge her palace; and for you to be lord and [9] draw close to her is not good indeed! If my lord were to follow those (such as) Uncle Kong, Yi of Yi, Shi of Qulu, Du of Yumi, these four persons, while they admonish my lord from the outside, Sir Zhan [10] reprimands from the inside. My lord's inability to make an effort is to the extent that it can be likened to not having a doctor when you are ill. If you do not ask, then you will also not hear. If you do not give out ▬, you will also not receive. [11] [Be warned,] lord! When I hear spoken of the state of Yin, Tang is talked about but Zhòu is talked about as well." [12]

Chapter Seven
Zi Fan Zi Yu 子犯子餘 Mr. Fan and Mr. Yu

The Manuscript

The *Zi Fan Zi Yu* 子犯子餘 narrates the story of Prince Chong'er 重耳 staying in Qin before taking power in Jin as Lord Wen of Jin 晉文公 (r. 636–628 BCE). The manuscript's fifteen slips are roughly 45 cm long and 0.5 cm wide and bound with three strings. The script is clear and arranged between the binds. There is only minor damage to slips 1, 4–6, 14. The verso of the first slip of the manuscript contains the title written in the same hand as the main text. The last slip of manuscript contains a thick hook-shaped punctuation mark followed by the empty space at the end.

An important feature of the *Zi Fan Zi Yu* is its extensive use of punctuation. It carries twenty-three marks that are used not just to parse the text but also to place stress on particular elements of the dialogue. In a previous study, I have argued that punctuation in the *Zi Fan Zi Yu* is used to highlight a particular reading of the text.[1] Major shifts in the narrative tend to be furnished with large marks, while subclauses and formulas tend to be highlighted using smaller marks. The distribution of these marks suggests that the punctuator placed a particular emphasis on the replies of the advisors in the dialogues. This observation provides further substantiation to the analysis of the narrative structure and the division of discursive power noted

---

1 For an extensive discussion of the use of punctuation in the *Zi Fan Zi Yu* and **Jin Wen Gong ru yu Jin*, see Krijgsman, "Punctuation and Text Division in Two Early Narratives."

above. Indeed, the witty reversals of the ruler's remarks by Mr. Fan and Mr. Yu are marked consistently, and despite the formulaic language structuring the dialogue, the text is engaging and entertaining to read.

The punctuation therefore reveals a particular reading of the text, a reception of the story, rather than just delineating the proper parsing of sentences. Whether the punctuator was a scribe involved in the production of this or a previous instantiation of the manuscript, a proof-reader, or simply a reader cannot be established beyond doubt, but it does suggest that we should take seriously the aesthetic and intellectual life of these manuscripts before they were placed in what we assume was a grave.

Within the present selection of manuscripts, a majority of which share a hand with the *Zi Fan Zi Yu*, it is noteworthy that except for the **Jin Wen Gong ru yu Jin*, the other materials do not feature an equally avid use of punctuation to mark story components. Possibly, this suggests that the punctuation was added by an individual other than the scribe. Nevertheless, as the scribe in the **Zheng Wen Gong wen Tai Bo* materials displays a marked interest in copying the text *as written*, it is also entirely possible that in this case too, he merely copied punctuation marks already present in a base copy of *Zi Fan Zi Yu*. Either way, this would rule out the present scribe as the source of the punctuation marks.

The Text

As a narrative, the *Zi Fan Zi Yu* fills a gap in other accounts of Chong'er's peregrinations.[2] It provides an intimate view into dialogues that form the background to the support that Lord Mu of Qin gave to Chong'er in his bid for power. Perhaps not surprisingly, this background has a decidedly moral character. Not concerned with the narration of events, the

---

2   For studies and overviews on the narrative cycle, see Jeff Bissel, "Literary Studies of Historical Texts: Early Narrative Accounts of Chong'er, Duke Wen of Jin" (Ph.d. diss., Univ. of Wisconsin, 1996); David W. Pankenier, "Applied Field-Allocation Astrology in Zhou China: Duke Wen of Jin and the Battle of Chengpu (632 B.C.)," *Journal of the American Oriental Society* 119 (1999): 261–279; Khayutina, "Die Geschichte der Irrfahrt des Prinzen Chong'er und ihre Botschaft."

dialogue that makes up the main body of the text is concerned with refuting Lord Mu's notion that Chong'er and his advisors were not up to the task, and proceeds to show both the ability of the advisors in their skillful manipulation of the dialogue and the moral character of Chong'er in the perception of his peers. Uncle Jian, an older advisor at Lord Mu's court, is even more direct in his challenges of Lord Mu's wisdom and does not spare Chong'er either. If anything, the narrative is about the wit and knowledge of the advisors, juxtaposing it with rulers who are willful, ignorant, or indecisive. By comparison, the famous *Zuo* account on Chong'er's stay in Qin focuses on the future Lord Wen of Jin's "recompense" *bao* 報 of help and wrongdoings by the lords of other states during his peregrinations. The same court scene, which by narrative logic, would provide the might of Qin to back up Chong'er in his bid for power, was imagined in vastly different ways. They present two different stories built from the same raw materials (character, place, time) and, if anything, ought to alert us to the wide range of motivations and aims of the authors who produced these different texts rather than subscribing to one or the other as a historically accurate rendition of the encounter.

Zi Fan Zi Yu 子犯子餘
Mr. Fan and Mr. Yu

□□□巨自楚桓秣阝出三戠． 秣公弓訋孑軋秀龕生．
曰孑㒸公孑之宣㡱孑． 耆芣䢻又禍公孑亍鈬㞢生． 秀

□□□耳自楚迡秦尻女三㦱＿ 秦公乃訋子軋而龕女＿
曰子若公子之良庶子＿ 耆晉邦又禍公子不能㞢女＿ 而

□□□[公子重]耳自楚蹠秦，處焉三歲＿。秦公乃召子犯而問焉＿，曰："子若公子之良庶子＿，胡晉邦有禍，公子不能止焉＿，而 [一]

[Prince Chong'] Er went from Chu and took to Qin on his heels and resided there for three years ▂.[3] The lord of Qin thereupon summoned Mr. Fan and asked him ▂, saying: "Since you are such a good advisor[4] to your Prince ▂, why is it that when there was misfortune in the state of Jin, your Prince did not manage to stay there ▂ and [1]

---

3   Note that based on received texts, Chong'er resided in Qin for two years. (*Shi ji* "Jin shijia" 晉世家).
4   I translate *shuzi* 庶子 as "advisor" here in line with the following lines. Compare Chen Wei 陳偉, "Qinghua qi *Zi Fan Zi Yu* jiaodu" 清華七《子犯子餘》校讀, *Wuhan daxue jianbo yanjiu zhongxin wangzhan* 武漢大學簡帛研究中心網站, April 30, 2017, http://www.bsm.org.cn/?chujian/7532.html, who reads it as a designation for the Prince himself. The structure of the text speaks against this reading.

走去之母乃猷心是不欤也虖▮ 子軏會曰誠女宔君之
言▮ 虐宔好定而敬訏不秉禍利身不忍人古走去之

走去之，毋乃猷心是不足也乎▮？"子犯答曰："誠如主君之言▮。吾主好定而敬信，不秉禍利，身不忍人，故走去之，[二]

ran away from it; was it not in fact that his resourcefulness was lacking ▮ ?" Mr. Fan replied, saying: "It is exactly as milord says ▮ . My ruler prefers stability and respects trust, he does not use the misfortune (of others) for his own good,[5] and cannot bear (to see the suffering of) others; that is why he ran away from there, [2]

---

5 My understanding of this line is informed by Liu Zhao 劉釗, "Liyong Qinghua jian (qi) jiaozheng gushu yi ze" 利用清華簡（柒）校正古書一則, *Fudan daxue chutu wenxian yu guwenzi yanjiu zhongxin wangzhan* 復旦大學出土文獻與古文字研究中心網站, January 5, 2017, http://www.fdgwz.org.cn/Web/Show/3018.

以卽中於天宔女曰疾利女不阞諴我宔古弗秉▬ 省公
乃訋子余而䎽𠮷曰子若公子之良庶子▬ 晉邦又禍公

以節中於天。主如曰：'疾利焉不足，' 諴我主故弗秉▬。" 少公乃召子餘而問焉，曰：
"子若公子之良庶子▬，晉邦有禍，公 [三]

to let heaven come to a balanced decision.[6] If, milord would say: 'His (desire) to quickly[7] profit from this was lacking,' that is exactly why my lord did not use it. ▬ " After a while the lord then summoned Mr. Yu and asked him, saying: "Since you are such a good advisor of your Prince ▬ , when there was misfortune in the state of Jin, your Prince [3]

---

6 Interestingly, the rhyme in this section, *sins* 信, *nin* 人, *thîn* 天, is not marked with punctuation. See Zi Ju for notes on rhyme in the text; Zi Ju 子居, "Qinghua jian qi *Zi Fan Zi Yu* yundu" 清華簡七《子犯子餘》韻讀, *Zhongguo xianqin shi wangzhan* 中國先秦史網站, October 28, 2017, originally published at https://www.xianqin.tk/2017/10/28/405, now available at https://www.academia.edu/41579159/%E6%B8%85%E5%8D%8E%E7%AE%80%E4%B8%83_%E5%AD%90%E7%8A%AF%E5%AD%90%E4%BD%99_%E9%9F%B5%E8%AF%BB.

7 I follow Shi Xiaoli in "Qinghua qi zhengli baogao buzheng," who glosses as *ji* 急 "hasty."

Chapter Seven Zi Fan Zi Yu 子犯子餘 Mr. Fan and Mr. Yu

□□□ [子不能] 止焉，而走去之，毋乃無良左右也乎？"子餘答曰："誠如主之言▬。吾主之二三臣，不干良規，不敝有善，必出有 [四]

did not manage to stay there and ran away from it; is it not then, that he did not have good assistants?" Mr. Yu replied, saying: "It is exactly as milord says ▬. My lord's ministers do not infringe on the proper guidelines, they do not eclipse the capable and expel the [4]

□□□ 𧈧𦀘𧉟𦄼𦀊𦄼𦁊𢦏𦀊又𥘉𢆶𢼌𦀊𡥜_ 𢖠𡶎𦁊之.
𥃩又𣅥戌𢆶𦀊心亻𠦪年𠩺之. 𡈼𦀊𤔲𣅥𢎘𥱎𡢟𢆶

□□□ 於難𧈧𦄼 於志幸旻又利不忻蜀_ 欲皆𠩺之_
事又訛女不忻以人必身𠩺之_ 虖宝弱寺而𢎘志不

[惡, 吾主]⁸ 於難, 諤留於志。幸得有利不忻獨__, 欲皆僉之__。事有過焉, 不忻以人, 必身擅之__。吾主弱時而强志, 不[五]

[wicked] without fail. [When my lord is] in difficulty,⁹ (he) keeps straight in (his) intent. If he has the fortune to gain an advantage, he does not enjoy it on his own __ , and wants everyone to share in it __ . When there are errors in affairs, he is not willing to have it extend unto other people,¹⁰ and insists on bearing it by himself __ . My ruler had strong intent (even) when times were weak, and did not [5]

---

8 I follow Wang Ning 王寧, "Shi Qinghua jian Qi Zi Fan Zi Yu zhong de 'e zhou'" 釋清華簡七《子犯子餘》中的"愕籀," *Fudan daxue chutu wenxian yu guwenzi yanjiu zhongxin wangzhan* 復旦大學出土文獻與古文字研究中心網站, April 5, 2017, http://www.fdgwz.org.cn/Web/Show/3024.

9 I follow Chen Wei, "Qinghua qi *Zi Fan Zi Yu* jiaodu." An alternative translation would be to have the ministers be the subject of the whole section. I understand it to refer to Lord Wen here because of the recurrence of the words *zhi* 志 "intent" and *du* 獨 "single<solitary" in the final lines that unambiguously refer to the ruler.

10 I follow the interpretation of Feng Shengjun 馮勝君, "Qinghua jian *Zi Fan Zi Yu* pian 'bu xi' jie" 清華簡《子犯子余》篇"不忻"解, *Wuhan daxue jianbo yanjiu zhongxin wangzhan* 武漢大學簡帛研究中心網站, May 5, 2017, http://www.bsm.org.cn/?chujian/7537.html.

□□□, 顧監於禍, 而走去之。主如此謂無良左右, 誠縈獨其志▬。" 公乃召子犯、子餘曰: "二子事公子, 苟盡有 [六]

.. .. .. he observed there was to be misfortune, and ran away from it. If this is what milord would call 'not having good assistants,' then it is exactly because (my ruler) is single-minded in his intent ▬ ." The lord then summoned Mr. Fan and Mr. Yu, saying: "You two, in serving your Prince, given that you are fully of [6]

⺅中昌天豊邲䘏自公子 ⺄ 乃各䞣之鐱䋲衣常而敹之思䢗 ⺄ 公乃䨐𨸁於邘雩曰夫公子之不能居晉邦訏天

心女是天豊悡褐於公子▁ 乃各賜之鐱緇衣常而敹之思還▁ 公乃䨐 於邘雩曰夫公子之不能居晉邦訏天

心如是，天禮悔禍於公子▁。"乃各賜之劍帶衣裳而善之，使還▁。公乃問於蹇叔曰："夫公子之不能居晉邦，信天[七]

this heart, Heaven, in accord with ritual propriety, will repent this misfortune brought upon the Prince ▁."[11] Thereupon he bestowed upon each of them a sword belt and upper and lower garments, and praised them.[12] Then he sent them back ▁. The lord then asked Uncle Jian, saying: "That the Prince could not stay in the state of Jin, was that really mandated by Heaven? [7]

---

11 I follow Chen Wei 陳偉, "Qinghua jian qi *Zi Fa Zi Yu* 'Tianli huihuo' xiaoshi" 清華簡七《子犯子余》"天禮悔禍"小識, *Wuhan daxue jianbo yanjiu zhongxin wangzhan* 武漢大學簡帛研究中心網站, May 4, 2017, http://www.bsm.org.cn/?chujian/7522.html, in reading this passage.

12 I follow Chen Wei, "Qinghua qi *Zi Fan Zi Yu* Jiaodu."

Chapter Seven Zi Fan Zi Yu 子犯子餘 Mr. Fan and Mr. Yu

[bamboo-strip script image]

命 哉 割 又 僕 若 是 而 不 果 以 㪍 民 心 訐 難 成 也 哉 ＿ 邗 㫐
會 曰 訐 難 成 ＿ 殹 或 易 成 也 凡 民 秉 厇 耑 正 譖 忒 才 上 之

命哉？曷有僕若是而不果以國，民心信難成也哉＿？" 蹇叔答曰："信難成＿，抑或易成也。凡民秉度端正僭忒，在上之 [八]

When has there been a case of someone with servants[13] such as these who did not end up ruling the kingdom, are the hearts and minds of the people really that hard to win over ＿?" Uncle Jian replied, saying: "Yes, they are truly hard to win over ＿. Or they might be easy to win over. In general, whatever standard the people hold on to, whether straight or transgressive, comes down to the person on top. [8]

---

13 *Pu* 僕 is used most commonly for carriage drivers and other lower servants close to the lord; it need not designate someone who is a driver or servant by status. Compare the case in *Zuo* Ai 2 where the lord's son by a concubine is acting as a driver: "Previously, the Prince of Wei went roaming in the outskirts of the city, with Gongzi Ying as his driver" 初，衛侯遊于郊，子南僕; see, Durrant, Li, and Schaberg, *Zuo Tradition*, 1840–1841. Here, written with the *chen* 臣 signific, it likely refers to Master Fan and Master Yu in a more colloquial style, as opposed to the more respectful 'good advisors' / 'counsellors' used in direct address. In this section, *guo* 國 is used in the same way as *bang* 邦 in the earlier half of the text. Whether or not these slight lexical differences add up with the clear textual break to suggest that these two were originally separate texts is unclear. It may just reflect a change in register from the more formal and public conversation between the lord and Chong'er's advisors as opposed to that between the lord and his own advisor.

人上總不遵斤亦不遺＿公乃䎽於邗䇂曰䇂昔之舊
聖折人之䣙政命刑罰事眾若事一人不敎余敢䎽亓

人，上繩不失，斤亦不僭＿。"公乃問於蹇叔曰："叔，昔之舊聖哲人之敷政令刑罰，使衆若使一人，不穀余敢問其 [九]

If the one on top does not lose the (correct hold of) the plumb line, the axe (i.e., the people) will also not transgress ▂."[14] The lord then asked Uncle Jian, saying: "Uncle, when in times of yore the old sages and wise men promulgated their edicts and punishments, they employed the masses as if employing a single person. I, the one unable to cultivate,[15] I dare to ask [9]

---

14 I follow Chen Wei, "Qinghua qi *Zi Fan Zi Yu* Jiaodu."
15 The self-deprecatory address *bu gu* 不穀, "the one unable to cultivate" is not normally followed by a personal pronoun such as *yu* 余. Possibly this text uses it as an adverbial subclause to highlight the self-deprecation. Indeed, in what follows, Lord Mu further positions himself as a learning subject to Uncle Jian.

Chapter Seven *Zi Fan Zi Yu* 子犯子餘 Mr. Fan and Mr. Yu

[seal/bronze script line]

道系 女猷昏是䏦 遺老之言必尚語我才盉孤是勿能
用卑若從䭾狀虐尚觀亓風_ 邗昏會曰凡君斋=䏦

道奚如。猷叔是聞遺老之言，必當語我哉。寧孤是勿能用？譬若從雉然，吾當觀其風__。"蹇叔答曰："凡君之所問[+]

what their way was? Supposing that you have heard sayings of the elders, then you really ought to tell them to me![16] Or do you think that I the orphaned one alone would not be able to use them? Think of it rather as if I were chasing a pheasant, I should want to observe its habits __."[17] Uncle Jian replied, saying: "Of all that you my lord ask, [10]

---

16 This whole section is very informal, suggesting a more intimate relation between Lord Mu and his close advisor.
17 Compare *Huainanzi* "Lanming xun" 覽冥訓: "As to the *Documents of Zhou*, it says: "If you cannot catch the hidden pheasant, then you need to follow its habits." 夫《周書》曰:"掩雉不得，更順其風"; He Ning, *Huainan zi jishi*, 498.

[Chinese seal/bronze script characters]

莫可䎽▁ 昔者成湯以神事山川以悳和民四方凥莫
句與人面見湯若鴌雨方奔之而鹿雁女用果念政

莫可聞▁。""昔者成湯以神事山川，以德和民。四方夷莫後與人，面見湯，若濡雨方奔之而鹿膺焉，用果念政[十一]

nothing could be heard ▁." "In times of yore, Cheng Tang served the mountains and rivers with his spirit, and harmonized the people with his power. Of the peoples of the four directions, none wanted to be (placed) later than the others.[18] When they saw Tang head-on, it was like a nourishing

---

18 There is a lot of debate concerning these couple of lines. For an overview, see Yi Nuo 伊諾, "Qinghua qi *Zi Fan Zi Yu* jishi" 清華七《子犯子餘》集釋, *Fudan daxue chutu wenxian yu guwenzi yanjiu zhongxin wangzhan* 復旦大學出土文獻與古文字研究中心網站, January 18, 2018, http://www.fdgwz.org.cn/Web/Show/4210, 47–57. I follow the parsing of Ma Nan in "Qinghua qi zhengli baogao buzheng." The sense of this line suggested by the editors is to read in line with Mengzi 孟子, "Liang Hui Wang xia" 梁惠王・下, i.e., that none of the peoples wanted to be attacked last, as this would be an insult:

> "The *Book of History* says, 'In his punitive expeditions T'ang began with Ke.' With this he gained the trust of the Empire, and when he marched on the east, the western barbarians complained, and when he marched on the south, the northern barbarians complained. They all said, 'Why does he not come to us first?' The people longed for his coming as they longed for a rainbow in time of severe drought. Those who were going to the market did not stop; those who were ploughing went on ploughing. He punished the rulers and comforted the people, like a fall of timely rain, and the people greatly rejoiced. "The *Book of History* says, 'We await our Lord. When he comes we will be revived.'"
> 《書》曰："湯一征，自葛始。"天下信之。東面而征，西夷怨；南面而征，北狄怨。曰，"奚為後我？"民望之，若大旱之望雲霓也。歸市者不止，耕者不變。誅其君而弔其民，若時雨降，民大悅。《書》曰："徯我后，后來其蘇。"
> Jiao Xun 焦循 ann. Shen Wenzhuo 沈文卓 ed., *Mengzi Zhengyi* 孟子正義, 2 vols. (Beijing: Zhonghua shuju, 1987), 152, D.C. Lau, *Mencius: Translated with an Introduction by D.C. Lau* (London: Penguin, 1970), 69–70.

In this passage, Tang's expansions are described with reference to the *Documents*. Note the similar comparison of Tang with nourishing waters when faced with drought. This of course is a pun on the name Tang (lit. 'hot water'), which carries mythic overtones suggesting nourishment.

rain; they promptly rushed onward and deer-like responded to it.[19] Thus, in the end they longed for his governance, [11]

[seal script characters]

九 州 而 窜 君 之 遂 殜 㒸 受 之 身 殺 三 無 㚢 為 㮥 為 烙 殺
某 之 女 為 㮘 㮸 三 百 㙋 邦 之 君 子 無 少 大 無 遠 逐 見

九州而命君之。後世就紂之身，殺三無辜，為炮為烙，殺梅之女，為拳桔三百。殷邦之君子，無小大，無遠邇，見 [十二]

and the Nine Regions diligently took him as their ruler.[20] In later generations when we come to the person of Zhòu, he murdered the three innocents, and roasted and burned people. He murdered the daughters of Mei, and shackled over three hundred. The lords of the state of Yin, whether big or small, far or close, whenever they saw [12]

---

19 The original suggestion of the editors to read this in line with *Chu ci* 楚辭, "Tianwen" 天問. The Deer is understood as a wind spirit following upon the coming of the rains, "Ping[yi] calls forth the rain, how does he evoke it? Its body is conjoined from two sides, how does the deer carry it?" 蓱號起雨，何以興之。撰體協肋，鹿何膺之. Hong Xingzu 洪興祖, *Chu ci buzhu* 楚辭補註 (Beijing: Zhonghua shuju, 1983), 101–102.
20 I follow Chen Wei 陳偉, "Qinghua qi *Zi Fan Zi Yu* jiaodu (xu)" 清華七校讀（續）, *Wuhan daxue jianbo yanjiu zhongxin wangzhan* 武漢大學簡帛研究中心網站, May 1, 2017, http://www.bsm.org.cn/?chujian/7534.html.

受 若 大 陸 㱿 具 陞 方 走 去 之 思 不 死 型 以 及 于 毕 身 邦 乃
述 嵬＿ 用 凡 君 所 𩂪 莫 可 𩂪＿ 公 子 橦 耳 𩂪 於 邗 叔 曰 嵬

紂若大岸將顛崩，方走去之，懼不死刑以及于厥身，邦乃遂亡＿。" "用凡君所問莫可聞＿。" 公子重耳問於蹇叔曰："亡 [十三]

Zhòu it was like seeing a tall dike about to collapse, and they promptly ran off and left him. They feared that even if they were not killed, corporal punishment would be inflicted upon their bodies. The state was then consequently lost ＿." "That is why I said, 'All that you my lord ask of, cannot be heard ＿.'" Prince Chong'er asked Uncle Jian, saying: "I am bereft (of my country, i.e., in exile)[21] [13]

---

21 I read this as *sang* 喪; the graph is structured different from the way *wang* 亡 is written in the manuscript. The compound *sang ren* 喪人 is used as a form of address to describe Chong'er's exile in *Liji* 禮記 "Tangong xia" 檀弓下, see also *Zuo* Zhao 25.

Chapter Seven Zi Fan Zi Yu 子犯子餘 Mr. Fan and Mr. Yu

□ 𪜶不孫敢大膽𦖞天下之君子欲记邦㞋以欲亡邦㞋
以邗𠯑會曰女欲记邦則大甲與盤庚文王武王女欲

□ [人]不遜，敢大膽問：'天下之君子，欲起邦奚以？欲亡邦奚以？'" 謇叔答曰："如欲起邦，則大甲與盤庚、文王、武王，如欲 [十四]

and unabashed, I dare to brazenly ask: 'The lords of the world, when they want to raise a state, who do they follow? When they want to wreck a state, who do they follow?'" Uncle Jian replied, saying: "If one wants to start a state, then follow Da Jia and Pan Geng, Kings Wen and Wu; If one wants to [14]

亡邦則桀及受刺王幽王亦備才公子之心巳絭
䣜女。

亡 邦 則 桀 及 受 刺 王 幽 王 亦 備 才 公 子 之 心 巳 絭
䣜 女

亡邦，則桀及紂、厲王、幽王，亦備在公子之心已，奚勞問焉▬？"[十五]

lose a state,[22] then follow Jie and Zhòu, Kings Li and You. This too is all already present in your heart, why belabor me in asking about it ▬ ?"[23] [15]

---

22 *Bang* 邦 was added later, squeezed in between.
23 In the previous section, Lord Mu of Qin asks about the tools for governance that he does not possess for he does not have the proper character, and as such, he cannot hear about them. Chong'er does have the character so he should not even be asking.

Verso

𝔻 𝔻 𝔻 𝔻

子 軋 子 余

子犯子餘 [一背]

Mr. Fan and Mr. Yu [1V]

子犯子餘

子犯子餘 [一背]

[公子重] 耳自楚蹠秦，處焉三歲▇。
秦公乃召子犯而問焉▇，曰："子若公子之良庶子▇，胡晋邦有禍，公子不能止焉▇，而 [一] 走去之，毋乃猷心是不足也乎▇？"
子犯答曰："誠如主君之言▇。吾主好定而敬信，不秉禍利，身不忍人，故走去之， [二] 以節中於天。主如曰：'疾利焉不足，'誠我主故弗秉▇。"
少公乃召子餘而問焉，曰："子若公子之良庶子▇，晋邦有禍，公 [三] [子不能] 止焉，而走去之，毋乃無良左右也乎？"
子餘答曰："誠如主之言▇。吾主之二三臣，不干良規，不敝有善，必出有 [四] [惡，吾主] 於難，諤留於志。幸得有利不忻獨▇，欲皆僉之▇。事有過焉，不忻以人，必身擅之▇。吾主弱時而强志，不 [五] □□□，顧監於禍，而走去之。主如此謂無良左右，誠繫獨其志▇。"
公乃召子犯、子餘曰："二子事公子，苟盡有 [六] 心如是，天禮悔禍於公子▇？"
乃各賜之劍帶衣裳而善之，使還▇。
公乃問於蹇叔曰："大公子之不能居晋邦，信天 [七] 命哉？曷有僕若是而不果以國，民心信難成也哉▇？"
蹇叔答曰："信難成▇，抑或易成也。凡民秉度端正僭忒，在上之 [八] 人，上繩不失，斤亦不僭▇。"
公乃問於蹇叔曰："叔，昔之舊聖哲人之敷政令刑罰，使衆若使一人，不穀余敢問其 [九] 道奚如。猷叔是聞遺老之言，必當語我哉。寧孤是勿能用？譬若從雉然，吾當觀其風▇。"
蹇叔答曰："凡君之所問 [十] 莫可聞▇。"
"昔者成湯以神事山川，以德和民。四方夷莫後與人，面見湯，若濡雨方奔之而鹿膺焉，用果念政 [十一] 九州而命君之。後世就紂之身,殺三無辜,為炮為烙,殺梅之女,為拳梏三百。殷邦之君子,無小大,無遠邇,見[十二]紂若大岸將顛崩,方走去之,懼不死刑以及于厥身,邦乃遂亡▬。"

"用凡君所問莫可聞▬。"

公子重耳問於蹇叔曰:"亡[十三][人]不遜,敢大膽問:'天下之君子,欲起邦奚以?欲亡邦奚以?'"

蹇叔答曰:"如欲起邦,則大甲與盤庚、文王、武王,如欲[十四]亡邦,則桀及紂、厲王、幽王,亦備在公子之心已,奚勞問焉▬?"[十五]

Mr. Fan and Mr. Yu

Mr. Fan and Mr. Yu [IV]

[Prince Chong'] Er went from Chu and took to Qin on his heels and resided there for three years ▃ .

The lord of Qin thereupon summoned Mr. Fan and asked him ▃ , saying: "Since you are such a good advisor to your Prince ▃ , why is it that when there was misfortune in the state of Jin, your Prince did not manage to stay there ▃ and [1] ran away from it; was it not in fact that his resourcefulness was lacking ▃ ?"

Mr. Fan replied, saying: "It is exactly as milord says ▃ . My ruler prefers stability and respects trust, he does not use the misfortune (of others) for his own good, and cannot bear (to see the suffering of) others; that is why he ran away from there, [2] to let heaven come to a balanced decision. If, milord would say: 'His (desire) to quickly profit from this was lacking,' that is exactly why my lord did not use it ▃ ."

After a while the lord then summoned Mr. Yu and asked him, saying: "Since you are such a good advisor of your Prince ▃ , when there was misfortune in the state of Jin, your Prince [3] did not manage to stay there and ran away from it; is it not then, that he did not have good assistants?"

Mr. Yu replied, saying: "It is exactly as milord says ▃ . My lord's ministers do not infringe on the proper guidelines, they do not eclipse the capable and expel the [4] [wicked] without fail. [When my lord is] in difficulty, (he) keeps straight in (his) intent. If he has the fortune to gain an advantage, he does not enjoy it on his own ▃ , and wants everyone to share in it ▃ . When there are errors in affairs, he is not willing to have it extend unto other people, and insists on bearing it by himself ▃ . My ruler had strong intent (even) when times were weak, and did not [5] .. .. .. he observed there was to be misfortune, and ran away from it. If this is what milord would call 'not having good assistants,' then it is exactly because (my ruler) is single-minded in his intent ▬ ."

The lord then summoned Mr. Fan and Mr. Yu, saying: "You two, in serving your Prince, given that you are fully of [6] this heart, Heaven, in accord with ritual propriety, will repent this misfortune brought upon the Prince ▬ ." Thereupon he bestowed upon each of them a sword belt and upper and lower garments, and praised them. Then he sent them back ▬ .

The lord then asked Uncle Jian, saying: "That the Prince could not stay in the state of Jin, was that really mandated by Heaven? [7] When has there been a case of someone with servants such as these who did not end up ruling the kingdom, are the hearts and minds of the people really that hard to win over ▬ ?"

Uncle Jian replied, saying: "Yes, they are truly hard to win over ▬ . Or they might be easy to win over. In general, whatever standard the people hold on to, whether straight or transgressive, comes down to the person on top. [8] If the one on top does not lose the (correct hold of) the plumb line, the axe (i.e., the people) will also not transgress ▬ ."

The lord then asked Uncle Jian, saying: "Uncle, when in times of yore the old sages and wise men promulgated their edicts and punishments, they employed the masses as if employing a single person. I, the one unable to cultivate, I dare to ask [9] what their way was? Supposing that you have heard sayings of the elders, then you really ought to tell them to me! Or do you think that I the orphaned one alone would not be able to use them? Think of it rather as if I were chasing a pheasant, I should want to observe its habits ▬ ."

Uncle Jian replied, saying: "Of all that you my lord ask, [10] nothing could be heard ▬ ." "In times of yore, Cheng Tang served the mountains and rivers with his spirit, and harmonized the people with his power. Of the peoples of the four directions, none wanted to be (placed) later than the others. When they saw Tang head-on, it was like a nourishing rain; they promptly rushed onward and deer-like responded to it. Thus, in the end they longed for his governance, [11] and the Nine Regions diligently took him as their ruler. In later generations when we come to the person of Zhòu, he murdered the three innocents, and roasted and burned people. He murdered the daughters of Mei, and shackled over three hundred. The lords of the state of Yin, whether big or small, far or close, whenever they saw [12] Zhòu it was like seeing a tall dike about to collapse, and they promptly ran off and left him. They feared that even if they were not killed, corporal punishment would be inflicted upon their bodies. The state was then consequently lost ▬ ."

"That is why I said, 'All that you my lord ask of, cannot be heard ▬ .'"

Prince Chong'er asked Uncle Jian, saying: "I am bereft (of my country, i.e., in exile) [13] and unabashed, I dare to brazenly ask: 'The lords of the world, when they want to raise a state, who do they follow? When they want to wreck a state, who do they follow?'"

Uncle Jian replied, saying: "If one wants to start a state, then follow Da Jia and Pan Geng, Kings Wen and Wu; If one wants to [14] lose a state, then follow Jie and Zhòu, Kings Li and You. This too is all already present in your heart, why belabor me in asking about it ▬ ?" [15]

Chapter Eight

*Jin Wen Gong ru yu Jin 晋文公入於晋
*Lord Wen of Jin Entered Jin

The Manuscript and its Affiliation

The *Jin Wen Gong ru yu Jin* is a bit of an outlier among the narratives included in this volume. While its topic and materiality closely relate it to the others, it does not feature interlocutors and only presents the voice of Lord Wen of Jin taking command of his home state. Similar to the *Zi Fan Zi Yu*, the nine slips carrying the text are roughly 45 cm in length and 0.5 cm in width. The manuscript does not carry a title and given the close similarities both in materiality and topic with the *Zi Fan Zi Yu* which does carry a title, it has been suggested that the two originally formed a single manuscript.[1] Such an understanding is reinforced by a similar pattern of punctuation—barring differences stemming from the narrative form—in the *Zi Fan Zi Yu*. It is entirely possible that at the moment of punctuating the texts, they were either part of the same manuscript or punctuated by the same individual.

Despite likewise sharing the *Zi Fan Zi Yu*'s proclivity for formulaic language, this is not to say that the texts these manuscripts carried were also produced in the same setting. Given the differences in forms of address, the way the ruler is presented in command rather than in obeisance, and especially the use of monologic versus dialogic narrative, it is equally possible

---

1   For similarities to the *Zi Fan Zi Yu* and for the understanding that the *Jin Wengong ru yu Jin* is a sequel to it, see Li Xueqin, "Zai *Qinghua daxue cang Zhanguo zhujian (Qi)* chengguo fabuhui shang de jianghua" 在《清華大學藏戰國竹簡（柒）》成果發佈會上的講話, *Chutu wenxian* 出土文獻 11 (2017): 1–2.

that the two narratives were composed by different individuals. Some similarities with the other narratives included in this volume can nevertheless be observed. It shares the same basic structure with an opening frame placing the narrative in space and time before having the characters emerge on 'stage' and commence their speech. The narration of military innovations and the listing of victories for the ruler likewise fall in line with some of the other examples included in this volume, such as the *Zheng Wu Furen gui ruzi and the *Zheng Wen Gong wen Tai Bo. If we were to entertain the possibility that the *Jin Wen Gong ru yu Jin and the Zi Fan Zi Yu were actually companion pieces, say, a larger text in two parts, then the occurrence of a large monologic section at the end of such a composition would also not stand out and could likewise be likened to the long monologic endings of the *Zheng Wen Gong wen Tai Bo and the *Zhao Jianzi, for example.

Given all these considerations, it appears impossible to be sure what form these materials took. Possibly, they were punctuated within the same locale, and to some readers they may have belonged together. If we understand the narratives as a set, then the Chong'er from the Zi Fan Zi Yu, chided by Uncle Jian, and not appearing all that ready to take on the role history had in mind for him, is redeemed and presented as exercising the necessary reforms on taking charge of the state in the *Jin Wen Gong ru yu Jin.

The Text

The text opens with Lord Wen as a ruler not discriminating amongst the people seeking an audience. The state is presented as in need of "restoration" (xiu 修). Lord Wen commands the elders of the state to have the prisoners released, agricultural and sacrificial offerings prepared, and to have the army restored. As noted, the *Jin Wen Gong ru yu Jin does not feature dialogue and presents Lord Wen in full command. Dialogue, especially given the role of the advisors in these texts, implies consultation or being instructed on what to do. The *Jin Wen Gong ru yu Jin eschews this sense of dialogue, and there is not a single voice of dissent:

Chapter Eight *Jin Wen Gong ru yu Jin* 晉文公入於晉 *Lord Wen of Jin Entered Jin*

晉文公自秦入於晉，端冕□□□□□□□□ [王] 母，
毋察於好臧偏嬺，皆見。明日朝屬邦耆老，命曰："以孤
之久不得由二三大夫以修晉邦之政▬，命訟獄拘執釋，
滯責毋有賽，四封之內皆然▬。"

When Lord Wen of Jin entered Jin from Qin, he put on his purple robe and hat of office, ... [grand]mother, he refrained from distinguishing between the good and excellent, and the partial and lowly. They were all granted an audience. The following day he held court with the elders of the state, and he commanded: "Because I the orphaned one have long not been able [1] to rely on you high officials in the restoration of the governance of the state of Jin ▬, command the prisoners waiting for trial to be set free, to let accusations be put to rest and indemnities annulled; let it be so everywhere within the four borders ▬."

By comparison, the *Zuo* presents the Lord's first audience with two vignettes. One presents him granting an audience and waiving punishment of a minor official — but only after the narrative reveals a threat to the lord's reputation.[2] In the other vignette, Lord Wen is described as not rewarding a supporter, Jie Zhitui 介之推, causing the latter to go in hiding.[3] Both represent criticism of Lord Wen and provide counterpoise to the hero taking command. A similar dynamic is visible in the *Zuo*'s description of how the lord's policies came about. The original "instructions" of Lord Wen, probably referring to a similar set of commands related here in the *Jin Wen Gong ru yu Jin*, are elided. Instead, in the *Zuo*'s rendition of an episode two years after the narrative action in the manuscript, Mr. Fan (Hu

---

2   This vignette appears in *Zuo* Xi 24; Durrant, Li, and Schaberg, *Zuo Tradition* 376–377. The exemplary story describes Lord Wen's ability to forgive past crimes and grant an audience to a storehouse guardian who had stolen from the stores in his absence. It echoes *Jin Wen Gong ru yu Jin*'s opening lines, wherein the lord is described as granting everyone an audience and accusations are put to rest.

3   *Zuo* Xi 24; Durrant, Li, and Schaberg, *Zuo Tradition*, 378–379.

185

Yan) continuously advises his lord to the effect that his instructions have not yet taken effect, and that the people need to be shown duty, good faith, ritual propriety and so forth. In other words, the passage in the *Zuo* — if read in dialogue with the present text, seems to deny the lord's achievements and again locate his eventual success in the quality advice of Mr. Fan.

晉侯始入而教其民，二年，欲用之。子犯曰：「民未知義，未安其居。」於是乎出定襄王，入務利民，民懷生矣，將用之。子犯曰：「民未知信，未宣其用。」於是乎伐原以示之信。民易資者，不求豐焉，明徵其辭。公曰：「可矣乎？」子犯曰：「民未知禮，未生其共。」於是乎大蒐以示之禮，作執秩以正其官。民聽不惑，而後用之。出穀戍，釋宋圍，一戰而霸，文之教也。

From the moment the Prince of Jin had entered the domain, he had instructed his people. After two years, he wanted to put them to use. Hu Yan said, "The people do not yet understand their duty, and they are not yet peacefully settled in their abodes." So it was that he left Jin to stabilize the position of King Xiang, then came back to the domain and strove to benefit the people, and the people cherished their livelihood. He was about to put them to use as soldiers. Hu Yan said, "The people do not yet understand good faith, and they have not yet demonstrated that they can be put to use." So it was that he attacked Yuan to show them an example of good faith. The people who traded goods did not seek undue profits from this and openly stood by their words. The lord said, "Can we act yet?" Hu Yan said, "The people who traded goods did not seek undue profits from this and openly stood by their words. The lord said, "Can we act yet?" Hu Yan said, "The people do not yet know ritual propriety, and they have not developed respect." So it was that he organized the great spring hunt to show them an example of ritual and established the keeper of

Chapter Eight *Jin Wen Gong ru yu Jin* 晋文公入於晋 *Lord Wen of Jin Entered Jin*

ranks to put in order his officials. The people could then heed his commands and not be deluded, and it was only then that he put them to use. That they could drive the Chu army from the garrison of Gu, relieve the siege of Song, and in a single battle become overlord was due to Wen's instructions.[4]

While the passage ends in an acknowledgement of Lord Wen's instructions,[5] it is clear that in this rendition of the restoration of Jin, the driving force is again placed with his advisors.

After listing the commands of Lord Wen, the *Jin Wen Gong ru yu Jin* narrates a set of innovations in the military that take up the whole latter half of the text. Lord Wen first has innovations made in the flag signaling system for troop deployment, before putting these innovations to the text in an extensive military review.

> 乃為三旗以成：至遠旗死，中旗刑，近旗罰。成之以扶于郊三。因以大作▬。
>
> Thereupon, three flags were established to mark accomplishment: those (only) reaching the far flag were put to death; those reaching the middle flag were given corporal punishment; those reaching the near flag were fined. He completed it by having three caned in the outskirts of the city. As a result of (these reviews) he (accomplished) great success ▬.

Yang Kuan 楊寬 gives a broad picture of the potential scope and background of military reviews, *sou* 蒐 or *jiao* 校.[6] *Sou* 蒐 designates a specific, ritualized gathering of the war chariots and their troops for inspection. This rite seems to have included testing the familiarity of the troops with the

---

4 Durrant, Li, and Schaberg, *Zuo Tradition*, 404–405.
5 Note here different understandings of *wen zhi jiao* 文之教 by Kong Yingda 孔穎達 and Du Yu 杜預; see Durrant, Li, and Schaberg, *Zuo Tradition*, 405, n. 397.
6 See Yang Kuan 楊寬, "'Da sou li' xintan" "大蒐禮"新探, *Xueshu yuekan* 學術月刊 3 (1963): 48–56.

correct movements indicated by drum-beating and flag-waving. Yang's study includes copious references, including military reviews conducted under Lord Wen of Jin. Especially in the *Zhou li*, there is a reference to the *san biao* 三表 (three marks) that needed to be reached in a timely and orderly fashion.[7] It also mentions a final mark, likely signaling full completion of the exercise. Quite possibly, the passage in the **Jin Wen Gong ru yu Jin* discusses a similar exercise, but only refers to three of the marks. Failing to reach a final mark would therefore result in various degrees of punishment. These exercises would in earlier times be combined with a hunt, used to test troop movements; it is likely that this is reflected in the text's use of *jiao* 郊 (outskirts).

Cheng Hao 程浩 has noted the generic nature of these descriptions of military reviews.[8] Both in the *Zuo* and unearthed materials, there are several descriptions of individuals being caned or beheaded after a review. The *Zuo zhuan* mentions two military reviews, linking them to a prediction of Chen Dechen's (Mr. Yu) future failure:

> 楚子將圍宋，使子文治兵於睽，終朝而畢，不戮一人。子玉復治兵於蒍，終日而畢，鞭七人，貫三人耳。
>
> The Prince of Chu was going to lay siege to Song. He sent Dou Gouwutu to drill the soldiers at Kui. Dou Gouwutu finished at the end of the morning and had not punished a single man. Cheng Dechen also drilled the soldiers at Wei. Cheng Dechen finished at the end of the day and had whipped seven men and pierced the ears of three others.[9]

---

7 See the description in *Zhou li* 周禮, "Xiaguan Sima" 夏官司馬, Ruan Yuan 阮元 ed., *Shisan jing zhushu fu jiaokan ji* 十三經註疏附校勘記 (Beijing: Zhonghua shuju, 1980), 29.838.A.

8 Cheng Hao 程浩, "Qinghua jian di qi ji zhengli baogao shiyi" 清華簡第七輯整理報告拾遺, April 23, 2017, *Qinghua daxue chutu wenxian yanjiu yu baohu zhongxin wangzhan* 清華大學出土文獻研究與保護中心網站, https://www.ctwx.tsinghua.edu.cn/info/1081/2234.htm, 4.

9 *Zuo* Xi 27, Durrant, Li, and Schaberg, *Zuo Tradition* 400–401. For a parallel with interesting differences, see the fragmented Shanghai Museum **Cheng Wang wei Chengpu zhi*

Chapter Eight   *Jin Wen Gong ru yu Jin* 晋文公入於晋   *Lord Wen of Jin Entered Jin*

To the *Zuo*, the appropriateness of killing soldiers during a review was the principal concern, but in the *Jin Wen Gong ru yu Jin*, the great success of Lord Wen is directly related to the harsh punishments inflicted on those who failed. It is clear that the two renditions of Lord Wen's coming to power in Jin present very different concerns.

Where the morality of Lord Wen's actions is continuously challenged in the *Zuo*, it is not important to the *Jin Wen Gong ru yu Jin*. The unearthed narrative 'deals' with these concerns in its ideologically charged narration of the Lord in the first two lines of the text, and then proceeds to explore its main concern: a story of success. Likewise, where the *Zuo* account emphasizes the role of advisors and Lord Wen's response to their critiques and challenges, the manuscript's narrative brooks no dissent and is much more concerned with writing a story of unilateral command.

As such, while both relate a similar set of events, they present these in a very different light and tone, and with a different argument about moral right and discursive power. To bring across such a different message, the two texts structure their narratives in different ways. The form of the narrative informs the presentation of the characters and their qualities.

---

xing 成王為城濮之行. While not integrated into a narrative of prediction, it likewise has the king of Chu favor the 'light' review. There are several differences in the passage; important here is the number of people and with which method they were punished.

子文蒐師於睽，一日而畢，不戮一人。子 [甲1] 玉受師，出之蔿，三日而畢，斬三人。

Zi Wen reviewed the troops at Kui, he was finished after a day and did not punish a single person. Master [A1] Yu took charge of the troops, and sent them out to Wei, he was finished after three days and beheaded three people.

*Jin Wen Gong ru yu Jin 晉文公入於晋
*Lord Wen of Jin Entered Jin

[bronze/bamboo script line 1]

[bronze/bamboo script line 2]

晉 文 公 自 秦 内 於 晋 褍 星 □ □ □ □ □ □ □ □ [王] 母₌ 毋
於 妞 妝 嬩 盘 皆 見 昷 日 朝 逗 邦 利 老 命 曰 以 孤 之 舊 不

晉文公自秦入於晋，端冕□□□□□□□□[王]母，毋察於好臧偏嫉，皆見。明日朝屬邦耆老，命曰："以孤之久不 [一]

When Lord[10] Wen of Jin entered Jin from Qin, he put on his purple robe and hat of office,[11] . . . . [grand]mother,[12] he refrained from distinguishing between the good and excellent, and the partial and lowly.[13] They were all granted an audience. The following day he held court with the elders of the state, and he commanded: "Because I the orphaned one have long not been able [1]

---

10 *Gong* 公 was added after the copying of the text, in smaller script, and is likely a correction from the scribe or a proofreading.
11 I follow the editors' second suggestion and read as *mian* 冕 "cap."
12 It is not entirely clear from the image whether or not there is a duplication mark after 毋 as the slip is chipped off on the right side of the graph and the ink traces are slight. For now, I follow the punctuation of the editors. The presence of the mark determines the subject of the following sentence. If there was no mark, the line ought to be punctuated as follows: "王。毋察於" making Lord Wen the unambiguous subject of the examination, whereas with the repetition mark, the subject may well be his mother or grandmother. I do not think the editors' reading of his mother summoning court ladies is likely, as it does not integrate well with the remainder of the narrative. Instead, I choose to read it as a mark of Lord Wen's character that he saw both the good (i.e., those who may have favored and supported him on his return) and the partial or lowly (i.e. those belonging to other factions at court).
13 The editors' reading for the next two graphs, 嬩盘 as 褊斐, focuses on outward appearance "slight and ugly" whereas the previous two described character. I find this unlikely, and suggest reading the first as *pian* 偏 "partial" instead, as it echoes the divided allegiances at court often hinted at in the sources describing Chong'er's return. "Qinghua qi zhengli baogao buzheng," 4 reads as *xi* 嫉 (lowly). Shi Xiaoli's reading is phonologically closer and likewise describes a character trait instead of physical appearance.

Chapter Eight *Jin Wen Gong ru yu Jin* 晋文公入於晋 *Lord Wen of Jin Entered Jin*

旻 繇 弎 厽 夫= 以 攸 晋 邦 之 政 ▂ 命 訟 試 敀 执 罨 䢃 責 母 又
賓 四 圳 之 内 皆 肰 ▂ 或 昷 日 朝 命 曰 以 孤 之 舊 不 旻 繇 弎

得由二三大夫以修晋邦之政▂，命訟獄拘執釋，滯責毋有賽，四封之内皆然▂。"
或明日朝，命曰："以孤之久不得由二 [2]

to rely on you high officials in the restoration of the governance of the state of Jin ▂, command the prisoners waiting for trial to be set free, to let accusations be put to rest and indemnities annulled;[14] let it be so everywhere within the four borders ▂." The following day he held court again, and commanded: "Because I the orphaned one have long not been able to rely [2]

---

14 I follow Feng Shengjun, "'Jin Wengong ru yu Jin' shidu zaji yi ze," in the sense of stopping complaints and letting old debts be left unsettled.

厽 夫=以攸晉邦之祀 命肥蒭羊牛豢犬豕 具畚稷醴=以祀 四圶之內皆肰▁ 或昷日朝 命曰 為豩䆃古命洀舊

三大夫以修晉邦之祀，命肥蒭羊牛、豢犬豕，具黍稷酒醴以祀，四封之內皆然▁。"或明日朝，命曰："為稼穡故，命瀹舊[三]

on you high officials in the organization of the sacrifices of the state of Jin, command to have the goats and oxen fattened with grass, and the dogs and hogs with grain, and to prepare millets and alcohol to be offered; let it be so everywhere within the four borders ▁." The following day he held court again, and commanded: "For the sake of sowing and reaping, order the dredging (lit. "make flow") of the old [3]

Chapter Eight *Jin Wen Gong ru yu Jin* 晋文公入於晋 *Lord Wen of Jin Entered Jin*

溝增舊芳四[封]之內皆狀▄或昷日朝命曰以虐晉邦
之閒尻戠歔之閒命竁攸先君之蠭貪車虢四[封]之內

溝、增舊防，四封之內皆然▄。"或明日朝，命曰："以吾晉邦〈之間〉處仇讎之間，
蒐修先君之乘，飭車甲，四封之內 [四]

channels and the reinforcing of the old dikes; let it be so everywhere within the four borders ▄." The following day he held court again, and commanded: "Because our state of Jin is located between[15] enemies, we have to gather and repair the chariots of our previous rulers and put in order[16] war-chariots and armor; let it be so everywhere within the four borders ▄ ." [4]

---

15 The repetition of *zhi jian* 之間, "in between," results in bad grammar, I understand the first instance to be a copying error (forward eye-skip); if so, it is interesting that this was not remarked upon by the reader who added *gong* 公 on slip 1.

16 The punctuation and the reading as *chi* 飭 "to put in order" follows "ee" (nickname), post 4 on the *Jianbo luntan* 簡帛論壇 forum thread "Qinghua qi *Jin Wen Gong ru yu Jin* chudu" 清華七《晋文公入於晋》初讀, April 24, 2017, http://www.bsm.org.cn/forum/forum.php?mod=viewthread&tid=3457&extra=page%3D11.

皆肰▂乃乍為羿勿為陞龍之羿帀以進為降龍之羿帀以退▂為左□□□□□□□□□□□□□□□□

皆然▂。" 乃作為旗物：為升龍之旗，師以進；為降龍之旗，師以退▂。為左□□□□□□□□□□□□□□□[五]

Thereupon he instituted the use of flag insignia: with the flag of the rising dragon, the army would advance; with the flag of the descending dragon, the army would retreat ▂ . With the (flag of the …) left .. .. [5]

Chapter Eight *Jin Wen Gong ru yu Jin* 晉文公入於晉 *Lord Wen of Jin Entered Jin*

為𧢲龍之𰃮𱍣以戰為交龍之𰃮𱍣以豫為日月之𰃮
𱍣以舊為熊𰃮夫=出為豹𰃮士出為蕘葦之𰃮戠粮者

為角龍之旗，師以戰；為交龍之旗，師以舍；為日月之旗，師以久；為熊旗，大夫出；
為豹旗，士出；為蕘採之旗，侵糧者 [六]

With the flag of dragons (interlocking) horns,[17] the troops would engage; with the flag of rising and falling dragons, the troops would desist;[18] with the flag of the sun and moon, the troops would endure; with the flag of the bear, the high officers would ride out; with the flag of the leopard, the lower officers would ride out; with the flag of gathering firewood and grass,[19] the attackers of the supply lines would [6]

---

17 I follow Ma Nan, "'Jin Wengong ru yu Jin' shulüe," 91. Alternatively, the editors suggest reading this as *gou* 遘. In either case, the idea ought to be of two dragons interlocking horns in fight.
18 I follow Cheng Hao, "Qinghua jian di qi ji zhengli baogao shiyi," 130–131.
19 Pending a better solution, I tentatively follow the editors here.

出 乃 為 三 羿 以 成 至 遠 羿 死 中 羿 荆 忻 羿 罰 成 之 以 象 于
嵩 三 因 以 大 乍＿ 元 年 克 㠯＿ 五 年 啟 東 道 克 曹 五 麋

出。乃為三旗以成：至遠旗死，中旗刑，近旗罰。成之以抶于郊三。因以大作＿。元年克原＿，五年啟東道，克曹、五鹿，[七]

ride out. Thereupon, three flags were established to mark accomplishment: those (only) reaching[20] the far flag were put to death; those reaching the middle flag were given corporal punishment; those reaching the near flag were fined. He completed it by having three caned[21] in the outskirts of the city. As a result of (these reviews) he (accomplished) great success ＿ . In the first year he conquered Yuan ＿ .[22] In the fifth year he opened the Eastern Road, conquering Cao and Wu Lu, [7]

20 I punctuate before *zhi* 至, since, as far as I know, there is no example in pre-Qin literature of *yi cheng zhi* 以成至 as a phrase.
21 Cheng Hao, "Qinghua jian di qi ji zhengli baogao shiyi," 4, reads as *chi* 抶 "to cane," in line with similar descriptions of 1, 3, or 7 punished individuals after a military review.
22 *Zuo* places this in the second year.

Chapter Eight *Jin Wen Gong ru yu Jin* 晋文公入於晋 *Lord Wen of Jin Entered Jin*

敗 楚 師 於 城 僕 ▃ 畫 衛 成 宋 回 譻 反 奠 之 庫 ▃ 九 年 大 旻 河 東 之 者 侯 ▃

敗楚師於城濮▃，建衛，成宋，圍許，反鄭之陣▃，九年大得河東之諸侯▃。[八]

and defeated the Chu armies at Chengpu ▃. He set up Wei, pacified (the situation in) Song, besieged Xu, and overturned the parapet wall of Zheng ▃. In the ninth year he greatly gained (the loyalty of) the lords east of the River ▃. [8]

晋文公入於晋

晋文公自秦入於晋，端冕☐☐☐☐☐☐☐☐[王]母，毋察於好臧偏娭，皆見。

明日朝屬邦耆老，命曰："以孤之久不[一]得由二三大夫以修晋邦之政■，命訟獄拘執釋，滯責毋有賽，四封之内皆然■。"

或明日朝，命曰："以孤之久不得由二[二]三大夫以修晋邦之祀，命肥篘羊牛、豢犬豕，具黍稷酒醴以祀，四封之内皆然■。"

或明日朝，命曰："為稼穡故，命瀹舊[三]溝、增舊防，四封之内皆然■。"

或明日朝，命曰："以吾晋邦處仇讎之間，蒐修先君之乘，飭車甲，四封之内[四]皆然■。"

乃作為旗物：為升龍之旗，師以進；為降龍之旗，師以退■。為左☐☐☐☐☐☐☐☐☐☐☐☐☐[五]為角龍之旗，師以戰；為交龍之旗，師以舍，為日月之旗，師以久；為熊旗，大夫出；為豹旗，士出；為蕘採之旗，侵糧者[六]出。

乃為三旗以成：至遠旗死，中旗刑，近旗罰。成之以抶于郊三。因以大作■。

元年克原■，五年啟東道，克曹、五鹿，[七]敗楚師於城濮■，建衛，成宋，圍許，反鄭之陴■，九年大得河東之諸侯■。[八]

Chapter Eight *Jin Wen Gong ru yu Jin* 晋文公入於晋 *Lord Wen of Jin Entered Jin

*Lord Wen of Jin Entered Jin

When Lord Wen of Jin entered Jin from Qin, he put on his purple robe and hat of office, ... [grand]mother, he refrained from distinguishing between the good and excellent, and the partial and lowly. They were all granted an audience.

The following day he held court with the elders of the state, and he commanded: "Because I the orphaned one have long not been able [1] to rely on you high officials in the restoration of the governance of the state of Jin ▬, command the prisoners waiting for trial to be set free, to let accusations be put to rest and indemnities annulled; let it be so everywhere within the four borders ▬."

The following day he held court again, and commanded: "Because I the orphaned one have long not been able to rely [2] on you high officials in the organization of the sacrifices of the state of Jin, command to have the goats and oxen fattened with grass, and the dogs and hogs with grain, and to prepare millets and alcohol to be offered; let it be so everywhere within the four borders ▬."

The following day he held court again, and commanded: "For the sake of sowing and reaping, order the dredging (lit. "make flow") of the old [3] channels and the reinforcing of the old dikes; let it be so everywhere within the four borders ▬."

The following day he held court again, and commanded: "Because our state of Jin is located between enemies, we have to gather and repair the chariots of our previous rulers and put in order war-chariots and armor; let it be so everywhere within the four borders ▬." [4]

Thereupon he instituted the use of flag insignia: with the flag of the rising dragon, the army would advance; with the flag of the descending dragon, the army would retreat ▬. With the (flag of the …) left .. .. [5] With the flag of dragons (interlocking) horns, the troops would engage; with the flag of rising and falling dragons, the troops would desist; with the flag of the sun and moon, the troops would endure; with the flag of the bear, the high officers would ride out; with the flag of the leopard, the lower officers would ride out; with the flag of gathering firewood and grass, the attackers of the supply lines would [6] ride out.

Thereupon, three flags were established to mark accomplishment: those (only) reaching the far flag were put to death; those reaching the middle flag were given corporal punishment; those reaching the near flag were fined. He completed it by having three caned in the outskirts of the city. As a result of (these reviews) he (accomplished) great success ▬ .

In the first year he conquered Yuan ▬ . In the fifth year he opened the Eastern Road, conquering Cao and Wu Lu, [7] and defeated the Chu armies at Chengpu ▬ . He set up Wei, pacified (the situation in) Song, besieged Xu, and overturned the parapet wall of Zheng ▬ . In the ninth year he greatly gained (the loyalty of) the lords east of the River ▬ . [8]

Chapter Nine
*Zhao Jianzi 趙簡子 *Zhao Jianzi

The Manuscript

The *Zhao Jianzi manuscript is composed of eleven slips. According to the source publication, the slips measure roughly 41.6 cm in length and 0.6 cm in width.[1] There is no numbering or title on the back of the slips, but there are carved lines, probably part of the production process. The title was chosen by the editors based on the first words of the text. Slips 4 and 11 are damaged; especially the latter slip is lacking about 10–11 graphs.[2] From the use of punctuation, and given the form of the narrative, it appears that the text is otherwise complete.[3] The calligraphy is clearly legible and there are not many problems in the reading of the text.

Because of similarities in the calligraphy of this manuscript with the others included in this study, Li Songru 李松儒 has suggested that they may have been written by the same scribe but at a different moment.[4] She notes

---

1 Li Songru, "Qinghua qi Zi Fan Zi Yu yu Zhao Jianzi deng pian ziji yanjiu," 178, measures 41.8 cm.
2 This is based on the amount of space left for writing on the missing parts of the slip.
3 The text is closed with a pronounced, hook-shaped punctuation mark, as is the first section ending on slip 4. Possibly, the text contained other sections, but given the fact that the question asked is fully answered, and ends on (what is likely) a rhetorical question, it is likely that no further slips are missing.
4 Li Songru, "Qinghua qi Zi Fan Zi Yu yu Zhao Jianzi deng pian ziji yanjiu," 178–179, has argued that the texts collected in this volume were written by the same scribe. She also includes *Huang Men from volume 1 of the Tsinghua manuscripts. She further notes that the present manuscript and the *Yue Gong qi shi are executed more carefully than especially the Zi Fan Zi Yu and *Jin Wen Gong ru yu Jin. She ascribes these differences to time and possibly to the material (brush etc.). It should be noted that in the examples adduced, while highly similar in overall look of the graphs, use and spacing of components etc., there are still minor differences in the execution of components that seem to

that the present manuscript and *Yue Gong qi Shi* 越公其事 are executed more carefully than the *Zi Fan Zi Yu* and **Jin Wen Gong ru yu Jin*, and ascribes these differences to time and material factors (different brush etc.). It should be noted that in the examples adduced, while highly similar in overall appearance of the graphs, use, and spacing of components, etcetera, there are still minor differences in the execution of components that seem to support a division between a group composed of the **Zhao Jianzi* and **Yue Gong qi shi* on the one hand, and the other manuscripts included here, on the other hand. I assume for now that these manuscripts at least came out of the same workshop, possibly by a single or two closely related scribes. The length of the present manuscript, 41.6 cm slips is close to the **Zi Yi*'s 41.7cm, and the **Yue Gong qi Shi*'s 41.6 cm; they are thus also closely related in terms of materiality, but contrast with the other 45 cm-long slip manuscripts in this volume.

The Text

The text is framed within the context of Zhao Jianzi 趙簡子 (Zhao Yang 趙鞅, served 497–475 BCE) being made a general and receiving a remonstrance from his senior, Fan Xianzi 范獻子 (Shi Yang 士鞅, served 509–497 BCE).[5] Both served Lord Ding of Jin 晉定公 (r. 511–475 BCE) as

---

support a division between a group composed of the **Zhao Jianzi* and **Yue Gong qi shi* and the others. I assume for now that these manuscripts at least came out of the same workshop, and possibly were the work of a single or two closely related scribes. The present manuscript and the **Yue Gong qi shi* are closely related in terms of materiality, featuring similar slip lengths and widths, contrasting with the other manuscripts in this volume featuring slips roughly 45 cm in length.

5 For discussions of the text, the historical background, and the manuscript, see Gu Shikao 顧史考 (Scott Cook), "*Zhao Jianzi* chutan"《趙簡子》初探, *Bulletin of the Jao Tsung-I Academy* 饒宗頤學院院刊 6 (2019): 361–375; Zhao Ping'an 趙平安 and Shi Xiaoli 石小力, "Cheng Zhuan ji qi yu Zhao Jianzi de wendui — Qinghua jian *Zhao Jianzi* chutan" 成鱄及其與趙簡子的問對——清華簡《趙簡子》初探, *Wenwu* 文物 2017.3: 85–89; Xie Huiting 謝輝亭, "Qinghua jian *Zhao Jianzi* shiling — jianlun qi wenxianxue jiazhi" 清華簡《趙簡子》拾零——兼論其文獻學價值, *Handan xueyuan xuebao* 邯鄲學院學報 2018.2, 32–37; Zi Ju 子居, "Qinghua jian qi *Zhao Jianzi* jiexi" 清華簡七《趙簡子》解析, published on May 29, 2017 at *Zhongguo Xianqin shi wangzhan* 中國先秦史網站, http://www.xianqin.tk/2017/05/29/383, link is now inactive, retrieved July 11, 2022 at https://www.academia.edu/41579163/%E6%B8%85%E5%8D%8E%E7%AE%80%E

chief ministers (*guo qing* 國卿). Zhao Jianzi had emerged as a powerful high official in the Jin power struggles between landed gentry and high officials. Later in life he battled with the Fan clan, and succeeded Fan Xianzi as chief minister. He became known for his reforms, especially of the penal system and taxation. A tell-tale anecdote foreboding future tension between Zhao Jianzi and the Fan clan is presented in *Zuo*:

> 冬，晉趙鞅、荀寅帥師城汝濱，遂賦晉國一鼓鐵，以鑄刑鼎，著范宣子所謂刑書焉。仲尼曰："晉其亡乎！失其度矣。[……]" 蔡史墨曰："范氏、中行氏其亡乎？中行寅為下卿，而干上令，擅作刑器，以為國法，是法姦也。又加范氏焉，易之，亡也。其及趙氏，趙孟與焉。然不得已，若德，可以免。"

> In Winter, Zhao Yang and Zhonghang Yin of Jin led out an army and built walls on the banks of the Ru River. They then levied one drum-measure of iron from the domain of Jin and used it to cast the so-called penal cauldron, upon which they inscribed the penal code that Fan Gai had composed.
> Confucius said: "Jin will perish, for it has lost its standards. […]" (followed by an argument as to why the cauldron is problematic.)
> The scribe Mo of Cai said: "The Fan and Zhonghang lineages will likely perish! As a low-rank minister, Zhonghang Yin has interfered in his superiors' issuing of commands and has taken it upon himself to create a vessel for the penal code that is to be the legal norm for the domain. This is a perversion of legal norms. And he has moreover implicated the Fans in his actions. Because he has now made the changes, they will perish. Insofar

---

4%B8%83_%E8%B5%B5%E7%AE%80%E5%AD%90_%E8%A7%A3%E6%9E%90; Zhang Mingzhu 張明珠 provides a convenient volume of collected interpretations and a translation into modern Chinese; see Zhang Mingzhu, "*Qinghua daxue cang Zhanguo zhujian (qi) Zhao Jianzi* jishi, yizhu"《清華大學藏戰國竹簡（柒）·趙簡子》集釋、譯註 (Master Thesis, Wuhan University, 2019).

as it affects the Zhaos, Zhao Yang will have a part in it. But he had no choice, and if he is virtuous, he will be able to escape."[6]

The present text does not seem to pick up on this potential area of contention, but merely presents Fan Xianzi in the familiar role of an older advisory figure. While the remonstrance itself is presented in no unclear terms, cautioning Zhao Jianzi to take responsibility for his actions and comport himself properly, there is no explicit linkage made to historical events.[7] While the use of historical precedent in the second half of the text is similar to some of the other materials in this volume, e.g., the *Zheng Wu Furen gui ruzi*, and the *Zheng Wen Gong wen Tai Bo*, the ending focuses on a more philosophical point. In this respect, the present text appears slightly different from the other texts in this volume that more carefully integrating their main message within a historical context, and the frame here seems to operate more as a pretext for a philosophical point. In all likelihood, this text was cobbled together from materials surrounding the figure of Zhao Jianzi.

The opening frame of the present narrative provides a context in which the appointment of Zhao Jianzi sets up the question of how to comport oneself. This section is concluded with a saying which suggests the importance of excellence in one's behavior so that one will attract excellence. This section is visually marked off by a punctuation mark, while the remainder of the slip is left blank. The second section of the text features a dialogue with Cheng Zhuan 成剸. Zhao Jianzi asks him why the lords of Qi lost power in Jin and the Chen 陳 (i.e., Tian 田) clan gained it. This second section has a particular focus on the economy and extravagance in spending.

Other than Zhao Jianzi, there is no obvious link between the two sections, whether in terms of time, space, or narrative progression. The two

---

6 See *Zuo* Zhao 29; Durrant, Li, and Schaberg, *Zuo Tradition*, 1702–1703. Other than references in the *Zuo* and *Shi ji*, there are also several anecdotes surrounding Zhao Jianzi collected in *Han Feizi* and *Shuo Yuan*.
7 Note that Gu Shikao, "*Zhao Jianzi* chutan," 364 follows Zi Ju in understanding the "excellent" 善人 as referring to concrete historical figures; this would provide at least a weak link.

themes — self-caution and the virtue of economy — are weakly linked by collocating the two scenes. This collocation occurs in the placement of the two sections on the manuscript, but other than a shared main character, there is no explicit textual link that places the texts within a single narrative. The forms of the sections are also different. The first section starts with a narrative description, followed by the admonishment by Fan Xianzi. Zhao Jianzi has no voice in this section, and is only described as present for the appointment in court. The second section features Zhao Jianzi in a more active role. Here he actively inquires with Cheng Zhuan and what follows is a simple back-and-forth question and answer. It is likely that in the final damaged slip, either Cheng Zhuan, or more likely Zhao Jianzi summarizes the lesson with a rhetorical question.

As in some of the other texts in this volume, Cheng Zhuan at first denies knowledge of relevant historical precedent, before answering after a specification of the question. This dynamic is also visible in an anecdote in the "Shan shuo" 善説 chapter of *Shuo yuan* 說苑:

趙簡子問於成摶曰：「吾聞夫羊殖者，賢大夫也，是行奚然？」對曰：「臣摶不知也。」簡子曰：「吾聞之子與友親，子而不知，何也？」摶曰：「其為人也數變，其十五年也，廉以不匿其過；其二十也，仁以喜義，其三十也，為晉中軍尉，勇以喜仁，其年五十也，為邊城將，遠者復親。今臣不見五年矣。恐其變，是以不敢知。」簡子曰：「果賢大夫也，每變益上矣。」

Zhao Jianzi asked Cheng Tuan, saying: "I heard that this Yang Zhi was a virtuous high official; was this because of his behavior?" He replied, saying: "Your servant Tuan does not know it." Jianzi said: "I heard that you were close with your friend, but you do not know it; why is that?" Tuan said: "As a person he changed many times. When he was fifteen, he was upright in not hiding his mistakes; when he was twenty, he was humane in delighting in propriety; when he was thirty, he was a military official of the middle, and was brave in delighting in humanness; when he was fifty, he was a general of the border city, and those far off renewed their kinship. Now your servant has not seen him for five years and I am afraid he has changed; that is why I dare not claim knowledge." Jianzi said: "Indeed he is a virtuous high officer; whenever he changes, he improves."[8]

It is not because Cheng Tuan (Zhuan) does not know Yang Zhi that he claims no knowledge, but rather because he knows him so well. Different from the *Zhao Jianzi, and indeed the other narratives collected in this volume, the anecdote from the Shuo yuan gives a clear explanation as to why Cheng Tuan is not willing to share his knowledge. As a literary conceit, this unwillingness is meant to draw the characters (and by extension, the audience) in and have them guessing at the profundity of the question. Yang Zhi was virtuous to the extent that it required extensive explanation and could not simply be related in a bite-sized answer. The fall of the clan of the lord of Qi and the rise of the Chen clan were likewise questions that involved so many aspects that it required further specification.

Another aspect that becomes clear from comparison is that other than the additional story heading the narrative and the opening frame placing it in historical time and space, there is not much that sets the narrative of the *Zhao Jianzi apart from such anecdotes as those collected in the Shuo yuan. In line with Du Heng's observations regarding the Han Feizi "Chu shuo" chapters,[9] the fundamental difference is one of paratextual embedding. And while it is clear that the narrative of the *Zhao Jianzi does not encapsulate the dialogues as neatly as, for instance, the Zi Fan Zi Yu or the *Zheng Wu

---

8   Liu Xiang 劉向, Xiang Zonglu 向宗魯 ed., Shuo yuan jiao zheng 説苑校正 (Beijing: Zhonghua shuju, 1987), 291. Zhao Ping'an and Shi Xiaoli pick up on this common model in the question-and-answer format; see their "Cheng Zhuan ji qi yu Zhao Jianzi de wen dui," 87.

9   Du Heng, "The Mastery of Miscellanea: Information Management and Knowledge Acquisition in the 'Chu shuo' Chapters of the Hanfeizi," Journal of the American Oriental Society 140.1 (2020): 115–142.

Furen gui ruzi, this simple observation should alert us to the possibility that many of the texts covered in the volume at hand may have simply been historically 'framed' and expanded renditions of common anecdotes, rather than seeing them as contemporary records, or historically authentic descriptions of Springs and Autumns events. Ultimately, the narratives told *a story* meant to draw in readers and have them experience — as if present — a past that was increasingly going out of reach for a Warring States audience.

Zhao Jianzi 趙簡子
Zhao Jianzi

[ancient script line 1]

[ancient script line 2]

盅朿子既受寎牂軍才朝軏獻子進諫曰昔虐子之
牂方少女又訛則非子之咎帀保

趙簡子既受命將軍。在朝，范獻子進諫曰："昔吾子之將方少，如有過，則非子之咎，師保[一]

Zhao Jianzi had just been made[10] a general. When he was at court, Fan Xianzi[11] offered a remonstrance, saying: "In former times, when my master was still[12] young, if you made a mistake, then it was not[13] your fault; it was your teachers and guardians' [1]

---

10 I read 寎 as *ming* 命 following Yang Mengsheng, in "Qinghua jian qi zhengli baogao buzheng." Some, such as Chen Zhijun 陳治軍, "Qinghua jian *Zhao Jianzi* zhong cong 'meng' zi shili" 清華簡《趙簡子》中从"甿"字釋例, *Fudan daxue chutu wenxian yu guwenzi yanjiu zhongxin wangzhan* 復旦大學出土文獻與古文字研究中心網站 April 29, 2017, http://www.fdgwz.org.cn/Web/Show/3017, have tried to argue that the appointment of Zhao Jianzi concerned the position of Upper General 上將軍 specifically. Cheng Hao, "Qinghua jian di qi ji zhengli baogao shiyi," reads *meng* 孟, the phonology of which is more apt. However, given the other instance of the graph in the *Zi Fan Zi Yu*, it seems likely that *ming* 命 is the better reading. See Chen Wei 陳偉, "Ye shuo Chujian cong 'meng' zhi zi" 也說楚簡从"甿"之字, April 29, 2017, *Wuhan daxue jianbo yanjiu zhongxin wangzhan* 武漢大學簡帛研究中心網站, http://www.bsm.org.cn/?chujian/7531.html.

11 The editors note that Fan Xianzi ought to have been higher ranked than Zhao Jianzi, and as such, his use of terms such as "my master" 吾子 and "to offer a remonstrance" 進諫 are problematic and should perhaps be taken as a sign of respect.

12 I follow Gu Shikao, "*Zhao Jianzi* chutan," 364. He notes that *jiang fang* 將方 is a temporal construction and that *jiang* should not to be understood as "general."

13 *Fei* 非 was added later and squeezed in-between the surrounding graphs.

Chapter Nine   *Zhao Jianzi* 趙簡子 *Zhao Jianzi*

之罪也。就吾子之將長，如有過，則非子之咎，傅母之罪也。今吾子既爲命將軍已，如有過，[二]

fault. When my master was growing up, if you made a mistake, then it was your governess' fault. Now my master has already been made a general; if you make a mistake, [2]

則非人之罪牆子之咎＿ 子𫝀造於善則善人至不
善人退子𫝀造於不善則不善人至善

則非人之罪，將子之咎＿。子始造於善，則善人至，不善人退。子始造於不善，則不善人至，善[三]

then it is not somebody else's fault, but your own mistake ＿. When you work towards excellence from the beginning, then the excellent will come, and the inferior will retreat. When you work towards inferiority from the beginning, then the inferior will come, and the excellent [3]

Chapter Nine *Zhao Jianzi* 趙簡子 *Zhao Jianzi*

人 退 用 緐 今 以 㞷 虐 子 㴂 不 可 以 不 戒 已 ▄

人退。用由今以往，吾子將不可以不戒已▄！" [四]

will retreat. In what comes from now on, you my master cannot but caution yourself ▄ !"[14] [4]

---

[14] This mark is followed by a blank slip end and indicates a hard division between the two sections, roughly comparable to a paragraph. These breaks often occur between sections that could, at least theoretically, have stood on their own.

趙簡子問於成鄦曰:"齊君失政,陳氏得之,敢問齊君失之奚由? 陳氏得之奚由▅?" 成鄦答曰:"齊 [五]

Zhao Jianzi asked Cheng Zhuan, saying: "The lord of Qi lost power, and the Chen clan gained it; I dare to ask how it came about that the lord of Qi lost it? How did it come about that the Chen clan gained it ▅?" Cheng Zhuan responded, saying: "The lord of Qi [5]

Chapter Nine *Zhao Jianzi* 趙簡子 *Zhao Jianzi*

[bamboo slip characters]

君失正臣不旻龍亓所繇陳是旻之臣亦不旻龍亓
所繇▄归昔之旻之與逨之皆又繇也▄盆朿

君失政，臣不得聞其所由，陳氏得之，臣亦不得聞其所由▄。抑昔之得之與失之，皆有由也▄。」趙簡 [六]

lost power; your servant did not manage to hear how it came about.[15] The Chen[16] clan gained it; your servant also did not manage to hear how it came about.[17] But the gains and losses of the past, they all come about for a reason ▄ ." Zhao Jian [6]

---

15 *Suo* 所 was added later, squeezed in between and to the side.
16 I here simply follow the manuscript's use of Chen 陳; in later sources, the clan is referred to as Tian 田.
17 Compare here the phrase "Of all that you my lord ask, nothing could be heard" 凡君之所問，莫可聞 on slip 11 of the *Zi Fan Zi Yu*. The phrase is a trope suggesting the exclusive nature of knowledge and the (discursive) power of the advisor.

ᙠ ᖛ ᔍ ᖨ ᓮ 豊 而 ᓪ 之 成 ᓬ 會 ᖛ ᓭ 虐 ᔬ 尻 ᕫ 公 是
ᔋ ᘎ ᔧ ᔕ 厇 ᓰ ᛊ ᖳ ᔑ ᘌ ᙑ ᛚ

子 曰 亓 所 繇 豊 可 䎽 也 成 剶 會 曰 昔 虐 先 君 獻 公 是
尻 掌 又 二 厇 之 室 以 好 士 庶 子 車 甲 外

子曰：“其所由禮可聞也？” 成剶答曰：“昔吾先君獻公是居，掌有二宅之室，以好士庶子車甲，外 [七]

zi said: "Can I hear the manners of how it came about?" Cheng Zhuan responded, saying: "Of old, when our former ruler Lord Xian was presiding, he held the chamber of two residences,[18] and appeased the sons of the gentry and the troops,[19] the outer [7]

---

18 There are numerous opinions as to how to interpret this line. The editors suggest it refers to the two major cities and power centers of Jin: Quwo 曲沃 and the capital Yi 翼. As an alternative reading, they suggest that the ruler had a house with two cracks or just two room-chambers. Both of these alternatives seem stretched. Most likely the line is indicative of the rift in Jin.
19 The sentence division follows Ma Nan, "Qinghua jian qi zhengli baogao buzheng." The editors note that *shi shuzi* 士庶子 refers to the sons of high officials and gentry that were stationed in the capital as an honor guard of sorts. Note the similarity to the *Zi Fan Zi Yu*'s use of *liang shuzi* 良庶子. I assume it suggests that the ruler was keeping his friends close against potential local uprising.

六寶溋▂ 宮中六窑并六祀狀則曼桶相周室亦智
者侯之愬豪虐先君襄公親冒虡覃以

六府盈▂，宮中六竈并六祀，然則得輔相周室，亦知諸侯之謀。就吾先君襄公，親冒甲冑，以 [八]

six bureaus had a surplus ▂, the six stoves of the inner palace were integrated into the six[20] sacrifices, and thus he managed to assist the governing of the Zhou royal house and knew of the plans of the lords of the states as well. When we come to our former ruler Lord Xiang, he personally donned his armor, in order to [8]

---

20 *Liu* 六 was added later, squeezed in between. According to the editors, this section supposedly refers to a method of economizing on ritual expenditure in making offerings. Given the repetition below, it may be an allusion to being able to keep both the interests of the palace and the nation aligned. Alternatively, it might indicate a means of putting the allotment for ritual spending into the coffers.

綍 河 淒 之 闕 之 矞 ▬ 各 不 裘 頸 不 張 籔 不 飤 濡 肉 宮
中 六 竈 并 六 祀 肰 則 旻 楠 相 周 室 兼

治河濟之閒之亂▬。冬不裘，夏不張箑，不食濡肉，宮中六竈并六祀，然則得輔相周室，兼 [九]

subdue the unrest between the Yellow River and the Ji ▬.[21] In the winter he did not don furs, and in the summer he did not spread a fan. He did not eat soft-boiled meats, the six stoves of the inner palace were integrated into the six sacrifices, and thus he managed to assist the governing of the Zhou royal house and stand as [9]

---

21 According to the editors, this refers to the battle at Xiao that opens the *Zi Yi*.

Chapter Nine *Zhao Jianzi 趙簡子 *Zhao Jianzi

敀者侯彙虖先君坪公宮中卅₌里駝馬四百駟奢亓
衣尚孚亓飤宮中三臺是乃俴巳肰

霸諸侯。就吾先君平公，宮中三十里，馳馬四百駟，奢其衣裳，飽其飲食，宮中三臺，是乃俴已，然 [十]

hegemon among the lords of the states. When we come to our former ruler Lord Ping,[22] the inner palace grounds (grew to) thirty *li*, he had four hundred teams of thoroughbred steeds, he was extravagant in his clothing, was satiated in food and drink, and the three platforms in the inner palace were used to indulge himself. Thus [10]

---

22 Lord Ping of Jin was noted for his lavish expenditure and waste; see for instance the prediction in *Zuo* Zhao 3; Durrant, Li, and Schaberg, *Zuo Tradition*, 1351:

> 叔向曰：＂然。雖吾公室，今亦季世也。戎馬不駕，卿無軍行，公乘無人，卒列無長。庶民罷敝，而宮室滋侈。＂
> Shuxiang said: "That is true. Even our lord's house is now also in its last generations. His war horses are not harnessed, and his ministers participate in no military campaigns. The lord's chariot has no riders; the infantry ranks have no captains. The common people are exhausted, while the palaces and mansions are ever more extravagant."

As noted by Zi Ju, "Qinghua qi *Zhao Jianzi* jiexi," Lords Hui 惠 and Wen 文 are elided in the text.

則遊敀者侯不智周室之☒會之欨☒□欨之會唐＿

則失霸諸侯，不知周室之……儉之侈……侈之儉乎＿？" [十一]

he lost the hegemony over the lords of the states, and did not know of the affairs of the Zhou royal house ... an excess of frugality ... or a frugality of excess ▬ ?" [11]

趙簡子

趙簡子既受命將軍。在朝，范獻子進諫曰："昔吾子之將方少，如有過，則非子之咎，師保[一]之罪也。就吾子之將長，如有過，則非子之咎，傅母之罪也。今吾子既爲命將軍已，如有過，[二]則非人之罪，將子之咎▅。子始造於善，則善人至，不善人退。子始造於不善，則不善人至，善[三]人退。用由今以往，吾子將不可以不戒已▅！"[四]

趙簡子問於成剬曰："齊君失政，陳氏得之，敢問齊君失之奚由？陳氏得之奚由▅？"

成剬答曰："齊[五]君失政，臣不得聞其所由，陳氏得之，臣亦不得聞其所由▅。抑昔之得之與失之，皆有由也▅。"

趙簡[六]子曰："其所由禮可聞也？"

成剬答曰："昔吾先君獻公是居，掌有二宅之室，以好士庶子車甲，外[七]六府盈▅，宮中六竈并六祀，然則得輔相周室，亦知諸侯之謀。就吾先君襄公，親冒甲胄，以[八]治河濟之間之亂▅。冬不裘，夏不張箑，不食濡肉，宮中六竈并六祀，然則得輔相周室，兼[九]霸諸侯。就吾先君平公，宮中三十里，馳馬四百駟，奢其衣裳，飽其飲食，宮中三臺，是乃侈已，然[十]則失霸諸侯，不知周室之……儉之侈……侈之儉乎▅？"[十一]

*Zhao Jianzi

Zhao Jianzi had just been made a general. When he was at court, Fan Xianzi offered a remonstrance, saying: "In former times, when my master was still young, if you made a mistake, then it was not your fault; it was your teachers and guardians' [1] fault. When my master was growing up, if you made a mistake, then it was your governess' fault. Now my master has already been made a general; if you make a mistake, [2] then it is not somebody else's fault, but your own mistake ▃ . When you work towards excellence from the beginning, then the excellent will come, and the inferior will retreat. When you work towards inferiority from the beginning, then the inferior will come, and the excellent [3] will retreat. In what comes from now on, you my master cannot but caution yourself ▃ !" [4]

Zhao Jianzi asked Cheng Zhuan, saying: "The lord of Qi lost power, and the Chen clan gained it; I dare to ask how it came about that the lord of Qi lost it? How did it come about that the Chen clan gained it ▃ ?"

Cheng Zhuan responded, saying: "The lord of Qi [5] lost power; your servant did not manage to hear how it came about. The Chen clan gained it; your servant also did not manage to hear how it came about. But the gains and losses of the past, they all come about for a reason ▃ ."

Zhao Jian [6] zi said: "Can I hear the manners of how it came about?"

Cheng Zhuan responded, saying: "Of old, when our former ruler Lord Xian was presiding, he held the chamber of two residences, and appeased the sons of the gentry and the troops, the outer [7] six bureaus had a surplus ▃ , the six stoves of the inner palace were integrated into the six sacrifices, and thus he managed to assist the governing of the Zhou royal house and knew of the plans of the lords of the states as well. When we come to our former ruler Lord Xiang, he personally donned his armor, in order to [8] subdue the unrest between the Yellow River and the Ji ▃ . In the winter he did not don furs, and in the summer he did not spread a fan. He did not eat soft-boiled meats, the six stoves of the inner palace were integrated into the six sacrifices, and thus he managed to assist the governing of the Zhou royal house and stand as [9] hegemon among the lords of the states. When we come to our former ruler Lord Ping, the inner palace grounds (grew to) thirty li, he had four hundred teams of thoroughbred steeds, he was extravagant in his clothing, was satiated in food and drink, and the three platforms in the inner palace were used to indulge himself. Thus [10] he lost the hegemony over the lords of the states, and did not know of the affairs of the Zhou royal house ... an excess of frugality ... or a frugality of excess ▬ ?" [11]

Chapter Ten
*Zi Yi 子儀 *Mr. Yi

The Manuscript

The *Zi Yi manuscript is composed of twenty slips. There is reason to believe that some slips may be missing. The slips are between 40.9 and 41.7 cm long and 0.6 cm wide. The manuscript was bound with three strings, some space having been left in the place of the middle binding string (except for the repetition mark placed on slip 6). Other than a small mark at the end of the text and the use of repetition marks, no punctuation is present.

There are no numbers or a title on the back of the slips, for which reason the order of the slips has been debated. In the original source publication, the editors stated that possibly slips were missing between slips 15 and 16, and between 19 and 20. Shortly after publication, suggestions were made to change the order of the slips. Zi Ju (pen name) suggested rearranging the slips as follows: 1, 15, 2–11, 17–19, 16, 12–14, 20.[1] Of these changes, the consensus agrees that slip 15 ought to be placed between slips 1 and 2.[2] The other suggestions by Zi Ju remain contested. Ma Nan, one of the editors responsible for the original sequence has been particularly convincing in arguing against these other changes, basing herself on narrative logic and historical background.[3] In the current edition, I follow Ma Nan and only

---

1 Zi Ju, "Qinghua jian *Zi Yi* jiexi."
2 See, for instance, Yu Houkai 尉侯凱, "*Qinghua jian 6 Ziyi* bianlian xiaoyi"《清華簡（陸）·子儀》編連小議, *Wuhan daxue jianbo yanjiu zhongxin wangzhan* 武漢大學簡帛研究中心網站, May 23, 2016 http://www.bsm.org.cn/?chujian/6717.html.
3 Ma Nan 馬楠, "Qinghua jian *Zi Yi* xiangguan shishi yu jianwen bianlian shidu" 清華簡《子儀》相關史事與簡文編連釋讀, *Jianbo* 簡帛 20 (2020), 31–38.

move slip 15 between slips 1 and 2.

Hostage or Emissary

A major debate surrounding the text is whether it describes events just after the battle at Xiao 殽 (627 BCE) or in the seventh year after the event (621 BCE). This battle saw the defeat of Qin at the hand of Jin, even though Qin had answered earlier calls by Jin for grain support. Qin had its armies drastically reduced in size and the text narrates how Lord Mu and his counselors introduced reforms to strengthen the army beyond its original size. In what follows, Lord Mu meets Chu emissary Mr. Yi 子儀 at Xing to talk about the possibilities of an alliance against Jin. This encounter takes up the lion's share of the text.

The editors argue that the text refers to the returning of the hostages Mr. Yi from Chu and Sui Hui 隨會 from Jin, in order to repair relations. Zhao Ping'an and Zi Ju argue that while the main gist of this position is correct, it should be placed seven years after the battle.[4] Ma Nan corrects this position and notes that the historical timeline does not fit. She argues that there is no Jin emissary present in the text, and that instead the narrative is about Lord Mu of Qin explaining his release of a Chu captive called Ma 獁 to the Chu emissary Mr. Yi, wanting to use the opportunity to repair relations with Chu.[5]

My own reading follows Ma Nan in terms of the general structure and historical timeline of the narrative, but follows Shan Yuchen 單育辰 in reading the graph "Ma" 獁 as ji 羈 "restrained," referring to a captive from the past more generally without making claims regarding their identity. It makes good sense of the sentence without introducing an unknown figure into the narrative.[6]

---

4   Zhao Ping'an 趙平安, "Qin Mu Gong fang gui Zi Yi kao" 秦穆公放歸子儀考, *Guwenzi yu gudaishi* 古文字與古代史 5 (Taipei: Institute of History and Philology, Academia Sinica, 2017), 287–294.

5   Ma Nan, "Qinghua jian *Zi Yi* xiangguan shishi yu jianwen bianlian shidu," 33–35.

6   Shan Yuchen 單育辰, "*Zi Yi* shiwen shangque"《子儀》釋文商榷, *Chutu wenxian yanjiu* 出土文獻研究 16 (2017), 33.

The Structure of Song

The meeting between Lord Mu of Qin and Mr. Yi is presented in the context of an archery rite with accompanying music and songs.[7] The encounter opens with Lord Mu suggesting that Qin and Chu work together to tip the power balance in their favor, to form a united front against Jin. In the songs and dialogue that follow, Lord Mu of Qin expresses his regrets at not doing so earlier, and that he desires Mr. Yi to bring his message of cooperation to the Chu king. Because the songs are rife with allusion, and the referents of the metaphors are not always clear, there has been a variety of interpretations. To compound this problem, the paratext of the songs does not clearly delineate either their structure or who is speaking at what moment. In my understanding of the passage, slips 4–10 read as follows:

> Then a large target was set up outside of the Eastern Corner, and an (archery) rite was held for Mr. Yi. There was no alcohol or gifts, but he was presented with singing and dancing (instead).

---

7   The locus classicus describing the archery ritual is *Shi jing* 詩經 "Bin zhi chu yan" 賓之初筵:

> When the guests first approach the mats, they take their places on the left and the right in an orderly manner. The dishes of bamboo and wood are arranged in rows, With the sauces and kernels displayed in them. The spirits are mild and good, And they drink, all equally reverent.
> The bells and drums are properly arranged; And they raise their pledge-cups with order and ease. [Then] the great target is set up; The bows and arrows are made ready for the shooting;
> The archers are matched in classes. "Show your skill in shooting," [it is said].
> "I shall hit that mark," [it is responded], "And pray you to drink the cup."
> 賓之初筵，左右秩秩。籩豆有楚，殽核維旅。酒既和旨，飲酒孔偕。鐘鼓既設，舉醻逸逸。大侯既抗，弓矢斯張。射夫既同，獻爾發功。發彼有的，以祈爾爵。

Ruan Yuan 阮元 ed., *Shisan jing zhushu fu jiaokan ji* 十三經註疏附校勘記 (Beijing: Zhonghua shuju, 1980), 484–487; James Legge, *The Chinese classics with a translation, critical and exegetical notes*, vol. 4, *The She King* (London: Trübner, 1871), 395–396.

For (somewhat idealized) descriptions of the archery ritual, see *Zhou li* 周禮 "Chunguan zongbo" 春官宗伯; *Li Ji* 禮記 "She yi" 射義; and *Yi Li* 儀禮 "Xiang she li" 鄉射禮. Note the similarities with the present text in having a predilection for the rite taking place in the east, the necessity to offer alcohol, and the use of musical (bell) performances. Note too that the Qin is never mentioned.

Chapter Ten　*Zi Yi 子儀 *Mr. Yi

The Lord ordered (music masters) Qiong Wei and Sheng Qin to strike the bells, and sing: "Slowly, winding, I go where the broker traveled, again stopping in hamlets, my words rambling."

The harmonizing song went: "The Wei River! I gaze afar, looking back at my achievements and mistakes. The Qian (river) is brimming, the Wei (river) is torrential, poplar and willow grow lush, the vastness beneath them. This is my painful cry of grief, that I have not attained it despite my planning, and I cry because I still seek. To change my expression of lament and sadness, and rest in beauty, I rely on you in my request."

Then he ordered Sheng Qin to sing to Mr. Yi, and harmonize it with Chu music. It went: "The bird flies, going further away. With what corded-arrow could I reach it? A person from far away, about to leave your lodge; my lord, I have words seeking an audience. Who will I think of to tell them? The bow is strong, and is drawn to its end; the corded-arrow pursues and reaches them; if you did not go, how could I place my words? I am afraid that he will doubt them and not trust me. Who will I think of to mediate my words? In the hunts of the past, I did not participate. Now (if) in this hunt, I was not to participate, (would this not be) exercising my duties and exerting myself in my task, yet not seeing it to completion. How could I offer at the altar of grain?"

Lord Mu orders his music masters to present Mr. Yi with song (*ge* 歌) and harmonizing song (*he ge* 和歌, *chu yue he zhi yue* 楚樂和之曰). Because the introduction of the second song, "Then he ordered Sheng Qin to sing to Mr. Yi, and harmonize it with Chu music. It went" 乃命升琴歌於子儀, 楚樂和之曰 (7, 8), is not conclusive about who presents the harmonizing song,[8] and given the familiar practice of "presenting odes" (*fu shi* 賦詩) in the *Zuo*, it is tempting to interpret this as a call and response format, with Mr. Yi answering Lord Mu.[9]

Nevertheless, the content of the text speaks against this. The allusions clearly indicate the need to find the right person (i.e., Mr. Yi) to transmit the intention of an alliance to Chu, the speaker of the second song therefore needs to be Lord Mu. With that in mind, the referents of the first song gain clarity. The 'broker' refers to Mr. Yi, whom Lord Mu seeks to meet. The hamlet points to the site of the meeting, Xing, and the unclear rambling of the speaker can be understood as the veiled allusion that characterizes the songs. In other words, it is a reflexive opening statement, a reading key, for the remainder of the song. The rivers in the responding song that follows are all metonymic references to Qin, and we picture Lord Mu looking back at his mistakes of the past, decrying that he still needs to seek an ally, making him "rely on you (Mr. Yi) in my request."

I therefore suggest that "song" and "harmonizing song" should be understood as the opening and closing parts of the same song, i.e., a purely formal distinction. In that sense, the opening song sketches an image, followed by a reflexive comment carrying the message to Mr. Yi. In that light, it makes sense to understand the second song as composed of two parts as well, the reflexive, "harmonizing" component likely starting with "In the hunts of the past ... ," which introduces a more general reflection on Lord Mu's need to seal an alliance.

---

8   The line could equally indicate that only the harmony is rendered in the text. Similar problems of identification occur in other song texts, such as the *Zhou Gong zhi qin wu 周公之琴舞, particularly in its use of *qi* 啟 and *luan* 亂; see the volume by David Lebovitz in this series.

9   One could argue that for the second instance, only the harmonizing song is presented in the text.

*Zi Yi 子儀
*Mr. Yi

𢾅 𢾅 伲 簹 㠯 中 亼 𠔏 𨒌 㝵 古 戠 𢝊 中 所 侌 亓 㫐 不
㯂 公 炂 𠬝 三 䇂 尃 之 北 土 不 飤 耄 勥

既敗於唐, 恐民之大病, 逐易古戠。欲民所安, 亓亶不㯂。公益及三謀尃之, 靡土不飤, 耄幼 [一]

既敗於殽, 恐民之大病, 移易故職。欲民所安, 其亶不更。公益及三謀輔之, 靡土不食, 耄幼 [一]

Having been defeated at Xiao, (Lord Mu of Qin) feared that the people would be greatly distressed,[10] and would move and alter their former occupations.[11] He wanted what would pacify the people, and that their trust would not change.[12] The Lord increasingly joined[13] with the three counselors to support them; there was no area that was not fed, and the elderly and infants [1]

---

10 I read *bing* 病 "distressed" instead of *fang* 方. This reading was noted as an alternative by the editors, and later taken up by Yang Mengsheng, "Qinghua liu *Zi Yi* pian jianwen jiaodu ji" and Ma Nan, "Qinghua jian *Zi Yi* xiangguan shishi yu jianwen bianlian shidu," 32.
11 The punctuation follows an alternative offered by the editors, as followed also by Yang Mengsheng, Ma Nan and others. I also follow interpretations by Zi Ju, "Qinghua jian *Zi Yi* jiexi," and Wang Ning, "Qinghua jian liu *Zi Yi* shiwen jiaodu."
12 For the readings of this line, I follow the alternatives offered by the editors, and taken up as well by Ma Nan.
13 The use of *yi ji* 益及 is very uncommon. Several suggestions revolve around reading *yi* adverbially and *ji* as a full verb, in the sense of "often – increasingly," as per the editors and Wang Ning, "Qinghua jian liu *Zi Yi* shiwen jiaodu." *Ji* 及 in turn ought to read either as "reach" or as "together with." Zi Ju, "Qinghua jian *Zi Yi* jiexi" suggests reading it as *ji* 急, which is unlikely in light of the parallel on slip 15.
   There is some debate concerning the identification of the three counselors 三謀. The editors suggest Meng Mingshi 孟明視, Xi Qishu 西乞術, and Bai Yibing 白乙丙; Zi Ju suggests Gongsun Zhi 公孫枝, Baili Xi 百里奚, and Uncle Jian 蹇叔.

才 公 陰 者 思 昜= 者 思 陰 民 惡 不 寔 乃 毀 裳 各 敄 降 上
品 之 攴 官 相 弋 乃 又 見 工 公 及 三

在公。陰者思陽，陽者思陰，民恒不實，乃毀常各務。降上品之，辨官相代，乃有見功。公及三 [十五]

were taken care of at public expense.[14] (But) those in the shade desired the sun, and those in the sun desired shade,[15] the people were continuously restless,[16] and this ruined the regularity of everyone's duties. (Lord Mu and his counselors) demoted superiors and evaluated them, and they differentiated officials to replace them, then they achieved results.[17] The lord joined with the three[18] [15]

---

14 Ma Nan, "Qinghua jian *Zi Yi* xiangguan shishi yu jianwen bianlian shidu," 36 suggests that this line refers to the maximizing of human resources by taking care of the elderly and young with public resources. My understanding is that the text reflects a moral ideal rather than a concerted argument towards the maximizing of resources.
15 The referent of this line is unclear, it may refer to locations vis-à-vis a mountain, or simply sun and shade, but I have not found comparable examples in the received literature.
16 Liu Gang 劉剛, "Cong Qinghua jian tan 'wan wu jiang zi bin'" 從清華簡談《老子》的 "萬物將自賓," *Wenshi* 文史 2014.4: 271–274, reads *zhi* 寘 "to place."
17 I read *gong* 功 for *gong* 公, following Ma Nan, "Qinghua jian *Zi Yi* xiangguan shishi yu jianwen bianlian shidu."
18 The placement of slip 15 here follows Zi Ju, "Qinghua jian *Zi Yi* jiexi." The punctuation follows Ma Nan, "Qinghua jian *Zi Yi* xiangguan shishi yu jianwen bianlian shidu," 32, 37.

㵖 慶 而 賞 之 乃 关 冊 秦 邦 之 豎 余 自 蠶 月 爭=眡 窒 備
女 取 及 七 年 車 臲 於 舊 䎽 三 百

謀慶而賞之。乃券冊秦邦之羨餘，自蠶月至于秋至備焉。聚及七年，車逸於舊數三百，[二]

counsellors to laud and reward them. Then they registered the manpower and surplus[19] of the Qin state, they completed (the register) from the Month of the Silkworm (i.e., the height of spring) up to the Height of Autumn.[20] They gathered (manpower and surplus) up to the 7th year (after the battle),[21] and chariots exceeded previous numbers by three hundred, [2]

---

19 "Qinghua liu zhengli baogao buzheng," notes Ma Nan who reads 豎 as *xian* 羨 "reservists," which I follow but interpret more generally as "surplus."
20 For this reading as *qiu zhi* 秋至 "Height of Autumn", see Chen Weiwu 陳偉武, "Du Qinghua jian di liu ce xiaozha" 讀清華簡第六冊小札, *Chutu wenxian* 出土文獻 11 (2017): 205–209.
21 I follow Zi Ju, "Qinghua jian *Zi Yi* jiexi," and Ma Nan, "Qinghua jian *Zi Yi* xiangguan shishi yu jianwen bianlian shidu."

徒逸于舊典六百以㝱楚子義於杏會公曰義父不
教繻左右絚繻右左絚女權之

徒逸於舊典六百，以示楚子儀於杏會。公曰："儀父，不穀擩左，右絚，擩右，左絚，如權之[三]

and troops exceeded the previous registers by six hundred. They showed[22] them to Mr. Yi of Chu during the meeting at Xing. The lord said: "Sir Yi,[23] if I, the one unable to cultivate, pull[24] to the left, the right (string) draws taut, and if I pull to the right the left draws taut. It is as when the scales [3]

---

22 The reading *shi* 示 follows "Musilang" 暮四郎, post no. 11 in the thread "Qinghua liu *Zi Yi* chudu" 清華六《子儀》初讀, April 17, 2016 on the *Jianbo luntan* 簡帛論壇 forum, http://www.bsm.org.cn/forum/forum.php?mod=viewthread&tid=3343&extra=page%3D2&page=2. The idea is that the power balance between Qin and Chu had shifted, and that the two states entered the meeting on more or less equal terms.

23 *Fu* 父~甫 is an honorific suffix for senior, high-ranking males. Here I translate as "Sir" to preserve its paternal overtones. See Schuessler, *ABC Etymological Dictionary*, 243.

24 The reading of *ru* 繻 as *ru* 擩 "pull" follows Zhu Zhongheng, "Qinghua daxue cang Zhanguo zhujian (liu) jishi," 111. However, I read *geng* 絚 as *geng* 緪 "draw tightly." The words refer to the pulling of rope and have been used to describe the drawing of a stringed musical instrument; see Wang Yi's annotation to the passage in *Chu ci* "Jiu ge" 九歌 'Dong jun' 東君：" 緪瑟兮交鼓" "Geng is to rapidly pull a snare" 緪, 急張絃也. Hong Xingzu, *Chu ci buzhu*, 75. Here, it likely describes "manipulating" (*zuoyou* 左右, in the sense of moving with one's hands) the many lords. By working together, Qin and Chu could tip the balance in their favor.

Chapter Ten *Zi Yi* 子儀 *Mr. Yi

[ancient script line 1]
[ancient script line 2]

又 加 橈 也 君 及 不 敎 剚 心 穆 力 以 左 右 者 侯 則 可 爲
而 不 可 乃 張 大 医 於 東 奇 之 外 豊

有加，橈也。君及不榖專心戮力以左右諸侯，則何爲而不可？"乃張大侯於東阿之外，禮 [四]

have something added, the balance is upset.[25] If you sir, and I, the one unable to cultivate, focus our minds and join our strength to move the many lords left and right, then what could we not achieve?" Then a large target was set up outside of the Eastern Corner,[26] and an (archery) rite [4]

---

[25] See the discussion in Zhou Boqun, "Mechanical Metaphors in Early China," esp. 61–66; Vankeerberghen, "Choosing Balance," 47–89; For the scales, compare *Mozi* 墨子 "Jing shuo xia" 經説下, Sun Yirang 孫怡讓 ed., *Mozi jiangu* 墨子間詁, vol. 1 (Beijing: Zhonghua shuju, 2001), 10.369:

> （衡）：加重於其一旁必捶，權重相若也。相衡則本短標長，兩加焉重相若，則標必下，標得權也。
> (The Beam.) The side of it on which you lay a weight will necessarily decline, because the two sides are equal in weight and leverage. If you make them level, the tip will be longer than the butt; and when you lay equal weights on both sides the tip will necessarily fall, because the tip has gained in leverage.

Quoted from Vankeerberghen, "Choosing Balance," 51–52, which in turn adapts Angus C. Graham, *Later Mohist Logic, Ethics and Science* (Hong Kong: The Chinese University Press, 1978), 387–390.

[26] I follow Ma Nan's earlier reading of *e* 阿 in "Qinghua liu zhengli baogao buzheng." An alternative proposed by Fan Changxi 范常喜, "Qinghua jian *Zi Yi* suo ji 'da sou' shi kaoxi" 清華簡《子儀》所記"大蒐"事考析, *Chutu wenxian* 出土文獻 2020.4: 68–71, reads this as an example of a military review: *da sou* 大蒐 or *da yue/jiao* 大閱/校.

子義亡豊縈貨以贛公命窮韋陞盩奏甬霓曰裎₌可
䛯₌可徒僧所遊又步里謓

子儀。無禮賄貨，以贛。公命窮韋、升琴奏鏞，歌曰："遲遲兮，委委兮，徒儈所遊，
又止里謓₍₅₎

was held for Mr. Yi. There was no alcohol or gifts, but he was presented with singing and dancing (instead).[27] The lord ordered (music masters) Qiong Wei and Sheng Qin to strike the bells,[28] and sing: "Slowly, winding, I go where the broker[29] traveled, again stopping in hamlets, my words rambling."[30] [5]

---

27 There is a great discrepancy in the parsing of this problematic passage. The editors read 禮子儀，無禮隋貨，以贛，wherein Sui Hui 隋貨 (or: 會) refers to a Jin emissary. Both the timeline and the sudden introduction of another emissary into the narrative is problematic, as noted in Ma Nan, "Qinghua jian *Zi Yi* xiangguan shishi yu jianwen bianlian shidu," 34. She reads 乃張大侯於東奇之外，豊。子儀無豊，縈貨以贛, instead, but does not translate. In "Qinghua qi zhengli baogao buzheng" she offers several alternatives, including reading as 豊子儀，無豊賄貨以貢, and reading *li* 豊 as *li* 醴. Other interpretations include Yang Mengsheng, "Qinghua jian *Zi yi* pian jianwen jiaodu ji," 禮子儀<以>亡(舞)，禮隨貨以贛.
    My interpretation follows the syntax of the editors, but with interpretations from Ma Nan in "Qinghua qi zhengli baogao buzheng," reading the second *li* 豊 as *li* 醴. In this reading, the explicit absence of alcohol and gifts places stronger emphasis on the content of the performance.
28 For a study of this passage, see He Jiaxing 何家興, "Cong Qinghua jian *Zi Yi* tan Chunqiu zou yue" 從清華簡《子儀》談春秋奏樂, *Zhongguo wenxue yanjiu* 中國文學研究 2018.2: 99–103.
29 I read *kuai* 儈 in its sense of "intermediary-broker."
30 This sentence is problematic. I tentatively follow Zi Ju, "Qinghua jian *Zi Yi* jiexi," who reads *lou lian* 謱譠 as a reversal of *lian lou* 譠謱, "rambling words," in light of *Chu ci* "Jiu si" 九思: "The intermediary stoops, her words rambling." 媒女詘兮譠謱. Hong Xingzu, *Chu ci bu zhu*, 317–318. The opening of the song seems to suggest an alliance between Chu and Qin, with Zi Yi as its intermediary.

Chapter Ten *Zi Yi 子儀 *Mr. Yi

灘也和晃曰漳水可遠䞭逆昗達化开可非₌渭可滔₌
楊㯱可依₌亓下之浧₌此恖之昜僮

讘也。"和歌曰："漳水兮遠望，逆視達過。开兮霏霏，渭兮滔滔，楊柳兮依依，其下之浩浩。此愠之傷慟，[六]

The harmonizing song went: "The Wei River![31] I gaze afar, looking back at my achievements and mistakes. The Qian (river) is brimming, the Wei (river)[32] is torrential, poplar and willow grow lush, the vastness[33] beneath them. This is my painful cry of grief, [6]

---

31 The modern-day Wei 渭 river flows through what used to be the plains towards the southeast of the Qin capital Yong 雍. Given that the final part of the text makes reference to Qin with this river, it seems likely that it refers to Qin.
32 The Qian and Wei rivers are important rivers in Qin, and stand for Qin as a whole; see Li Xueqin 李學勤, "You guan Chunqiu shishi de Qinghua jian wu zhong zongshu," 82–83.
33 I follow the editors' second suggestion to read this as *hao* 浩, likely referring to the vastness of Qin.

是不孜而猶僅是尚求弔昜之怍尻虐以休萬子是
救乃命陞盞訶於子義楚樂和

是不孜而猷，慟是尚求。蟄惕之怍，處吾以休，賴子是求。"乃命升琴歌於子儀，楚樂和。[七]

I have not attained it despite my planning,[34] and I cry because I still seek. To change my expression of lament and sadness, and rest in beauty, I rely on you in my request."[35] Then he ordered Sheng Qin to sing to Mr. Yi, and harmonize it with Chu music. [7]

---

34 Alternatively, this line is about Lord Mu's inability to "hold back" (*han* 馯) Jin, and that he still blames himself for it, reading *you* 猶 as *you* 訧 "blame."
35 The punctuation here follows the rhyme as per Wang Ning, "Qinghua jian liu *Zi Yi* shiwen jiaodu," while the reading follows Zi Ju, "Qinghua jian *Zi Yi* jiexi."

Chapter Ten *Zi Yi* 子儀 *Mr. Yi*

[seal script characters]

之曰鳥飛可䧹永余可矰以遏之遠人可麗佰君又
䜣言余隼思于告之弜弓可縵亓䋃

之，曰："鳥飛兮適永，余何矰以就之？遠人兮離宿，君有尋言，余誰思于告之？強弓兮挽其絕[八]

It went: "The bird flies going[36] further away. With what corded-arrow could I reach it? A person from far away, about to leave your lodge;[37] you my lord, I have words seeking an audience.[38] Who will I think of to tell them? The bow is strong, and is drawn to its end, [8]

---

36 Yang Mengsheng, "Du Qinghua liu *Zi Yi* biji wuze—fu *Zheng Wen Gong Wen Tai Bo yi ze*," reads this as *shi* 適; the interpretation follows Mu Silang 暮四郎, post no. 45 in the thread "Qinghua liu *Zi Yi* chudu" 清華六《子儀》初讀, April 20, 2016 on the *Jianbo luntan* 簡帛論壇 forum, http://www.bsm.org.cn/forum/forum.php?mod=viewthread&tid=3343&extra=page%3D2&page=5.

37 I follow Shan Yuchen, "*Zi Yi* shiwen shangque," 32, who reads *li* 離. I follow Ma Nan, "Qinghua jian *Zi Yi* xiangguan shishi yu jianwen bianlian shidu," in reading *ke* 可 as *xi* 兮. The whole song seems to be hinting at the use of Master Yi to send a message to the Chu king; for this reading, see Ji Xusheng 季旭昇, "*Qinghua liu Zi Yi* 'niao fei zhi ge' shijie" 《清華六·子儀》"鳥飛之歌"試解, *Wuhan daxue jianbo yanjiu zhongxin wangzhan* 武漢大學簡帛研究中心網站, April 27, 2016, http://www.bsm.org.cn/?chujian/6694.html.

38 I follow Ma Nan in "Qinghua liu zhengli baogao buzheng."

丄 𦉢 𨒰 𣆗 㦰 丄 𤯔 㥈 可 山 𠂤 雩 余 𤝇 亓 或 𣏟 㠯 訐 余
𤯔 㦰 于 𦉢 丄 䍐 丄 䴩 而 余 㠯 䇯 勹 𢆶

也，矰追而𣏟之莫𨒰可。以寅言余𤝇亓或而不訐余
隼思于䇯之昔之𤡊可余不與今兹

也，矰追而及之；莫往兮何以寅言？余畏其忒而不信，余誰思于協之。昔之獵兮余不與，今兹 [九]

the corded-arrow pursues and reaches them;[39] if you did not go, how could I place my words?[40] I am afraid that he will doubt them and not trust me.[41] Who will I think of to mediate my words? In the hunts of the past, I did not participate.[42] Now (if) in this [9]

---

39 For reading 𣏟 as ji 及, see Shan Yuchen, "Zi Yi shiwen shangque," 32.
40 There is a debate whether 雩 writes yan 言 or yin 音. I follow the former option offered by the editors, Ji Xusheng, "Qinghua liu Zi Yi 'niao fei zhi ge' shijie" favors the latter.
41 I follow Mu Silang 暮四郎, post no. 56 in the thread "Qinghua liu Zi Yi chudu" 清華六《子儀》初讀, April 21, 2016 on the Jianbo luntan 簡帛論壇 forum, http://www.bsm.org.cn/forum/forum.php?mod=viewthread&tid=3343&extra=page%3D2&page=6.
42 I follow Ji Xusheng, "Qinghua liu Zi Yi 'niao fei zhi ge' shijie."

之襘余或不與攷之練可而勯之織紝之不成虐可
以祭稷竉明公遣子義公曰義

之獵余或不與，施之責兮而奮之職，任之不成，吾何以祭稷？"翌明，公送子儀。
公曰："儀[十]

hunt, I were not to participate, (would this not be) exercising my duties and exerting myself in my task, yet not seeing it to completion. How could I offer at the altar of grain?"[43] The next morning, the lord sent off Mr. Yi. Lord (Mu) said: "Sir Yi, [10]

---

43 The editors provide minimal annotation and suggest interpreting the previous section in light of the *la* 臘 sacrifice, a reading that is rendered problematic by the obvious use of hunting imagery.
  For this line, I tentatively follow Ji Xusheng, "*Qinghua liu Zi Yi* 'niao fei zhi ge' shijie." Another option is presented in an augmented version of Wang Ning's reading by Zhu Zhongheng, "Qinghua daxue cang Zhanguo zhujian (liu) jishi," 125, reading as follows: (it is as if) making a thread and working it into a weave, but if the weave is unfinished, how could I offer at the altar of grain? 施之績兮而奮之，織紝之不成，吾何以祭稷, wherein the weaving metaphor is used to reinforce the idea of a job not finished (i.e. aligning with Chu in the fight against Jin). While the reading is possible, the sudden introduction of a new weaving metaphor appears problematic to me.

父 以 不 教 之 攸 遠 於 君 可 爭 而 不 好 辟 之 女 兩 犬 縴
河 敆 而 奰 敉 惌 不 歁 心 則 不

父，以不穀之修遠於君，何爭而不好，譬之如兩犬沿河，啜而猌。豈畏不足，心則不[十一]

I, the one unable to cultivate, am so far from you oh lord, why fight and not have good relations? Liken it to two dogs following along the river, they bare their teeth at each other while drinking. How could we fear there is not enough, and not examine our hearts? [11]

毀 救 兄 弟 以 見 東 方 之 者 侯 歔 曰 奉 晉 軍 以 相 南 面
之 事 先₌又 言 曰 咎 者 不 元 昔 䋃

察？求兄弟以見東方之諸侯，豈曰奉晉軍以相南面之事？先人有言曰：'咎者不怨。'
昔䋃 [十二]

I hope we can appear before the many lords of the east as brothers;[44] how could they say that they support the Jin armies in ministering the affairs of the one facing south? The elders had a saying that went: 'Do not harbor a grudge against those who committed an offense.'[45] In the past when the hostage[46] [12]

---

44 I follow Shan Yuchen, "*Zi Yi* shiwen shangque," 33.
45 I follow Shan Yuchen, "*Zi Yi* shiwen shangque," 33.
46 The discussion centers on whether this graph should be read as a word roughly meaning hostage, or, whether it is a name. The editors read it as *zhi* 質 "hostage." Shan Yuchen, "*Zi Yi* shiwen shangque," 33 reads it as *ji* 羈 "restrained." Ma Nan, "Qinghua jian *Zi Yi* xiangguan shishi yu jianwen bianlian shidu," 34–35, reads the graph as the name of a Chu hostage. I tentatively follow Shan Yuchen since this makes the most sense paleographically (note the use of the *si* 糸 signific in 䋃) and does not involve the naming of a previously unknown figure as in Ma Nan's reading. While the referent of the "restrained" is not made explicit in this text, the editors are correct in surmising that this refers to the hostage-taking of the Jin heir apparent Yu by Lord Mu, an event significant enough to merit a prediction and three references in *Zuo* Xi 15, 17, and 22. Lord Mu married a daughter to Yu, and lodged the prince at Lingtai 靈臺, suggesting an intent to offer the ruler to the God on High. (*Zuo*, Xi 15.4) This sequence of events is tightly linked to Qin's famine relief efforts that were unrequited by Jin. For a discussion, see Durrant, Li, and Schaberg, *Zuo Tradition*, 315ff.

之 悊 之 未 㱾 佰 之 需 吾 㦣 年 皇 之 亦 唯 㕛 之 古 公
曰 等 父 㮣 氏 多 聯 緍 秝 不 緖

之 㱾 也 不 教 佰 之 需 吾 厭 年 而 見 之 亦 唯 咎 之 古 公
曰 義 父 溫 氏 多 絲 緍 而 不 繹

之來也，不穀宿之靈陰，厭年而見之，亦唯咎之故。" 公曰："儀父！嬴氏多聯婚而不續，[十三]

came, I, the one unable to cultivate, lodged him at Lingyin and only saw them after a year, that is the source of the offense." Lord (Mu) said: "Sir Yi, the Ying family intermarried many times (with Jin),[47] yet they did not continue (this goodwill); [13]

---

47 I follow Yang Mengsheng, "Du Qinghua liu *Zi Yi* biji wuze."

Chapter Ten *Zi Yi* 子儀 *Mr. Yi*

[ancient script line 1]
[ancient script line 2]

級織不能官凥占夢亶永不休鼍上又兔橮枳堂櫺
犯客而誸之子義曰君欲汽丹

給職不能官處，占夢適永不休。臺上有兔，橮枝當棬，娭客而宴之。"子儀曰："君欲乞丹[十四]

we offered officers that could not take up their post,[48] and the dream prognostications never had a good outcome. On the platform there is a rabbit, and bent branches make its vessel; I wait upon the guest to feast on it."[49] Mr. Yi said: "If you want to request[50] (an alliance) with the Cinnabar region (i.e. the south, i.e. Chu), [14]

---

48 This possibly refers to Qin placing officials in former Jin territories ceded to Qin according to the treaty at Han. This area was returned to Jin within two years, see *Zuo* Xi 15, 17.
49 Su Jianzhou 蘇建洲, "*Qinghua liu* wenzi bushi《清華六》文字補釋, *Wuhan daxue jianbo yanjiu zhongxin wangzhan* 武漢大學簡帛研究中心網站, April 20, 2016, http://www.bsm.org.cn/?chujian/6684.html transcribes 橮 as *jiu* 橮 and reads 櫺 as *quan* 棬 "crooked-wood drinking vessel." Wang Ning, "Qinghua jian liu *Zi Yi* shiwen jiaodu," notes that 誸 can be read as 宴 "feast." Note that Yang Mengsheng, "Du Qinghua liu *Zi Yi* biji wuze," points to the use of rabbits as an ominous omen (see also *Chijiu zhi ji tang zhi wu* 赤鳩之集湯之屋) and as such it could be understood as an extension of the dream prognostication. Another reading is suggested by Wang Ning, arguing that the line reads as an invitation for Master Yi (the guest) to present the treaty (the rabbit) to his liege. None of these explanations makes full sense of this difficult passage. I tentatively read it as a segue into Master Yi's response. Possibly, this draws on *Shi jing* "Hu ye" 瓠葉: "There is but a single rabbit, Baked, or roasted. [But] the superior man, from his spirits, Fills the cup and presents it [to his guests]" 有兔斯首、炮之燔之。君子有酒、酌言獻之. Ruan Yuan, *Shisanjing zhushu*, 499; Legge, *The Chinese Classics*, vol.4, 420.
50 I read *qi* 乞 "ask" for *qi* 汽 following Zi Ju, "Qinghua jian *Zi Yi* jiexi," and Ma Nan, "Qinghua jian *Zi Yi* xiangguan shishi yu jianwen bianlian shidu," 37.

方 豢 狂 冋 夲 鐕 虎 忶 漳 之 川 屛 亦 夲 㡯 䣙 䖿 仔 之 楷
之 公 曰 篆 父 㝫 䋿 之 㱃 夲 勢 諂

方者邘君不贍皮泹漳之川屛而不盧殹䏁尼之櫓
也公曰義父昔焉之行不教欲

方，諸任君不瞻彼沮漳之川開而不闠，抑虜夷之楷也。" 公曰："儀父！昔羈之行，不穀欲 [十六]

the rulers do not look highly upon the Ju and Zhang plain (i.e., border area Qin and Chu) being open and not closed off (to each other), yet it is the model for this captured barbarian."[51] Lord (Mu) said: "Sir Yi, previously upon the departure of the hostage, I, the one unable to cultivate, desired [16]

---

51 The plains between the Ju and Zhang rivers form a corridor from Qin to Chu. The area being open and not closed to each other signals an alliance. The captured barbarian here ought to be a form of self-address by Master Yi, referring to his previous capture by Qin and the old trope of Chu being barbarians. For the use of *yi* 夷 to refer to people from Chu, see *Mengzi*, "Teng Wen Gong shang" 滕文公上: "I have heard of the Chinese converting barbarians to their ways, but not of their being converted to barbarian ways. Ch'en Liang was a native of Chou. Being delighted with the way of the Duke of Chou and Confucius, he came north to study in the Central Kingdoms." 吾聞用夏變夷者，未聞變於夷者也。陳良，楚產也。悦周公、仲尼之道，北學於中國. *Mengzi Zhengyi*, 393; Lau, *Mencius*, 103.

Chapter Ten *Zi Yi 子儀 *Mr. Yi

裕 我 亡 反 副 尚 耑 項 瞻 遊 目 以 昏 我 秦 邦 不 穀 敢 炁
糧 公 曰 義 父 歸 女 丌 可 言 子 義

裕，我亡反復。尚端項瞻，遊目以盰我秦邦。不穀敢愛糧？"公曰："儀父！歸，汝其何言？"子儀 [十七]

magnanimity,[52] I did not turn back on this. When I stretch my neck and look up, and allow my eyes to wander for a gander at our state of Qin, how could I, the one unable to cultivate, dare to covet provisions?[53] The lord said: "Sir Yi, when you return, what will you say?" Mr. Yi [17]

---

52 I follow Ma Nan, "Qinghua jian *Zi Yi* xiangguan shishi yu jianwen bianlian shidu," 37. She notes that the release of the captive by Qin was a sign of goodwill (i.e. tolerance 裕).

53 Yang Mengsheng, "Du Qinghua liu *Zi Yi* biji wuze," suggests this refers to Qin supporting Jin with provisions when the population was starving despite an earlier betrayal; Zi Ju, "Qinghua jian *Zi Yi* jiexi," suggests it is a statement of intent, and that the provisions are to be understood as war preparations. Ma Nan suggests that the captive (Ma, in her reading) sneaked a peak at the war provisions of Qin. I understand it as Lord Mu of Qin suggesting that his magnanimity extends to his grain supply. Alternatively, with the editors, it refers to the grain transports from Qin to Jin, but that reading would require the "restrained" to refer to a captive from Jin.

曰 臣 觀 於 湋 澋 見 敢 鵠 踦 淒 不 夂 需 鵠 臣 亓 歸 而 言
之 臣 見 二 人 戜 競 一 人 至 辭 於 儷 獄

曰:"臣觀於湋溢,見屬鵠踦濟,不終需鵠,臣其歸而言之;臣見二人仇競,一人至,辭於儷,獄 [十八]

said: "I, your minister, touring along the Wei and Shi rivers, saw a type of crane that wanted to cross over on one foot. It did not reach the end and had to wait for another (to do it together).[54] That is what I will say when I return. I saw two people fighting, another person arrived and adjudicated between the pair.[55] The case [18]

---

54 This is another enigmatic reference. According to the editors (p. 134), it refers to the crane, often seen standing on one foot, or, with Zi Ju, "Qinghua jian *Zi Yi* jiexi," a *man* 鸛 bird which only has one foot, one wing, and one eye, and needs another to fly.
55 This should refer to Chu weighing in on the fight between Qin and Jin; see Zi Ju, "Qinghua jian *Zi Yi* jiexi."

乃 成 臣 亓 歸 而 言 之 臣 見 遺 者 弗 復 翼 明 而 反 之 臣
亓 歸 而 言 之 公 曰 君 不 尚 芒 䣂

乃成，臣其歸而言之；臣見遺者弗復，翌明而叛之，臣其歸而言之；公曰'君不尚荒隔，[十九]

was then solved. That is what I will say when I return. I saw someone giving something that was not given back. The next day they were betrayed. That is what I will say when I return. When you, milord, say:[56] 'If you do not value desolate separation (between our states), [19]

---

56 Jia Lianxiang, "Qinghua liu zhengli baogao buzheng" reads this as a quote, which seems to solve the supposed "missing slip between 19-20" problem.

王 之 北 𣳚 迵 之 于 虖 道 敚 于 孫= 若 臣 亓 遲 而 言 之

王之北没，通之於殽道', 豈於子孫若? 臣其歸而言之▬。" [二十]

and do not want the (territories) north of your king lost,[57] and connected to the Xiao corridor,[58] can we really leave that to our sons and grandsons? That is what I will say when I return ▬." [20]

---

57 In other words, the situation if Qin did not receive help from Chu against Jin.
58 I.e., right up to Jin's doorstep.

子儀

　　既敗於殽，恐民之大病，移易故職。欲民所安，其宣不更。

　　公益及三謀輔之，靡土不食，耄幼[一]在公。陰者思陽，陽者思陰，民恒不實，乃毀常各務。降上品之，辨官相代，乃有見功。公及三[十五]謀慶而賞之。乃券册秦邦之羨餘，自蘁月至于秋令備焉。聚及七年，車逸於舊數三百，[二]徒逸于舊典六百，以視楚子儀於杏會。

　　公曰："儀父，不穀擩左，右緺，擩右，左緺，如權之[三]有加，橈也。君及不穀專心戮力以左右諸侯，則何爲而不可？"

　　乃張大侯於東阿之外，禮[四]子儀。無醴賄貨，以竷。公命窮韋、升琴奏鏞。

　　歌曰：

　　"遲遲兮，委委兮，徒儈所遊，又止里譨[五]譿也。"

　　和歌曰：

　　"漳水兮遠望，逆視逵過。汧兮霏霏，渭兮滔滔，楊柳兮依依，其下之浩浩。此愠之傷慟，[六]是不攽而猶，慟是尚求。蹙惕之怍，處吾以休，賴子是求。"

　　乃命升琴歌於子儀，楚樂和[七]之，曰：

　　"鳥飛兮適永，余何矰以就之？遠人兮離宿，君有尋言，余誰思于告之？强弓兮挽其絶[八]也，矰追而及之；莫往兮何以寅言？余畏其忒而不信，余誰思于協之。昔之獵兮余不與，今茲[九]之獵余或不與，施之責兮而奮之職，任之不成，吾何以祭稷？"

　　翌明，公送子儀。

　　公曰："儀[十]父，以不穀之修遠於君，何爭而不好，譬之如兩犬沿河，啜而欶，豈畏不足，心則不[十一]察？求兄弟以見東方之諸侯，豈曰奉晉軍以相南面之事？先人有言曰：'咎者不怨。'昔羈[十二]之來也，不穀宿之靈陰，厭年而見之，亦唯咎之故。"

　　公曰："儀父！嬴氏多聯婚而不續，[十三]給職不能官處，占夢適永不休。臺上有兔，樛枝當棬，唉客而宴之。"

　　子儀曰："君欲乞丹[十四]方，諸任君不瞻彼沮漳之川開而不闔，抑虜夷之楷也。"

公曰:"儀父!昔羈之行,不穀欲[十六]裕,我亡反復。尚端項瞻,遊目以盱我秦邦。不穀敢愛糧?"

公曰:"儀父!歸,汝其何言?"

子儀[十七]曰:"臣觀於漳滋,見屬鸛踦濟,不終需鸛,臣其歸而言之;臣見二人仇競,一人至,辭於儷,獄[十八]乃成,臣其歸而言之;臣見遺者弗復,翌明而返之,臣其歸而言之;公曰'君不尚荒隔,[十九]王之北沒,通之於殽道',豈於子孫若?臣其歸而言之▬。"[二十]

Chapter Ten   *Zi Yi 子儀 *Mr. Yi

*Mr. Yi

Having been defeated at Xiao, (Lord Mu of Qin) feared that the people would be greatly distressed, and would move and alter their former occupations. He wanted what would pacify the people, and that their trust would not change. The Lord increasingly joined with the three counselors to support them; there was no area that was not fed, and the elderly and infants [1] were taken care of at public expense. (But) those in the shade desired the sun, and those in the sun desired shade, the people were continuously restless, and this ruined the regularity of everyone's duties. (Lord Mu and his counselors) demoted superiors and evaluated them, and they differentiated officials to replace them, then they achieved results. The lord joined with the three [15] counsellors to laud and reward them. Then they registered the manpower and surplus of the Qin state, they completed (the register) from the Month of the Silkworm (i.e., the height of spring) up to the Height of Autumn. They gathered (manpower and surplus) up to the 7th year (after the battle), and chariots exceeded previous numbers by three hundred, [2] and troops exceeded the previous registers by six hundred. They showed them to Mr. Yi of Chu during the meeting at Xing.

The lord said: "Sir Yi, if I, the one unable to cultivate, pull to the left, the right (string) draws taut, and if I pull to the right the left draws taut. It is as when the scales [3] have something added, the balance is upset. If you sir, and I, the one unable to cultivate, focus our minds and join our strength to move the many lords left and right, then what could we not achieve?"

Then a large target was set up outside of the Eastern Corner, and an (archery) rite [4] was held for Mr. Yi. There was no alcohol or gifts, but he was presented with singing and dancing (instead). The lord ordered (music masters) Qiong Wei and Sheng Qin to strike the bells, and sing: "Slowly, winding, I go where the broker traveled, again stopping in hamlets, my words rambling." [5]

The harmonizing song went: "The Wei River! I gaze afar, looking back at my achievements and mistakes. The Qian (river) is brimming, the Wei (river) is torrential, poplar and willow grow lush, the vastness beneath them. This is my painful cry of grief, [6] that I have not attained it despite my planning, and I cry because I still seek. To change my expression of lament and sadness, and rest in beauty, I rely on you in my request."

Then he ordered Sheng Qin to sing to Mr. Yi, and harmonize it with Chu music. [7] It went: "The bird flies, going further away. With what corded-arrow could I reach it? A person from far away, about to leave your lodge; my lord, I have words seeking an audience. Who will I think of to tell them? The bow is strong, and is drawn to its end, [8] the corded-arrow pursues and reaches them; if you did not go, how could I place my words? I am afraid that he will doubt them and not trust me. Who will I think of to mediate my words? In the hunts of the past, I did not participate. Now (if) in this [9] hunt, I were not to participate, (would this not be) exercising my duties and exerting myself in my task, yet not seeing it to completion. How could I offer at the altar of grain?"

The next morning, the lord sent off Mr. Yi. Lord (Mu) said: "Sir Yi, [10] I, the one unable to cultivate, am so far from you oh lord, why fight and not have good relations? Liken it to two dogs following along the river, they bare their teeth at each other while drinking. How could we fear there is not enough, and not examine our hearts? [11] I hope we can appear before the many lords of the east as brothers; how could they say that they support the Jin armies in ministering the affairs of the one facing south? The elders had a saying that went: 'Do not harbor a grudge against those who committed an offense.' In the past when the hostage [12] came, I, the one unable to cultivate, lodged him at Lingyin and only saw them after a year, that is the source of the offense."

Lord (Mu) said: "Sir Yi, the Ying family intermarried many times (with Jin), yet they did not continue (this goodwill); [13] we offered officers that could not take up their post, and the dream prognostications never had a good outcome. On the platform there is a rabbit, and bent branches make

Chapter Ten *Zi Yi 子儀 *Mr. Yi

its vessel; I wait upon the guest to feast on it."

Mr. Yi said: "If you want to request (an alliance) with the Cinnabar region (i.e. the south, i.e. Chu), [14] the rulers do not look highly upon the Ju and Zhang plain (i.e. border area Qin and Chu) being open and not closed off (to each other), yet it is the model for this captured barbarian.

Lord (Mu) said: "Sir Yi, previously upon the departure of the hostage, I, the one unable to cultivate, desired [16] magnanimity, I did not turn back on this. When I stretch my neck and look up, and allow my eyes to wander for a gander at our state of Qin, how could I, the one unable to cultivate, dare to covet provisions?

The lord said: "Sir Yi, when you return, what will you say?"

Mr. Yi [17] said: "I, your minister, touring along the Wei and Shi rivers, saw a type of crane that wanted to cross over on one foot. It did not reach the end and had to wait for another (to do it together). That is what I will say when I return. I saw two people fighting. Another person arrived and adjudicated between the pair. The case [18] was then solved. That is what I will say when I return. I saw someone giving something that was not given back. The next day they were betrayed. That is what I will say when I return. When you, milord, say: 'If you do not value desolate separation (between our states), [19] and do not want the (territories) north of your king lost, and connected to the Xiao corridor,' can we really leave that to our sons and grandsons? That is what I will say when I return ▬." [20]

Works Cited

Allan, Sarah. *The Way of Water and Sprouts of Virtue.* Albany: State University of New York Press, 1997.

———. *The Heir and the Sage: Dynastic Legend in Early China.* San Francisco: Chinese Materials Center, 1981.

Bal, Mieke. *Narratology: Introduction to the Theory of Narrative, Third Edition.* Toronto: University of Toronto press, 2009.

Bakhtin, Mikhail M., Vern W. McGee trans. "The Problem of Speech Genres." In *Speech Genres and Other Late* Essays. Austin: University of Texas Press, 2010, 60–102.

Bauer, Wolfgang. *Der chinesische* Personenname. Wiesbaden: Harrassowitz, 1959.

Bissel, Jeff. "Literary Studies of Historical Texts: Early Narrative Accounts of Chong'er, Duke Wen of Jin." PhD dissertation. University of Wisconsin, 1996.

Chao Fulin 晁福林. "Tan Qinghua jian *Zheng Wu Furen gui ruzi* de shiliao jiazhi" 談清華簡《鄭武夫人規孺子》的史料價值. *Qinghua daxue xuebao (zhexue shehui kexue ban)* 清華大學學報（哲學社會科學版）2017.3: 128–129.

Chen Wei 陳偉. "Zheng Bo ke Duan 'qianzhuan' de lishi xushi" 鄭伯克段"前傳"的歷史敘事. *Zhongguo shehui kexue bao* 中國社會科學報 30 May 2016.

———. "Qinghua jian qi *Zi Fa Zi Yu* 'Tianli huihuo' xiaoshi" 清華簡七《子犯子餘》"天禮悔禍"小識. *Wuhan daxue jianbo yanjiu zhongxin wangzhan* 武漢大學簡帛研究中心網站. At http://

www.bsm.org.cn/?chujian/7522.html. Posted 4 May 2017.

———. "Qinghua qi *Zi Fan Zi Yu* jiaodu (xu)" 清華七校讀（續）. *Wuhan daxue jianbo yanjiu zhongxin wangzhan* 武漢大學簡帛研究中心網站. At http://www.bsm.org.cn/?chujian/7534.html. Posted 1 May 2017.

———. "Qinghua qi *Zi Fan Zi Yu* jiaodu" 清華七《子犯子餘》校讀. *Wuhan daxue jianbo yanjiu zhongxin wangzhan* 武漢大學簡帛研究中心網站. At http://www.bsm.org.cn/?chujian/7532.html. Posted 30 April 2017.

———. "Ye shuo Chujian cong 'meng' zhi zi" 也説楚簡从"黽"之字. *Wuhan daxue jianbo yanjiu zhongxin wangzhan* 武漢大學簡帛研究中心網站, At http://www.bsm.org.cn/?chujian/7531.html. Posted 29 April 2017.

———. *Xin chu Chujian yandu* 新出楚簡研讀 (Wuhan: Wuhan daxue, 2010).

Chen Weiwu 陳偉武, "Du Qinghua jian di liu ce xiaozha" 讀清華簡第六冊小札, *Chutu wenxian* 出土文獻 11 (2017): 205–209.

Chen Yawen 陳雅雯 and Wang Lingjuan 王玲娟. "'bu gu' xintan" "不穀"新探. *Heihe xueyuan xuebao* 黑河學院學報 2019.12: 154–157.

Chen Zhijun 陳治軍. "Qinghua jian *Zhao Jianzi* zhong cong 'meng' zi shili" 清華簡《趙簡子》中从"黽"字釋例. *Fudan daxue chutu wenxian yu guwenzi yanjiu zhongxin wangzhan* 復旦大學出土文獻與古文字研究中心網站. At http://www.fdgwz.org.cn/Web/Show/3017. Posted 29 April 2017.

Cheng Hao 程浩. "Qinghua jian di qi ji zhengli baogao shiyi" 清華簡第七輯整理報告拾遺. *Qinghua daxue chutu wenxian yanjiu yu baohu zhongxin wangzhan* 清華大學出土文獻研究與保護中心網站. At https://www.ctwx.tsinghua.edu.cn/info/1081/2234.htm. Posted 23 April 2017.

Cheng Yan 程燕. "Qinghua liu kaoshi san ze" 清華六考釋三則. *Wuhan daxue jianbo yanjiu zhongxin wangzhan* 武漢大學簡帛研究中心網站. At http://www.bsm.org.cn/?chujian/6683.html. Posted 19

April 2016.

de Jong, Irene. *Narratology and Classics: A Practical Guide*. Oxford: Oxford University Press, 2014.

———. *Narrators and Focalizers: The Presentation of the Story in the Iliad*. London: Bloomsbury Academic, 2004 [1987].

de Jong, Irene. René Nünlist, and Angus Bowie eds., *Narrators, Narratees, and Narratives in Ancient Greek Literature*. Leiden: Brill, 2004.

Defoort, Carine. "Heavy and Light Body Parts: The Weighing Metaphor in Early Chinese Dialogues." *Early China* 38 (2015): 55–77.

Di Biase-Dyson, Camilla, and Markus Egg. *Drawing Attention to Metaphor: Case Studies Across Time Periods, Cultures and Modalities*. Amsterdam: John Benjamins, 2020.

Du Heng. "The Mastery of Miscellanea: Information Management and Knowledge Acquisition in the 'Chu shuo' Chapters of the *Hanfeizi*." *Journal of the American Oriental Society* 140.1 (2020): 115–142.

Durrant, Stephen, Li Wai-Yee, and David Schaberg trans. *Zuo Tradition / Zuozhuan* 左傳: *Commentary on the "Spring and Autumn Annals."* Seattle: University of Washington Press, 2016.

Egan, Ronald. "Narratives in Tso Chuan." *Harvard Journal of Asiatic Studies* 37.2 (1977): 323–352.

Elman, Benjamin. "Philosophy (*I-Li*) versus Philology (*K'ao-cheng*): The *Jen-hsin tao-hsin* Debate." *T'oung Pao* 2nd ser. 69.4–5 (1983):175–222.

Ekstrom, Martin S. "Does the Metaphor Translate?" In Ming Dong Gu and Rainer Shulte eds. *Translating China for Western Readers: Reflective, Critical, and Practical Essays*. Albany: State University of New York Press, 2014, 45–70.

Eisenberg, Andrew. *Kingship in Early Medieval China*. Leiden: Brill, 2008.

Fan Changxi 范常喜. "Qinghua jian *Zi Yi* suo ji 'da sou' shi kaoxi" 清華簡《子儀》所記"大蒐"事考析. *Chutu wenxian* 出土文獻 2020.4: 68–71.

Feng Shengjun 馮勝君. "Qinghua jian *Zi Fan Zi Yu* pian 'bu xi' jie" 清華簡《子犯子余》篇"不忻"解. *Wuhan daxue jianbo yanjiu zhongxin wangzhan* 武漢大學簡帛研究中心網站. At http://www.bsm.org.cn/?chujian/7537.html. Posted 5 May 2017.

Foster, Christopher J. "Introduction to the Peking University Han Bamboo Strips: On the Authentication and Study of Purchased Manuscripts." *Early China* 40 (2017): 167–239.

Gandolfo, Stefano. "Metaphors of Metaphors: Reflections on the Use of Conceptual Metaphor Theory in Premodern Chinese Texts." *Dao* 18.3 (2019), 323–345.

Geaney, Jane. "Self as Container? Metaphors We Lose by in Understanding Early Chinese Texts." *Antiquorum Philosophia* 5 (2012): 11–30.

Genette, Gérard, Jane E. Lewin trans. *Paratexts: Thresholds of Interpretation.* Cambridge: Cambridge University Press, 1997.

——, Jane E. Lewin trans., *Narrative Discourse: An Essay in Method.* Ithaca: Cornell University Press, 1980.

Giele, Enno. "Using Early Chinese Manuscripts as Historical Source Materials." *Monumenta Serica* 51 (2003): 409–438.

Graham, Angus C. *Later Mohist Logic, Ethics and Science.* Hong Kong: The Chinese University Press, 1978.

Grethlein, Jonas. *Experience and Teleology in Ancient Historiography: 'Futures Past' from Herodotus to Augustine.* Cambridge: Cambridge University Press, 2013.

Grethlein, Jonas. and Antonios Rengakos eds. *Narratology and Interpretation The Content of Narrative Form in Ancient Literature.* Berlin: Walter de Gruyter, 2009.

Gu Shikao 顧史考 (Scott Cook). "*Zhao Jianzi* chutan"《趙簡子》初探. *Bulletin of the Jao Tsung-I Academy* 饒宗頤學院院刊 6 (2019): 361–375.

Guo Jue. "Western Han Funerary Relocation Documents and the Making of the Dead in Early Imperial China." *Bamboo and Silk* 2.2 (2019): 141–273.

Harbsmeier, Christoph. "*Xunzi* and the Problem of Impersonal First Person Pronouns." *Early China* 22 (1997): 181–220.

He Jiaxing 何家興. "Cong Qinghua jian *Zi Yi* tan Chunqiu zou yue" 從清華簡《子儀》談春秋奏樂. *Zhongguo wenxue yanjiu* 中國文學研究 2018.2: 99–103.

He Ning 何寧 ann. *Huainan zi jishi* 淮南子集釋. Beijing: Zhonghua shuju, 1998.

He Youzu 何有祖. "Du Qinghua jian liu zhaji (er ze)" 讀清華簡六札記（二則）. *Chutu wenxian* 出土文獻 10 (2017): 119–123.

Hong Xingzu 洪興祖. *Chu ci buzhu* 楚辭補註. Beijing: Zhonghua shuju, 1983.

Hu Pingsheng 胡平生. "Lun jianbo bianwei yu liushi jiandu qiangjiu" 論簡帛辨偽與流失簡牘搶救. *Chutu wenxian yanjiu* 出土文獻研究 9 (2010): 76–108.

Huang Dekuan 黃德寬 and Xia Hanyi 夏含夷 (Edward L. Shaughnessy) ed.-in-chief. *Qinghua daxue cang Zhanguo zhujian jiaoshi* 清華大學藏戰國竹簡校釋. Beijing: Shangwu yinshuguan, 2024.

Jauss, Hans Robert, Elizabeth Benzinger trans. "Literary History as a Challenge to Literary Theory." *New Literary History* 2.1 (1970): 7–37.

Ji Xusheng 季旭昇. "*Qinghua liu Zi Yi* 'niao fei zhi ge' shijie"《清華六・子儀》"鳥飛之歌"試解》. *Wuhan daxue jianbo yanjiu zhongxin wangzhan* 武漢大學簡帛研究中心網站. At http://www.bsm.org.cn/?zhujian/6694.html. Posted 27 April 2016.

Jia Lianxiang 賈連翔. "Qinghua jian *Zheng Wu Furen Gui Ruzi* pian de zai bianlian yu fuyuan" 清華簡《鄭武夫人規孺子》篇的再編連與復原. *Wenxian* 文獻 2018.3: 54–59.

——— . *Zhanguo zhushu xingzhi ji xiangguan wenti yanjiu—yi Qinghua Daxue cang Zhanguo zhujian wei zhongxin* 戰國竹書形制及相關問題研究——以清華大學藏戰國竹簡為中心. Shanghai: Zhong Xi shuju, 2015.

Jiao Xun 焦循 ann. Shen Wenzhuo 沈文卓 ed. *Mengzi Zhengyi* 孟子正義, 2 vols. (Beijing: Zhonghua shuju, 1987).

Jiang Guanghui 姜廣輝, "Qinghua jian jianding keneng yao jingli yige changqi guocheng — Zai tan dui Baoxun pian de yiwen" 清華簡鑒定可能要經歷一個長期過程——再談對保訓篇的疑問. *Guangming ribao* 光明日報, 8 June 2009.

———. "Baoxun yiwei xinzheng wuze" 保訓疑偽新證五則. *Zhongguo zhexueshi* 中國哲學史 2010.3: 30–34.

Jiang Guanghui 姜廣輝, Fu Zan 付贊 and Qiu Mengyan 邱夢燕. "Qinghua jian Qiye wei weizuo kao" 清華簡耆夜為偽作考. *Gugong bowuyuan yuankan* 故宮博物院院刊 4.168 (2013): 86–94.

Jiang Guanghui 姜廣輝 and Fu Zan 付贊, "Qinghua jian Yingao xian yi" 清華簡尹誥獻疑, *Hunan daxue xuebao (shehui kexue ban)* 湖南大學學報（社會科學版）28.3 (2014): 109–114.

Jingmen shi bowuguan 荊門市博物館 ed. *Guodian Chu mu zhujian* 郭店楚墓竹簡 (Beijing: Wenwu chubanshe, 1998).

Goldin, Paul R. "*Heng Xian* and the Problem of Studying Looted Artifacts." *Dao* 12.2 (2013): 153–160.

Grebnev, Yegor. "The *Yi Zhoushu* and the *Shangshu*: The Case of Texts with Speeches." In Martin Kern and Dirk Meyer eds. *Origins of Chinese Political Philosophy: Studies in the Thought and Composition of the* Shangshu. Leiden: Brill, 2017, 249–280.

Hills, David. "Metaphor," *The Stanford Encyclopedia of Philosophy* (Fall 2017 Edition), Edward N. Zalta ed. At https://plato.stanford.edu/archives/fall2017/entries/metaphor/. Accessed 21 June 2022.

Huadong Shifan daxue zhongwen xi chutu wenxian yanjiu gongzuo shi 華東師範大學中文系出土文獻研究工作室. "Du *Qinghua daxue cang Zhangguo zhujian (liu) Zheng Wen Gong wen Tai Bo* shu hou (yi) 讀《清華大學藏戰國竹簡（陸）·鄭文公問太伯》書後（一）. *Wuhan daxue jianbo yanjiu zhongxin wangzhan* 武漢大學簡帛研究中心網站. At http://www.bsm.org.cn/?chujian/6685.html. Posted 20 April 2016.

Khayutina, Maria. "Die Geschichte der Irrfahrt des Prinzen Chong'er und ihre Botschaft." In Heiner Roetz ed. *Kritik im alten und modernen*

China: Jahrbuch der Deutschen Vereinigung für Chinastudien 2. Wiesbaden: Harrassowitz, 2006, 20–47.

Krijgsman, Rens. "Punctuation and Text Division in Two Early Narratives: The Tsinghua University *Jin Wen Gong ru yu Jin* 晉文公入於晉 and *Zi Fan Zi Yu* 子犯子餘 Manuscripts." *Journal of the American Oriental Society* 143.1 (2023): 109–124.

———. "Elision and Narration: Remembering and Forgetting in Some Recent Unearthed Historiographical Manuscripts." In Albert Galvany ed. *The Craft of Oblivion: Aspects of Forgetting and Memory in Ancient China*. Honolulu: University of Hawaii Press, 2023, 49–69.

———. "Cultural Memory and Excavated Anecdotes in 'Documentary' Narrative: Mediating Generic Tension in the *Baoxun* Manuscript." In Paul van Els and Sarah Queen eds., *Between History and Philosophy: Anecdotes in Early China*. New York: SUNY, 2017, 301–329.

Krijgsman, Rens and Paul Nicholas Vogt. "The One Text in the Many: Separate and Composite Readings of an Early Chinese Historical Manuscript." *Bulletin of the School if Oriental and African Studies* 82.3 (2019): 473–492.

Lakoff, George and Mark Johnson, *Metaphors We Live By*. Chicago: Chicago University Press, 1980.

Lau, D.C. *Mencius: Translated with an Introduction by D.C. Lau*. London: Penguin, 1970.

Legge, James. *The Chinese Classics*. 7 vols. London: Trübner & Co., 1871.

Li Ling 李零. *Jianbo gushu yu xueshu yuanliu* 簡帛古書與學術源流. Beijing: Shenghuo · Dushu · Xinzhi Sanlian shudian, 2004.

Li Shoukui 李守奎. "*Zheng Wu furen gui ruzi* zhong de sangli yongyu yu xiangguan de lizhi wenti"《鄭武夫人規孺子》中的喪禮用語與相關的禮制問題. *Zhongguo shi yanjiu* 中國史研究 2016.1: 11–18.

———. "Shi Chu jian zhong de 'gui' — jianshuo 'zhi' yi 'gui' zhi biaoyi chuwen" 釋楚簡中的"規"——兼說"支"亦"規"之表意初文,

Fudan xuebao (shehui kexue ban) 復旦學報（社會科學版）2016.3: 80–86.

Li Songru 李松儒. "Qinghua qi *Zi Fan Zi Yu* yu *Zhao Jianzi* deng pian ziji yanjiu" 清華七《子犯子餘》與《趙簡子》等篇字迹研究. *Chutu wenxian* 出土文獻 15 (2019): 177–192.

Li Tianhong 李天虹. "Hubei chutu Chu jian (wuzhong) geshi chuxi" 湖北出土楚簡（五種）格式初析. *Jiang Han kaogu* 江漢考古 2011.4: 102–106.

Li, Wai-Yee. *The Readability of the Past in Early Chinese Historiography*. Cambridge: Harvard University Asia Center, 2007.

Li Xueqin 李學勤 ed.-in-chief, Qinghua daxue Chutu wenxian yanjiu yu baohu zhongxin 清華大學出土文獻研究與保護中心 ed. *Qinghua daxue cang Zhanguo zhujian (yi–ba)* 清華大學藏戰國竹簡(壹—捌). Shanghai: Zhong Xi shuju, 2010–2018.

———. "Zai *Qinghua daxue cang Zhanguo zhujian (Qi)* chengguo fabuhui shang de jianghua" 在《清華大學藏戰國竹簡（柒）》成果發佈會上的講話. *Chutu wenxian* 出土文獻 11 (2017): 1–2.

———. "Youguan Chunqiu shishi de Qinghua jian wuzhong zongshu" 有關春秋史事的清華簡五種綜述. *Wenwu* 文物 2016.3: 79–83.

———. *Chongxie xueshushi* 重寫學術史. Shijiazhuang: Hebei Jiaoyu chubanshe, 2002.

———. "Yigu sichao yu chonggou gu shi" 疑古思潮與重構古史. *Zhongguo wenhua yanjiu* 中國文化研究 1999.1: 2–5.

———. *Zouchu yigu shidai* 走出疑古時代. Shenyang: Liaoning daxue chubanshe, 1994.

Liu Gang 劉剛. "Cong Qinghua jian tan 'wan wu jiang zi bin'" 從清華簡談《老子》的"萬物將自賓." *Wenshi* 文史 2014.4: 271–274.

Liu Guang 劉光. "Qinghua jian *Zheng Wen Gong wen Tai Bo* suo jian Zhengguo chunian shishi yanjiu" 清華簡六《鄭文公問太伯》所見鄭國初年史事研究. *Dang'an yanjiu* 檔案研究 2016.6: 31–34.

Liu Guozhong. Christopher J. Foster and William N. French trans. *Introduction to the Tsinghua Bamboo-Slip Manuscripts*. Leiden: Brill, 2016,

51–54.

Liu Xiang 劉向. Xiang Zonglu 向宗魯 ed. *Shuo yuan jiao zheng* 説苑校正. Beijing: Zhonghua shuju, 1987.

Liu Zhao 劉釗. "Liyong Qinghua jian (qi) jiaozheng gushu yi ze" 利用清華簡（柒）校正古書一則. *Fudan daxue chutu wenxian yu guwenzi yanjiu zhongxin wangzhan* 復旦大學出土文獻與古文字研究中心網站. At http://www.fdgwz.org.cn/Web/Show/3018. Posted 5 January 2017.

Liao Mingchun 廖名春. "*Shangshu* 'ruzi' kao ji qita" 尚書"孺子"考及其他. *Wenxian* 文獻 2019.5: 76–89.

Ma Chengyuan 馬承源 ed. *Shanghai bowuguan cang Zhanguo Chu zhushu (yi)* 上海博物館藏戰國楚竹書（壹）Shanghai: Shanghai Guji chubanshe, 2001.

Ma Nan 馬楠. "Qinghua jian *Zi Yi* xiangguan shishi yu jianwen bianlian shidu" 清華簡《子儀》相關史事與簡文編連釋讀. *Jianbo* 簡帛 20 (2020): 31–38.

———. "Qinghua jian *Zheng Wen Gong wen Tai Bo* yu Zhengguo zaoqi shishi" 清華簡《鄭文公問太伯》與鄭國早期史事. *Wenwu* 文物 2016.3: 84–87.

Major, John S. "Tool Metaphors in the *Huainanzi* and Other Texts." In Sarah Queen and Michael Puett eds. *The* Huainanzi *and Textual Production in Early China*. Leiden: Brill, 2014, 153–198.

Maspero, Henri. "Notes sur la logique de Mo-tseu et de son école." *T'oung Pao*, Second Series, Vol. 25, No. 1/2 (1927): 1–64, esp. 32–33.

Meng Yuelong 孟躍龍. "Qinghua jian 'Yi jian' ji 'Yi que' shuo" 清華簡"伊閑"即"伊闕"説. *Wuhan daxue jianbo yanjiu zhongxin wangzhan* 武漢大學簡帛研究中心網站. At http://www.bsm.org.cn/?chujian/6679.html. Posted 15 April 2016.

Milburn, Olivia. "The *Xinian*: An Ancient Historical Text from the Qinghua University Collection of Bamboo Books." *Early China* 39 (2016): 53–109.

Mindlin, Murray, M. J. Geller, and J. Wansbrough eds. *Figurative Language in the Ancient near East.* London: School of Oriental and African Studies, 1987.

Pankenier, David W. "Applied Field-Allocation Astrology in Zhou China: Duke Wen of Jin and the Battle of Chengpu (632 B.C.)." *Journal of the American Oriental Society* 119 (1999): 261–279.

Pelliot, Paul. "Le *Chou King* en caractères anciens et le *Chang Chou che wen*." *Mémoires concernant l'Asie Orientale* 2 (1916): 123–177.

Pines, Yuri. *Zhou History Unearthed: The Bamboo Manuscript Xinian and Early Chinese Historiography.* New York: Columbia University Press, 2020.

———. "From Teachers to Subjects: Ministers Speaking to the Rulers from Yan Ying 晏嬰 to Li Si 李斯." In Garret Olberding ed. *Facing the Monarch: Modes of Advice in the Early Chinese Court.* Cambridge: Harvard University Asia Center 2013, 69–99.

———. "History as a Guide to the Netherworld: Rethinking the *Chunqiu shiyu*." *Journal of Chinese Religions* 31 (2003): 101–126.

———. "Friends or Foes: Changing Concepts of Ruler-Minister Relations and the Notion of Loyalty in Pre-Imperial China." *Monumenta Serica* 50 (2002): 35–74.

———. *Foundations of Confucian Thought: Intellectual Life in the Chunqiu Period.* Honolulu: University of Hawaii Press, 2002.

Propp, Vladimir. Laurence Scott trans. *Morphology of the Folktale.* Austin: University of Texas Press, 1968.

Puett, Michael, *The Ambivalence of Creation: Debates Concerning Innovation and Artifice in Early China* (Stanford: Stanford University Press, 2002).

Qinghua daxue chutu wenxian dushu hui 清華大學出土文獻讀書會. "Qinghua liu zhengli baogao buzheng" 清華六整理報告補正. Qinghua daxue chutu wenxian yanjiu yu baohu zhongxin wang 清華大學出土文獻研究與保護中心網. At https://www.ctwx.tsinghua.edu.cn/info/1081/2230.htm. Posted 16 April 2016.

———. "Qinghua qi zhengli baogao buzheng" 清華七整理報告補正.

Qinghua daxue chutu wenxian yanjiu yu baohu zhongxin wang 清華大學出土文獻研究與保護中心網. At https://www.ctwx.tsinghua.edu.cn/info/1081/2233.htm. Posted 23 April 2017.

"Qinghua qi *Jin Wen Gong ru yu Jin* chudu" 清華七《晋文公入於晋》初讀. *Jianbo luntan* 簡帛論壇 forum. At http://www.bsm.org.cn/forum/forum.php?mod=viewthread&tid=3457&extra=page%3D11.

"Qinghua liu *Zi Yi* chudu" 清華六《子儀》初讀. *Jianbo luntan* 簡帛論壇 forum. At http://www.bsm.org.cn/forum/forum.php?mod=viewthread&tid=3343&extra=page%3D2&page=2.

"Qinghua liu *Zheng Wu Furen gui ruzi* chudu" 清華六《鄭武夫人規孺子》初讀. *Jianbo luntan* 簡帛論壇 forum. At http://www.bsm.org.cn/forum/forum.php?mod=viewthread&tid=3345&extra=page%3D10&page=2.

Qiu Xigui 裘锡圭. "Chutu wenxian yu gudianxue chongjian" 出土文獻與古典學重建. *Chutu wenxian* 出土文獻 4 (2013): 1–18.

——— . "Shi Zhanguo Chujian zhong de 'ji' zi" 釋戰國楚簡中的"咠"字. In *Qiu Xigui xueshu wenji—Jiandu boshu juan* 裘錫圭學術文集·簡牘帛書卷, vol. 2. Shanghai: Fudan daxue chubanshe, 2012, 456–464.

——— . "Zhongguo gudianxue chongjian zhong yinggai zhuyi de wenti" 中國古典學重建中應該注意的問題. *Beijing daxue Zhongguo guwenxian yanjiu zhongxin jikan* 北京大學中國古文獻研究中心集刊 2 (2001): 1–14; See also, Qiu Xigui 裘錫圭. *Qiu Xigui xueshu wenji—Jiandu boshu juan* 裘錫圭學術文集·簡牘帛書卷. Shanghai: Fudan daxue chubanshe, 2012, 334–344.

Ready, Jonathan L. *Character, Narrator, and Simile in the Iliad*. Cambridge: Cambridge University Press, 2011.

Richter, Matthias. "Towards a Profile of Graphic Variation: On the Distribution of Graphic Variants within the Mawangdui Laozi Manuscripts." *Asiatische Studien / Etudes Asiatiques* 59.1 (2005): 169–207.

Ruan Yuan 阮元 ed., *Shisan jing zhushu fu jiaokan ji* 十三經註疏附校勘記.

Beijing: Zhonghua, 1980.

Schaberg, David. "Playing at Critique: Indirect Remonstrance and the Formation of *Shi* Identity." In Martin Kern ed. *Text and Ritual in Early China*. Seattle: University of Washington Press, 2005, 194–225.

———. *A Patterned Past: Form and Thought in Early Chinese Historiography*. Cambridge: Harvard University Asia Center, 2002.

———. "Song and the Historical Imagination in Early China." *Harvard Journal of Asiatic Studies* 59.2 (1999): 305–361.

———. "Remonstrance in Eastern Zhou Historiography." *Early China* 17 (1997): 133–179.

———. "Foundations of Chinese Historiography: Literary Representation in *Zuo zhuan* and *Guoyu*." PhD Dissertation. Harvard University, 1995.

Schuessler, Axel. *Minimal Old Chinese and Later Han Chinese—a Companion to Grammata Serica Recensa*. Honolulu: University of Hawaii Press, 2009.

———. *ABC Etymological Dictionary of Old Chinese*. Honolulu: University of Hawaii Press, 2006.

Sena, David M. "Arraying the Ancestors in Ancient China: Narratives of Lineage History in the 'Scribe Qiang' and 'Qiu' Bronzes." *Asia Major* 25.1 (2012): 63–81.

Shan Yuchen 單育辰. "*Zi Yi* shiwen shangque"《子儀》釋文商榷. *Chutu wenxian yanjiu* 出土文獻研究 16 (2017): 30–36.

Shaughnessy, Edward L. "The Tsinghua Manuscript **Zheng Wen Gong wen Tai Bo* and the Question of the Production of Manuscripts in Early China." *Bamboo and Silk* 3.1 (2020): 54–73.

———. *Rewriting Early Chinese Texts*. Albany, N.Y.: SUNY Press, 2006.

———. "The Duke of Zhou's Retirement in the East and the Beginnings of the Ministerial-Monarch Debate in Chinese Political Philosophy." *Early China* 18 (1993): 41–72.

Shen Pei 沈培. "Qinghua jian *Zheng Wu Furen gui ruzi* jiaodu wuze" 清華

简《鄭武夫人規孺子》校讀五則. *Hanzi Hanyu yanjiu* 漢字漢語研究 2018.4: 38–55.

Shi Xiaoli 石小力. "Qinghua jian di liu ji zhong de e zi yanjiu" 清華簡第六輯中的訛字研究. *Chutu wenxian* 出土文獻 2016.2: 190–197.

Shi Zhenying 史楨英. "Ye shuo Qinghua daxue cang Zhanguo zhujian (qi) shouxie wenti" 也説《清華大學藏戰國竹簡（七）》寫手問題. *Wuhan daxue jianbo yanjiu zhongxin wangzhan* 武漢大學簡帛研究中心網站. At http://www.bsm.org.cn/?chujian/7899.html. Posted 15 June 2018.

Slingerland, Edward G. *Effortless Action: Wu-wei as Conceptual Metaphor and Spiritual Ideal in Early China*. Oxford: Oxford University Press, 2003.

Su Jianzhou 蘇建洲. "*Qinghua liu Zheng Wen Gong Wen Tai Bo* "kui er bu er" bushuo《清華六·鄭文公問大伯》"饋而不二"補説. *Wuhan daxue jianbo yanjiu zhongxin wangzhan* 武漢大學簡帛研究中心網站. At http://www.bsm.org.cn/?chujian/6693.html. Posted 26 April 2016.

———. "*Qinghua liu* wenzi bushi《清華六》文字補釋. *Wuhan daxue jianbo yanjiu zhongxin wangzhan* 武漢大學簡帛研究中心網站. At http://www.bsm.org.cn/?chujian/6684.html. Posted 20 April 2016.

Sun Peiyang 孫沛陽. "Jiance bei hua xian chutan" 簡册背劃綫初探. *Chutu wenxian yu guwenzi yanjiu* 出土文獻與古文字研究 4 (2011): 449–462.

Sun Yirang 孫詒讓 ed. *Mozi jiangu* 墨子閒詁, 2 vols. Beijing: Zhonghua shuju, 2001.

Talmon, Shemaryahu. "Har and Midbār: An Antithetical Pair of Biblical Motifs." In Mindlin, et al. eds. *Figurative Language in the Ancient near East*, 105–126.

Thote, Alain. "Daybooks in Archaeological Context." In Donald Harper and Marc Kalinowski eds. *Books of Fate and Popular Culture in Early China: The Daybook Manuscripts of the Warring States, Qin, and*

Han. Leiden: Brill, 2017, 11–56.

UNESCO, "Convention on the Means of Prohibiting and Preventing the Illicit Import, Export and Transfer of Ownership of Cultural Property of 1970." At https://www.unesco.org/en/legal-affairs/convention-means-prohibiting-and-preventing-illicit-import-export-and-transfer-ownership-cultural.

Van Auken, Newell Ann. *Spring and Autumn Historiography: Form and Hierarchy in Ancient Chinese Annals.* New York: Columbia University Press, 2023.

Vankeerberghen, Griet. "Choosing Balance: Weighing (*quan* 權) as a Metaphor for Action in Early Chinese Texts." *Early China* 30 (2005–2006): 47–89.

Vogt, Paul Nicholas, "Towards a Metavocabulary of Early Chinese Deathbed Texts," paper presented at *The International Conference on the Tsinghua Bamboo Manuscripts* 清華簡國際研討會, Hong Kong and Macao, 26–28 October 2017.

von Falkenhausen, Lothar. "Social Ranking in Chu Tombs: The Mortuary Background of the Warring States Manuscript Finds." *Monumenta Serica* 51 (2003): 439–526.

Wang Guowei 王國維. *Gu shi xin zheng: Wang Guowei zuihou de jiangyi* 古史新證——王國維最後的講義. Beijing: Qinghua daxue chubanshe, 1994.

Wang Ning 王寧. "Shi Qinghua jian qi Zi Fan Zi Yu zhong de 'e zhou'" 釋清華簡七《子犯子餘》中的"愕籀." *Fudan daxue chutu wenxian yu guwenzi yanjiu zhongxin wangzhan* 復旦大學出土文獻與古文字研究中心網站. At http://www.fdgwz.org.cn/Web/Show/3024. Posted 5 April 2017.

——— . "Qinghua jian liu *Zi Yi* shiwen jiaodu" 清華簡六《子儀》釋文校讀. *Fudan daxue chutu wenxian yu guwenzi yanjiu zhongxin wangzhan* 復旦大學出土文獻與古文字研究中心網站. At http://www.fdgwz.org.cn/Web/Show/2824. Posted 9 June 2016.

——— . "Qinghua jian liu *Zheng Wen Gong wen Tai Bo* Jia ben shiwen jiaodu" 清華簡六《鄭文公問太伯》(甲本) 釋文校讀. *Fudan daxue chutu wenxian yu guwenzi yanjiu zhongxin wangzhan* 復旦大學出土文獻與古文字研究中心網站. At http://www.fdgwz.org.cn/web/show/2809. Posted 30 May 2016.

Wei Dong 魏棟. Qinghua daxue cang Zhanguo zhujian *jiaoshi di liu ji*《清華大學藏戰國竹簡》校釋第六輯. Beijing: Sanlian, *forthcoming*.

Weiss, Andrea. *Figurative Language in Biblical Prose Narrative: Metaphor in the Book of Samuel*. Leiden: Brill, 2006.

White, Hayden. *The Content of the Form: Narrative Discourse and Historical Representation*. Baltimore: Johns Hopkins University Press, 1990.

Xia Dekao 夏德靠. Guo yu *xushi yanjiu*《國語》敘事研究. Beijing: Zhishi chanquan, 2015.

Xia Lu 夏渌. "Gu, gua ren, bu gu xinquan" 孤，寡人，不穀新詮. *Zhongguo yuwen* 中國語文 1983.4: 288.

Xiao Yunxiao. "Mediating between Loss and Order: Reflections on the Paratexts of the Tsinghua Manuscripts." *Bamboo and Silk* 6.2 (2023): 186–237.

———. "Shilun Qinghua zhushu Yi Yin san pian de guanlian" 試論清華竹書伊尹三篇的關聯. *Jianbo* 簡帛 8 (2013): 471–476.

Xie Huiting 謝輝亭. "Qinghua jian *Zhao Jianzi* shiling — jianlun qi wenxianxue jiazhi" 清華簡《趙簡子》拾零——兼論其文獻學價值. *Handan xueyuan xuebao* 邯鄲學院學報 2018.2: 32–37.

Xing Wen 邢文. "New Light on the *Li Ji* 禮記: The *Li Ji* and the Related Warring States period Guodian Bamboo Manuscripts." *Early China* 37 (2014): 522–523.

———. "Beida jian Laozi bianwei" 北大簡老子辨偽. *Guangming ribao* 光明日報, 8 August 2016.

———. "Bianzheng zhi mei yu sandian toushi — Beida jian Laozi zai bianwei" 辯證之美與散點透視——北大簡老子再辨偽. *Guangming ribao*, 12 September 2016.

Xu Yuangao 徐元誥. *Guo yu jijie* 國語集解. Beijing: Zhonghua shuju, 2002.

Xu Zaiguo 徐在國. "Qinghua liu *Zheng Wen Gong wen Tai Bo* zhaji yi ze"

清華六《鄭文公問太伯》札記一則. *Zhongguo wenzi xuebao* 中國文字學報 8 (2017): 122–124.

Yan Ruoqu 閻若璩 (1636–1704). *Shang shu guwen shuzheng* 尚書古文疏證. In *Huang Qing jingjie xubian* 皇清經解續編, vols. 6-10. Jiangyin: Nanjing shuyuan, 1888.

Yang Kuan 楊寬. "'Da sou li' xintan" "大蒐禮"新探. *Xueshu yuekan* 學術月刊 3 (1963): 48–56.

Yang Lei. *Narrative Devices in the Shiji: Retelling the Past* (Albany: State University of New York Press, 2024).

Yang Mengsheng 楊蒙生. "Qinghua liu *Zi Yi* pian jianwen jiaodu ji" 清華六《子儀》篇簡文校讀記. *Qinghua daxue Chutu wenxian yanjiu yu baohu zhongxin wangzhan* 清華大學出土文獻研究與保護中心網站. At https://www.ctwx.tsinghua.edu.cn/info/1081/2228.htm. Posted 16 April 2016.

———. "Du Qinghua liu *Zi Yi* biji wuze — fu *Zheng Wen Gong wen Tai Bo* yi ze " 讀清華六《子儀》筆記五則——附《鄭文公問太伯》筆記一則. *Qinghua daxue Chutu wenxian yanjiu yu baohu zhongxin wangzhan* 清華大學出土文獻研究與保護中心網站. At https://www.ctwx.tsinghua.edu.cn/info/1081/2227.htm. Posted 16 April 2016.

Yi Nuo 伊諾. "Qinghua qi *Zi Fan Zi Yu* jishi" 清華七《子犯子餘》集釋. *Fudan daxue chutu wenxian yu guwenzi yanjiu zhongxin wangzhan* 復旦大學出土文獻與古文字研究中心網站. At http://www.fdgwz.org.cn/Web/Show/4210. Posted 18 January 2018.

Yu Houkai 尉侯凱. "Du Qinghua jian liu zhaji" 讀清華簡六札記（五則）. *Chutu wenxian* 出土文獻 10 (2017): 124–129.

———. "*Qinghua jian 6 Ziyi* bianlian xiaoyi"《清華簡（陸）·子儀》編連小議, *Wuhan daxue jianbo yanjiu zhongxin wangzhan* 武漢大學簡帛研究中心網站. At http://www.bsm.org.cn/?chujian/6717.html. Posted 23 May 2016.

Yu, Pauline, *The Reading of Imagery in the Chinese Poetic Tradition*. Princeton: Princeton University Press, 1987.

Zi Ju 子居. "Qinghua jian qi *Zi Fan Zi Yu* yundu" 清華簡七《子犯子餘》韻讀. *Zhongguo xianqin shi wangzhan* 中國先秦史網站. 28 October 2017. originally published at https://www.xianqin.tk/2017/10/28/405, now available at https://www.academia.edu/41579159/%E6%B8%85%E5%8D%8E%E7%AE%80%E4%B8%83_%E5%AD%90%E7%8A%AF%E5%AD%90%E4%BD%99_%E9%9F%B5%E8%AF%BB.

———. "Qinghua jian qi *Zhao Jianzi* jiexi" 清華簡七《趙簡子》解析. *Zhongguo Xianqin shi wangzhan* 中國先秦史網站, originally published on 29 May 2017 at http://www.xianqin.tk/2017/05/29/383, link is now inactive. Retrieved on 11 July 2022 at https://www.academia.edu/41579163/%E6%B8%85%E5%8D%8E%E7%AE%80%E4%B8%83_%E8%B5%B5%E7%AE%80%E5%AD%90_%E8%A7%A3%E6%9E%90.

———. "Qinghua jian *Zheng Wu Furen gui ruzi* jiexi" 清華簡《鄭武夫人規孺子》解析. *Zhongguo xianqin shi wangzhan* 中國先秦史網站，26 June 2016, original link expired, now available at https://www.academia.edu/41579308/%E6%B8%85%E5%8D%8E%E7%AE%80_%E9%83%91%E6%AD%A6%E5%A4%AB%E4%BA%BA%E8%A7%84%E5%AD%BA%E5%AD%90-%E8%A7%A3%E6%9E%90.

———. "Qinghua jian *Zi Yi* jiexi" 清華簡《子儀》解析. *Zhongguo Xianqin shi wangzhan* 中國先秦史網站, 11 May 2016, originally published at http://xianqin.byethost10.com/2016/05/11/333. Now available at, https://www.academia.edu/41579284/%E6%B8%85%E5%8D%8E%E7%AE%80_%E5%AD%90%E4%BB%AA_%E8%A7%A3%E6%9E%90.

Zhao Ping'an 趙平安. "Qin Mu Gong fang gui Zi Yi kao" 秦穆公放歸子儀考. *Guwenzi yu Gudaishi* 古文字與古代史 5. Taipei: Institute of History and Philology, Academia Sinica, 2017, 287–294.

Zhao Ping'an 趙平安 and Shi Xiaoli 石小力. "Cheng Zhuan ji qi yu Zhao Jianzi de wendui — Qinghua jian *Zhao Jianzi* chutan" 成鱄及

其與趙簡子的問對 ——清華簡《趙簡子》初探. *Wenwu* 文物 2017.3: 85–89.

Zhao Xiaobin 趙曉斌. "Jingzhou zaozhi jian *Wuwang Fuchai qi shi fa Yue* yu Qinghua jian *Yue Gong qi shi*" 荊州棗紙簡《吳王夫差起師伐越》與清華簡《越公其事》. Paper presented at the conference "Qinghua Zhanguo Chujian guoji xueshu yantaohui" 清華戰國楚簡國際學術研討會. Tsinghua University, Beijing, 19 November 2021.

Zhang Mingzhu 張明珠. "*Qinghua daxue cang Zhanguo zhujian (qi) Zhao Jianzi* jishi, yizhu" 《清華大學藏戰國竹簡(柒)·趙簡子》集釋、譯註. MA Thesis. Wuhan University, 2019.

Zhang Suqing 张素卿. Zuo zhuan *cheng shi yanjiu*《左傳》稱詩研究. Taipei: Guoli Taiwan daxue, 1991.

Zhou Boqun. "Subtle and Dangerous: The Crossbow Trigger Metaphor in Early China." *Early China* 44 (2021): 465–492.

Zhou Boqun. "Mechanical Metaphors in Early Chinese Thought." PhD Dissertation. University of Chicago, 2019.

Zhu Zhongheng 朱忠恒. "Qinghua daxue cang Zhanguo zhjian liu jishi" 清華大學藏戰國竹簡六集釋. MA Thesis. Wuhan University, 2016.

Zuern, Tobias, "Overgrown Courtyards and Tilled Fields: Image-Based Debates on Governance and Body Politics in the *Mengzi*, *Zhuangzi*, and *Huainanzi*." *Early China* 41 (2018): 297–332.

Index of Concepts

Allusion, 74, 80, 84, 215 n.20, 224, 226
Analogy, 73 n.9, 74, 76–80
Anecdote, 95–97, 203, 205, 206
Author, 45

Bao 報 "recompense," 43
Bi 比 "metaphor — simile — analogy," 73 n.9
Bronze inscriptions, 45
Bu gu 不穀 "the one unable to cultivate," 47 n.11, 65–66, 130, 170 n.15
Bo 伯 (suffix), 29

Chi 侈 "excess," 64
Chu mortuary culture, 41 n.33
Ci 賜 "bestows," 53
Collection, 36

Dialogue, 33, 42, 44–49, 53, 56, 58–69; Introduction of, 48, 52
Discourse markers, 74
Discursive power, 42–43, 46, 53, 80
Descriptive circumlocution, see Periphrasis

"Elders of the state" 屬邦耆老, 54, 68

Exclamation, 30

Focalization, 44, 46, 53, 65
Fu 父 (suffix), 29
Fu 賦 "exposition," 73 n.9
Fu shi 賦詩 "presenting odes," 226

Gong 公 (title), 29–30
Gu 孤 "the orphaned one," 65–67
Gui 規 "admonition," 50, 60
Guo qing 國卿, 203

Historiography, 40 n.32

Illocutionary force, 49
Image-based language, 30, 46, 70–93; Images of water, 78–79
Interlocutor, 33, 39, 43, 45 n.6, 52–53, 54 n.18, 58–59, 65, 68, 72, 94, 96, 183
Interpretive framework, 38
Intertextuality, 40
"Inventions" 作, 54

Ji 既 "After," 47
Jin jian yue 進諫曰 (speech genre marker), 49
Jian 儉 "frugality," 64
Jian 諫 "remonstrate," 60
Jun 君 (title), 29–30
Jun ruo yue 君若曰 "the ruler said to the effect," 48

lin 臨 "wail," 51

Metaphor, 70, 72–73, 73 n.9, 80–88; and discourse marker, 74

Motif, 72

Nai 乃 "then" (connective), 51

Narrative, 28, 39, 42–57, 100–102; Technique, 38; Unearthed, 38; Frame, 42, 46–49, 53; Narrator, 42, 44–45, 48–50, 53–56; Narratee, 46; Narration, 44–45, 52; Form of, 45–46; Deathbed, 48 n.12, 126; historiographical, 51, 88–89; Structure of, 94–97; Genre of, 42, 59, 74, 80, 88, 97

Narratology, 37

Paratextual encapsulation, 38

Paternal-advisory, 126

Periphrasis, 47, 58, 65–68

Pi 譬 "comparison," 73 n.9

Pi ru 譬如 "can be likened to" (discourse marker), 74

Pretext, 48

Punctuation marks, 52 n.17, 98, 104 n.12, 125, 159–160, 164 n.6, 183, 201, 204, 222

Qing 卿 "Chancellor," 59 n.3

Reception, 36–37, 41

Rhetorical question, 30

Ru 如 "like, as if" (discourse marker), 74

Ruler, 96; and minister, 42, 53, 58–65, 76; and former ruler, 88–92

Ruo 若 "as if" (discourse marker), 74

Ruo yue 若曰 (speech genre marker), 49

Ruzi 孺子 "young child," 47 n.11, 50

San biao 三表 "three marks," 188

Scene change, 45; and complexity, 49–53

Scribe, 35

Self-deprecatory modes of address, 30

Simile, 74–80

Shi 使 "send off," 53

Shi 寔 "verily," 75

Shu 叔 (birth sequence indicator), 29

Shu 書 "*writings*," 45

Si 殣 "temporary grave," 51

Sizi 嗣子 "heir," 50 n.11

sou 蒐 "military review," 187

Springs and Autumns 春秋, 32, 47–48, 97, 100–101; Translation of appellations of, 29; Narratives about, 36, 39, 88;

Style of text, 33

Transmitted texts, 40–41

Tenor, 74, 76, 80–81

Vehicle, 74, 76, 80

Vorlagen, 125

Wang ruo yue 王若曰 "the king said to the effect," 48

Warring States 戰國, 36, 100–101; Historiographical discourse, 39; Collective memory of, 40; Audience of, 41

Wen 問 "Ask," 47, 59–61

Wen 聞 "Hear," 47, 59–61

Wen 文 "Cultural attainment," 88

Workshop, 35

Wu 吾 "I," 65–66

Wu 武 "martial prowess," 88

Xi 昔 "in days of yore," 47

Xiao xiang 小祥 "the Minor Auspicious Sacrifice," 51, 82

Xing 興 "evocation," 73 n.9, 86

Yan 言 "speak," 60

Yu 余 "I" (mode of address), 65

Yu 喻 "explanation," 73 n.9

Yue 曰 "saying" (connective), 51

Zang 葬 "burial," 51

Zhao 召 "summon," 53

Zhe 謫 "reprimand," 60

Zi 子 ("courteous prefix"), 29

Index of Proper Names

Aristotle, 76

Bian fu 邊父 Sir Bian, 29, 50–51, 59, 82, 99, 126

Chao Fulin 晁福林, 30, 30 n.11
Chen clan, 204, 206
Chen Dechen, see Zi Yu 子玉
Chen Wei 陳偉. 100
Cheng Hao 程浩, 188
Cheng Tuan 成摶, see Cheng Zhuan
Cheng Zhuan 成剸, 49, 51, 59–60, 64, 204–206
Chong'er 重耳, 43, 52, 54, 60, 62–63, 90–91, 159–161, 174 n.21, 184–185, 187–188
Chu 楚, 32–33, 55, 68, 80, 85, 87, 223–226

Du Heng, 206

Edward Shaughnessy, 125

Fan Xianzi 范獻子, 49, 59, 202; and the Fan clan and Zhao Jianzi, 203–205

Gongshu Duan 共叔段, 100

275

Hu Yan, see Zi Fan

Jia Lianxiang 賈連翔, 98–99

Jian shu 蹇叔 Uncle Jian, 29, 52–53, 59, 62–63, 78, 161

Jie Zhitui 介之推, 185

Jin 晋, 32–33, 43, 52, 55, 87, 204, 223

Jonathan Ready, 71, 77

King Zhuang of Chu 楚莊王, 96–97, 101 n.8

Lady Wu of Zheng 鄭武夫人, 43, 49–50, 75, 99, 100

Li Shoukui 李守奎, 100

Li Songru 李松儒, 35, 201

Lord Ding of Jin 晉定公, 202

Lord Huan of Zheng 鄭桓公, 88–89

Lord Mu of Qin 秦穆公, 29, 53, 55–56, 61–64, 67, 78, 84–85, 160–161, 223–226

Lord Wen of Jin 晉文公, see Chong'er

Lord Wen of Zheng 鄭文公, 44, 47–48, 53, 60, 75–76, 126–127

Lord Wu of Zheng 鄭武公, 43, 49–50, 60, 75, 99–101

Lord Zhuang of Zheng 鄭莊公, 99–102

Ma Nan 馬楠, 222–223

Mi clan 羋氏, 127

Qin 秦, 32–33, 43, 52, 55, 68, 80, 85, 87, 159, 223–226

Qi 齊, 204, 206

Shemaryahu Talmon, 72

Shi Yang 士鞅, 202

Sui Hui 隨會, 223

Tai Bo 太伯 Grand Elder, 29, 47–48, 50, 58–59, 62, 75–77, 88, 126–127

Wai-Yee Li, 28, 43
Wei 衛, 75
Wei Dong 魏棟, 27, 28
Wu Jiang 武姜, see Lady Wu of Zheng

Xiao 敎, 223
Xing 杏, 223

Yang Kuan 楊寬, 187–188
Yang Mengsheng 楊蒙生, 87
Yang Zhi 羊殖, 205–206
Yi Fu 儀父 Sir Yi, see Zi Yi
Yu Houkai 尉侯凱, 99

Zhao Jianzi 趙簡子, 49, 51, 59, 64, 202–205
Zhao Ping'an 趙平安, 223
Zhao Yang 趙鞅, see Zhao Jianzi
Zheng 鄭, 32, 75
Zhu Zhongheng 朱忠恒, 28
Zi Fan 子犯 Mr. Fan, 29, 52, 185–186
Zi Ju 子居, 99, 222–223
Zi Yu 子玉, 188
Zi Yu 子餘 Mr. Yu, 52
Zi Yi 子儀 Mr. Yi, 29, 55–56, 61, 67–68, 84–86, 223–226
Ziren Chengzi 子人成子, 47, 126
Ziren Yu 子人語, see Ziren Chengzi

Index of Text Titles

Bao xun 保訓 "Treasured Instructions," 126

Chu ju 楚居, 40 n.32
Chunqiu 春秋 *Springs and Autumns*, 39
Chunqiu Shiyu 春秋事語, 40 n.32
Collated Interpretations 清華大學藏戰國竹簡校釋, 22; Volume 6, 27, 36

Guo yu 國語, 28, 36
Gao Di Shu 告地書, 39 n.3

"Chu shuo" chapters of *Han Feizi* 韓非子, 206
Huang Men 皇門, 35

Jin Wen Gong ru yu Jin 晉文公入於晉 *Lord Wen of Jin Entered Jin*, 32, 33, 34, 41, 53–54, 58, 60, 68, 90–91, 94–95, 185 n.2, 202; Basic manuscript data of, 35; Handwriting of, 35; The manuscript and its affiliation, 183–184; The text, 184–189; Slip-by-slip translation, 190–197; Full-text translation, 198–200

Kongzi Shilun 孔子詩論, 39 n.28
"Kang gao" 康誥, 45 n.6

"Luo gao" 洛誥, 45 n.6

Pingwang wen Zhengshou 平王問鄭壽, 40 n.32
Pingwang yu Wangzi Mu 平王與王子木, 40 n.32

Rongchengshi 容成氏, 40 n.32
Ruzi, see *Zheng Wu Furen gui ruzi

Shanghai Museum collection of Warring States bamboo manuscripts, 33, 39 n.28, 95
Shang shu 尚書, 45 n.6, 48, 58
"Shanshuo" 善說 chapter of the *Shuoyuan* 說苑, 73 n.9, 205–206
Shi jing 詩經, 66; *Daxu* 大序 "Major Preface," 71
Shi Qiang Pan 史墻盤, 45 n.6

Xinian 繫年, 40 n.32

Yue Gong qi Shi 越公其事, 35, 202
Zhao Jianzi 趙簡子 *Zhao Jianzi*, 32, 33, 41, 48–49, 58, 60, 64, 95, 97; Basic manuscript data of, 35; Handwriting of, 35; The manuscript, 201–202; The text, 202–207; Slip-by-slip translation, 208–218; Full-text translation, 219–221

Zhaowang huishi — Zhaowang yu Gong zhi Zhui 昭王毀室・昭王與龔之脽

Zheng Wen Gong wen Tai Bo 鄭文公問太伯 *Lord Wen of Zheng Asks Grand Elder*, 29, 34, 41, 48, 58–60, 75–77, 81–82, 88–89, 91–92, 95, 184, 204; Basic manuscript data of, 35; Handwriting of, 35–36; The manuscript, 125–126; The text, 126–127; Version A 甲本, 32, 46; Slip-by-slip translation of Version A, 128–141; Full-text translation of Version A, 142–144; Version B 乙本, 32, 76 n.13; Slip-by-slip translation of Version B, 145–155; Full-text translation of Version B; 156–158

Zheng Wu Furen gui ruzi 鄭武夫人規孺子 *Lady Wu of Zheng Admonished* her Young Child, 30, 32, 34, 41, 43, 49–52, 58–59, 64, 67, 75, 82–83, 94, 125–126, 184, 204, 206–207; Basic manuscript data of, 35; Handwriting of, 35; The manuscript, 98–99; The text, 99–102; Slip-by-slip translation of, 103–120; Full-text translation of, 121–124; Full-text translation, 178–182

Zhou Li 周禮, 188

Zhuangwang ji Cheng 莊王既成, 40 n.32, 95–97

Zi Fan Zi Yu 子犯子餘 Mr. Fan and Mr. Yu, 32–34, 41, 43, 52–53, 56, 59, 62, 64, 66, 72, 77–78, 94, 183–184, 202, 206; Basic manuscript data of, 35; Handwriting of, 35; The manuscript, 159–160; The text, 160–161; Slip-by-slip translation, 162–177; Full-text translation, 178–182

*Zi Yi 子儀 *Mr. Yi, 32, 33, 41, 54–56, 61, 67, 72, 79–80, 83–88, 94; Basic manuscript data of, 35, 38 n.26; The manuscript, 222–223; Hostage or emissary, 223; The structure of song, 224–226; Slip-by-slip translation, 227–246; Full-text translation, 247–251

Zuo zhuan 左傳 Zuo Tradtion, 28, 29, 36, 38, 40, 42–43, 71, 84, 87, 100, 161, 185–186, 188–189, 203–204

Images of the Manuscripts

圖片來源：北京，清華大學出土文獻研究與保護中心。

Source: Research and Conservation Center for Unearthed Texts, Tsinghua University, Beijing.

Zheng Wu Furen gui ruzi 鄭武夫人規孺子
Lady Wu of Zheng Admonished her Young Child, recto

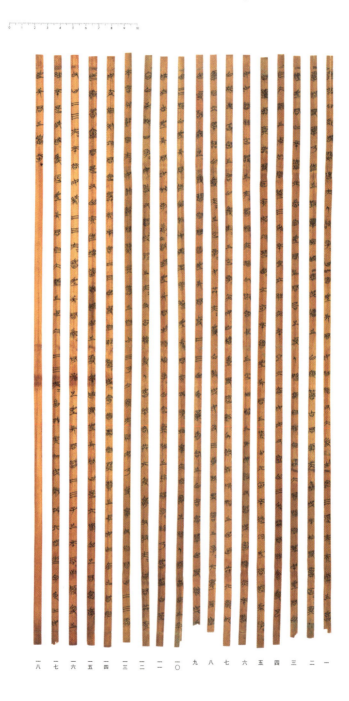

Zheng Wu Furen gui ruzi 鄭武夫人規孺子
Lady Wu of Zheng Admonished her Young Child, verso

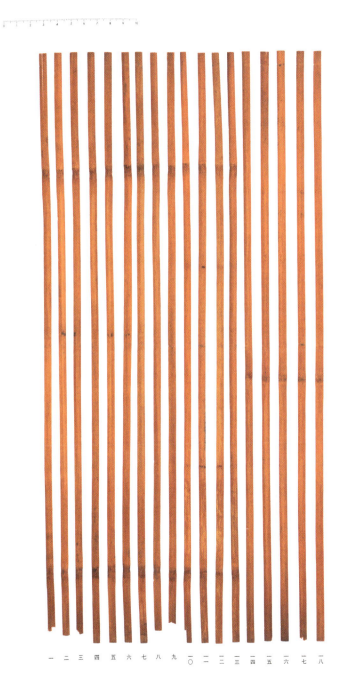

Zheng Wen Gong wen Tai Bo (A) 鄭文公問太伯（甲本）
Lord Wen of Zheng Asks Grand Elder (A), recto

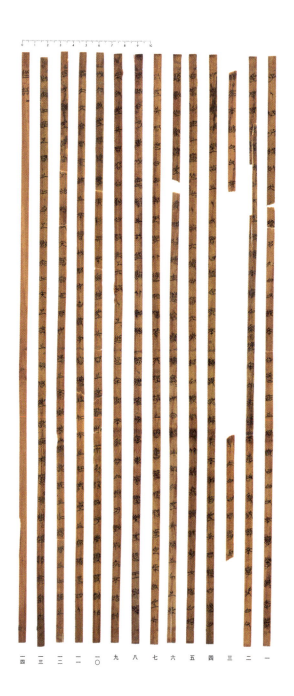

Zheng Wen Gong wen Tai Bo (A) 鄭文公問太伯（甲本）
Lord Wen of Zheng Asks Grand Elder (A), verso

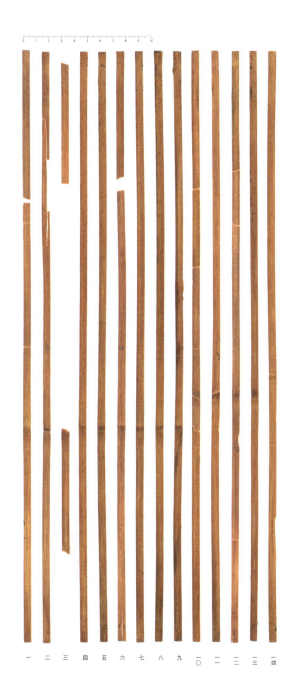

Zheng Wen Gong wen Tai Bo (B) 鄭文公問太伯（乙本）
Lord Wen of Zheng Asks Grand Elder (B), recto

Zheng Wen Gong wen Tai Bo (B) 鄭文公問太伯（乙本）
Lord Wen of Zheng Asks Grand Elder (B), verso

Zi Fan Zi Yu 子犯子餘
Mr. Fan and Mr. Yu, recto

Zi Fan Zi Yu 子犯子餘
Mr. Fan and Mr. Yu, verso

Jin Wen Gong ru yu Jin 晋文公入於晋
Lord Wen of Jin Entered Jin, recto

Jin Wen Gong ru yu Jin 晋文公入於晋

Lord Wen of Jin Entered Jin, verso

Zhao Jianzi 趙簡子 *Zhao Jianzi*, recto

Zhao Jianzi 趙簡子 *Zhao Jianzi*, verso

一 二 三 四 五 六 七 八 九 一〇 二一

*Zi Yi 子儀 *Zi Yi, recto

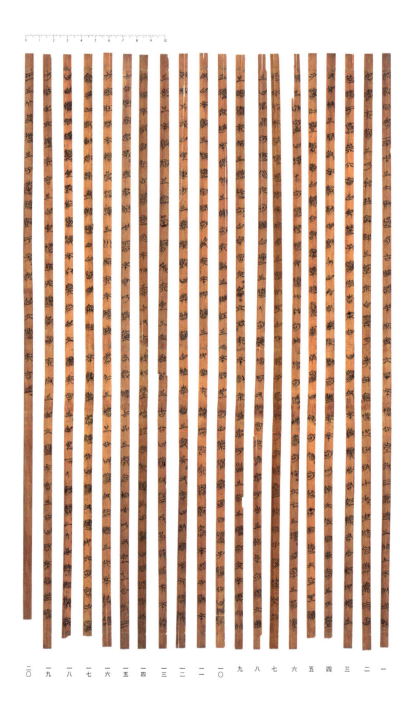

Zi Yi 子儀 *Zi Yi*, verso

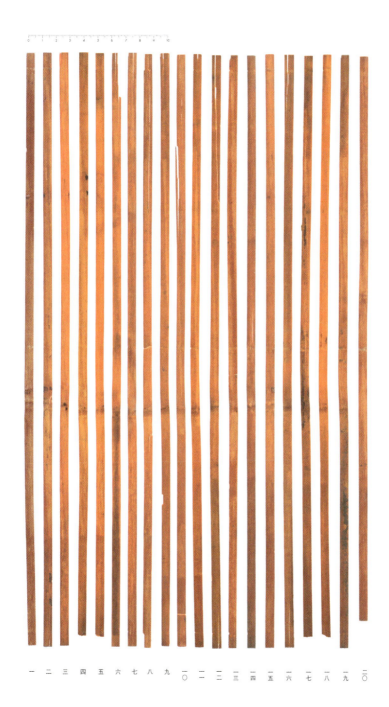